SIXTY YEARS OF MORAL THEOLOGY

Readings in Moral Theology No. 20

PREVIOUS VOLUMES IN THIS SERIES

SIXTY YEARS OF MORAL THEOLOGY

Readings in Moral Theology No. 20

Charles E. Curran

Paulist Press
New York / Mahwah, NJ

Permissions for previously published material may be found in the Acknowledgments.

Jacket and case design by Lynn Else

Library of Congress Cataloging-in-Publication Data
Names: Curran, Charles E, editor.
Title: Sixty years of moral theology / edited by Charles E Curran.
Description: New York : Paulist Press, 2020. | Series: Readings in moral theology ; 20 | Summary: "After a run of over forty years, the series Readings in Moral Theology comes to a close with this retrospective volume by one of the original editors, Charles E. Curran"— Provided by publisher.
Identifiers: LCCN 2019049452 (print) | LCCN 2019049453 (ebook) | ISBN 9780809106653 (hardcover) | ISBN 9781587689055 (ebook)
Subjects: LCSH: Christian ethics—Catholic authors.
Classification: LCC BJ1249 .S475 2020 (print) | LCC BJ1249 (ebook) | DDC 241—dc23
LC record available at https://lccn.loc.gov/2019049452
LC ebook record available at https://lccn.loc.gov/2019049453

ISBN 978-0-8091-0665-3 (hardcover)
ISBN 978-1-58768-905-5 (e-book)

Published by Paulist Press
997 Macarthur Boulevard
Mahwah, New Jersey 07430
www.paulistpress.com

Printed and bound in the
United States of America

To the staff of Paulist Press
Especially Kevin Lynch, CSP, and Mark-David Janus, CSP

Contents

PART THREE: THE ENSUING YEARS

    Lisa Sowle Cahill

Publisher's Note

Paulist Press first had the wisdom to publish Fr. Charles Curran in 1962. His first work was a pamphlet that began to unfold to the American scene theological developments in moral theology occasioned by the Second Vatican Council. Happily, we have enjoyed the privilege of publishing him on numerous occasions, most notably in the series he has edited and coedited: *Readings in Moral Theology*. This series has carefully curated some of the best and most timely writings from a wide range of moral theologians. It is fitting that this series concludes with volume 20, *Sixty Years of Moral Theology*, dedicated to his own writings and the development of his thought throughout his career.

Anyone who has met Fr. Charles Curran is immediately aware of his kindness, his catholicity, his penetrating intellect, his desire for honest dialogue with those of different points of view. As a seminarian I enjoyed the good fortune of having Fr. Curran as a professor. From Charlie we learned moral theology, the importance of theological method, the absolute necessity of mastering the tradition, and most importantly, how to think. To instruct the ignorant is one of the works of mercy, and I gratefully join the ranks of the recipients of Charlie's tender mercies.

In *Sixty Years of Moral Theology*, Fr. Curran has selected articles representing his thought and methodology. It is the work of a rigorous scholar, a pastoral priest, and loyal member of the Church. It is my privilege, on behalf of all at Paulist Press, to thank Fr. Charlie Curran for the honor of publishing this series.

Rev. Mark-David Janus, CSP, PhD
President and Publisher of Paulist Press

Foreword

A Moral Life

From 1979 to 1982, I was studying at Weston School of Theology, taking courses with Professors David Hollenbach, Lisa Sowle Cahill, Ed Vacek, and Sr. Mary Emil Penet. Ah, that last one, there's the surprise. "SME," as we called her, had been tutored by Josef Fuchs in Rome, and primarily through her, many of us were introduced subsequently to the world of fundamental moral theology. And for me, strangely, few things were more interesting.

In the United States, two people helped others like SME to introduce the rest of us to the emerging conciliar and postconciliar studies in moral theology: Richard ("Dick") McCormick and Charles ("Charlie") Curran. Dick became known for his "Moral Notes" that appeared from 1965 to 1984 in every March issue of *Theological Studies*; there he effectively presented and presided over some of the early discussions and debates among European and American scholars who were wrestling with the basic question of how to do moral theology after the Second Vatican Council. Later, Dick and Charlie together launched their Readings in Moral Theology series, which Charlie, with his fine narrative style and enduring clarity, describes in his preface here in this collection.

As Dick started writing the "Moral Notes," Charlie started publishing books. While Dick was weighing in on other's positions, Charlie began synthesizing, appropriating, and developing his own distinctive contributions. As he wrote these essays, putting together one collection after another, his own excitement about the developments became clear, his writing was extraordinarily accessible, and his vision was continuously growing in inclusivity.

From 1982, when I arrived in Rome to study with Josef Fuchs and Klaus Demmer, Charlie's writings became my companions. I would go to the Ancora bookstore adjacent to St. Peter's Square and buy his books, from the oldest to the newest, from *Christian Morality Today:*

The Renewal of Moral Theology, to *A New Look at Christian Morality* and, later, *Themes in Moral Theology*. My favorite, and the one that I bought before even arriving in Rome, was *Catholic Moral Theology in Dialogue*. It introduced me to a wide variety of what were once unimaginable discussions within the contemporary Church.

These books, with their lackluster titles, were gems: they were always an assortment of essays, sometimes well connected, sometimes not, but reading them, one could not help but get a sense of Charlie's own passion to communicate the embracing *spirit* of theology, and therein he conveyed all the signs of hope, wisdom, and compassion of the theology that he was sharing, articulating, and developing in the period following Vatican II, when the aggiornamento unfolded.

Biblical foundations, conscience at the center, the Christian in community, the moral life expressed in liturgy, the call to love, the in-breaking of the kingdom, the varied issues around the Church's teaching authority, and the movement of the Spirit, these themes are the fundamental theological interests that Charlie was bringing into our hearts and minds.

In order to go forward with the renewal, Charlie, like his peers, knew that the use of resources would derive from periods much further back in the history of the tradition. In fact, the further back one went, the richer and more relevant were the investigative yields.

But Charlie was not simply reporting, he was teaching, and in order to do so, he often put things into comparative categories, giving us taxonomies, whether of models, stances, settings, or strands. He wanted us to see how extensive the conversations, dialogues, and debates were following the council. And so, he grouped them into discernible categories, that we could see their breadth and depth, their comparatives and their contrasts.

These were not simple academic exercises. All along, Charlie has always been giving these lessons for personal and social impact: offering the tools in order to find, understand, and inevitably live the moral life. And because of this interest, in realizing the moral life, the real, the concrete, the empirical was always a necessity for any moral theological investigation.

As this incredibly fertile period of growth moved from the 1960s into and through the '80s, *Humanae vitae*'s own arrival on the scene became an evident and ongoing contradiction to much of the developments energizing the Church. Charlie sees, I think, the encyclical as first an interruption and then as an ongoing threat to the theological agenda that he so devotedly communicated. When it was promulgated, Charlie began reporting and teaching with the same athletic passion, the same appreciation of the immediacy of experience and the same concern for conscience and love that fed him before the encyclical's arrival. But now he took public stands, coordinating meetings, becoming, if you will, prophetic, reading for us the signs of the times. And while his early writings were mostly engaging proposals, these writings in the light of the birth control encyclical were critiques. He was, of course, not abandoning his propositional writing, but now he was writing on two very different fronts.

In this collection, Curran shares with us the now legendary statement of dissent that Rome never forgot, his own analysis of the encyclical, the evolution of the concept of dissent that he developed and would effectively embody, and finally, rather brilliantly, a comparative analysis of the differences in methodology among the different fields of theological ethics—fundamental, sexual, social, and so on. Clearly on this last point, Charlie the taxometer does not propose a variety of different methodologies, but rather shows and critiques how profoundly methodologically inconsistent and alienated the magisterium is when it teaches on sexuality.

Afterward, though he championed his dissent and stood clearly as a witness against the encyclical, he continued his critiques and proposals, digging deeper into the Catholic common good tradition, as he endorsed more inclusive, integrative, and sustainable theological claims.

Clearly, in all of this, Charlie is a churchman, 100 percent. Like his proposals, his critiques and dissents are always within the Church. His stance is not outside the Church but deeply within it, a point he makes clearly within his *Catholic Moral Theology: A Synthesis*. The Church is not only his starting point for doing his theology, it is the enduring locus of his reflection. Thus, he did not walk out of the Catholic University of America but fought to stay within it. And, after being forced out, he offered to another Catholic university in the same city the manuscripts he would write over the next twenty-five years. In fact, when one thinks of his more recent books that deal with the last three papacies, among other topics, one could say that Charlie is a lot more Roman than many think.

In the ensuing years, Charlie has continued his double task of critic and proponent, writing about our tradition as it tries to move forward, more and more mindful of the claims of the common good on us.

I remember the first time I met Charlie. It was either June 1988 or 1989. I had finished studies at Rome in 1987 and was then teaching at Fordham. My friend and former classmate at the Gregorian University, Thomas Kopfensteiner, and I were recruited by the USCCB's Committee on Doctrine to help with the revision of the Ethical and Religious Directives (ERDS) for Catholic Healthcare. Along with fifty other Catholic ethicists, Tom and I were invited by Dick McCormick to the University of Notre Dame; Dick had done this for a few years, but this was my first time being invited. I remember us all sitting around in a room, talking not only about the state of things but also providing some forecasts. And, when Charlie talked, he did with the same matter-of-factness with which he writes. Having read almost everything he had written, I was not surprised by the theologian. He spoke with ease, humor, narrative, clarity, intelligence, and passion. It was his stuff, but his stuff in the Church.

In the late afternoon, Charlie, it had been decided, would preside at the Eucharist. I was happily surprised by this. I remember to this day how moved I was by his celebration of the Eucharist, from the opening greeting to the closing blessing, by how pivotal in his life (and then how visible it was to me) was the Eucharist and his priesthood. His theology was not conceptual, but lived, with the same spirit and passion as he writes.

Later that night, we were all sitting around again. Charlie recounted how he received the first copy of *Humanae vitae*, before anyone else had in the United States. The interesting thing in recounting the story was his own agency. He talked more about what others did, not to convey himself as innocent, but to highlight how all the others were involved. Like any party that Charlie throws, he wanted to make sure no one gets left out of the narrative but rather becomes known or familiar.

As the evening wore on, someone remarked that he had heard that the bishops were going to try to revise the ERDS again. (The last time they tried that was thirteen years earlier when they had recruited, among others, Dick to help with the revisions.) Someone said he heard that the Bishops' Committee on Doctrine had decided to hire two very young, Roman-trained theologians, whom no one knew, to work on the revisions.

Others acknowledged hearing the same, but no one knew who the two were. Eventually, I looked at Tom and decided to admit it was us. It was for me a real coming-of-age moment, meeting Charlie face-to-face, beginning to tell my own story as he was just finishing his.

Roman-trained Charlie always made me feel welcomed wherever he was. He made everything familiar. But then, that's what his theology always was about, making Vatican II familiar, all its evolving agenda, as he has done and continues to do these sixty years. This descriptive, *familiar*, I think captures Charlie's style; his hospitality like his theology is familiar, and even the stories he tells, like the theology he teaches, become familiar to the listener. Even when I was studying in Rome, before meeting Charlie, whenever either Fuchs or Demmer returned from a trip to the States, they would tell me stories about Charlie. I think they liked him so much not only for what he wrote and did but also for his style: it is as refreshing as his theology.

Let me close with another story. In 2005, I needed to go to Aachen for a conference I was planning the next year. I learned that my mentor, Josef Fuchs, was in Altenheim. I was able to visit him, just five days before he died, as it turned out. When I first saw Joe that afternoon, I thought he seemed remarkably well, but after a little while I realized he was suffering from, among other things, a great deal of dementia. I stayed about two hours, but all during the time, Joe couldn't effectively talk or make sense, though I would occasionally say something to see if I could engage him. As I was about to leave I saw a photo album there and I looked through it (there were only a few photos) but one photo was surprising: Joe standing with Dick, Charlie, and Ken Himes at a reception, smiling, each holding his own drink. I said, "Joe, here's a picture of you, Dick, Ken, and Charlie." Joe's face lit up, and clear as a bell, he asked, "How's Charlie?" And he happily waited to hear what I had to say.

Making the moral life familiar, whether as it is in the Church, in its tradition in its theology, or as it's lived out, strikes me as the task of all theological ethicists, but Charlie has embodied that moral life, making it familiar.

James Keenan, SJ
Boston College

Preface

This book is volume 20 in the series of Readings in Moral Theology published by Paulist Press. This volume follows the approach of the earlier volumes by bringing together previously published academic essays. However, the subject matter of this volume is somewhat different from the previous volumes because it deals with my story of sixty years of moral theology.

The primary difficulty has been selecting the essays for this volume in light of all that I have written. As a result, the volume does not deal with any of the particular issues in moral theology in the areas of social, political, sexual, or bioethics. The volume deals with issues that are associated with fundamental moral theology and methodology.

I have frequently written about the history of moral theology, both in its broader Catholic perspective and in the United States. Unfortunately, this volume does not have room for any in-depth historical studies, but such historical research is very important both in itself and for what it tells us about moral theology today. History shows us, for example, that there has been no such thing as a coherent, consistent theory of natural law with an agreed-upon body of content existing throughout time. The current volume emphasizes the significant role that Vatican II had in calling for a different methodological approach and orientation in moral theology and replacing the manuals of moral theology that had been in existence for centuries. In an earlier study of U.S. moral theology at the turn of the twentieth century, I showed how there was a short flicker of intellectual creativity in moral theology in which Thomas Bouquillon of Catholic University strongly opposed the manuals of moral theology on the basis of his Thomistic approach. Likewise, John Baptist Hogan, a Sulpician priest associated with St. Mary's Seminary in Baltimore and St. John's Seminary in Boston, strongly criticized the manuals in light of his more inductive and historically conscious approach.[1] However, this brief flicker of intellectual creativity in moral theology and across the board in Catholic thought and theology was snuffed out by the strong antimodernist reaction after 1907 and the ultramontanist emphasis on the centrality of the Church under the Roman pontiff.

This volume is constructed chronologically beginning with the two events of the 1960s—Vatican II and *Humanae vitae*—that had significant effects on the development of moral theology down to the present. The reader should be attentive to the years in which these chapters were first published. I have resisted the temptation to change or eliminate any aspects that I understand differently today. I have occasionally deleted repetitious material, but in a volume such as this some repetition is unavoidable. Also, I have changed the exclusive language in the earlier writings.

The manuscript is divided into three parts—"Vatican II and Its Aftermath"; "*Humanae Vitae* and Its Aftermath"; and "The Ensuing Years." Each part begins with an "Introduction and Context" section, which deals with the context in which the material covered in the part unfolded and my personal involvements. Each of the three parts ends with a section on "Subsequent Developments" that brings the material up to date. These comments provide a more unified narrative, shaping how the thirteen chapters develop the reality of my story of sixty years of moral theology.

This will be the last volume in the series of Readings in Moral Theology. After sixty years working in the field of moral theology, my days are numbered—and the number is not large! In addition, the growth of moral theology as described in this volume shows why this series is not as significant and important today as it was when the first volume was published in 1978. The early volumes helped acquaint the new and growing number of professors of moral theology with the recent developments in the discipline. Some of the larger volumes (e.g., the six-hundred-page volume 8 on Catholic sexual ethics) were able to put between two covers the most important recent writings on a particular subject. The many citations of these volumes in the academic literature testify to how significant they were. As time went on, however, the number of moral theologians and the writings in moral theology grew exponentially. In this context, there was no longer as much need for this series. The more recent volumes did not sell as well as the earlier ones, but Paulist Press was still willing to subsidize what they saw as an important contribution to Catholic theology.

I am most grateful to Paulist Press for their strong support of this series. The first piece I ever published in moral theology was the pamphlet "Morality and the Love of God" in 1962, which was a part of the Paulist Doctrinal Pamphlet Series. Each pamphlet sold for fifteen cents. One of my friends claimed my pamphlet was not worth the price! This series showed the serious effort of Paulist Press to make Catholics aware of recent developments in theology even before the first session of Vatican II. In the late 1970s, Dick McCormick and I met with Kevin Lynch, CSP, the president of Paulist Press, and out of these conversations came the idea for Readings in Moral Theology. Subsequent presidents of the press, down to Mark-David Janus, CSP, the present president, have continued to strongly support the series. Paulist Press sees this series as a way to contribute to the important role of theology in the Church. The staff of the Press, especially including Donna Crilly, the editor of the present volume, have been both helpful and efficient in the publication of the twenty volumes in this series.

This series would never have existed without the work of my closest colleague and friend, Richard A. McCormick. Dick and I collaborated on the first eleven volumes until his death in 2000. Dick's good friend, Leslie Griffin, and I coedited volume 12 in honor of Dick. I then edited a few volumes myself before coediting a volume on marriage with Julie Hanlon Rubio. The last four volumes I have had the privilege of coediting with Lisa Fullam, who is both a former student and friend.

Finally, I publicly express my gratitude to Southern Methodist University, which has provided me a congenial and challenging academic environment with many good colleagues for the last thirty years. I am privileged to hold the Elizabeth Scurlock University Chair of Human Values, generously endowed by Jack S. and Laura Lee Blanton in honor of her mother. Laura Lee Blanton passed away some years ago, but her memory lives on at SMU thanks to the many benefactions of the Blanton family. The Bridwell Library and its accomplished and friendly librarians continue to facilitate my research. My most immediate cooperator is my associate, Lisa Hancock, who, with the "help" of her infant son Angus, skillfully prepared this manuscript for publication and assisted me in many ways with her efficient and friendly help.

Notes

1. Charles E. Curran, *The Origins of Moral Theology in the United States* (Washington, DC: Georgetown University Press, 1997), 210–95.

Acknowledgments

I am grateful to all the publishers who have made my writings available over the years. A special word of thanks goes to Fides Publishers of Notre Dame, which no longer exists but published the first two chapters in this volume and was my first publisher.

In addition, from the legal perspective, I am grateful to the following publishers who have the copyrights for my work published in this volume:

Curran, *Themes in Fundamental Moral Theology* (Notre Dame, IN: University of Notre Dame Press, 1977), 202–32. ©1977 by the University of Notre Dame. Reprinted with permission.

Curran, *Catholic Moral Theology in the United States: A History* (Washington, DC: Georgetown University Press, 2008), 106–24. ©2008 by Georgetown University Press. Reprinted with permission. www .press.georgetown.edu.

Curran, *Tensions in Moral Theology* (Notre Dame, IN: University of Notre Dame Press, 1988), 87–109. ©1988 by The University of Notre Dame. Reprinted with permission.

Curran, *American Catholic Moral Theology* (Notre Dame, IN: University of Notre Dame Press, 1987), 20–42. ©1987 by the University of Notre Dame. Reprinted with permission.

Curran, *Moral Theology: A Continuing Journey* (Notre Dame, IN: University of Notre Dame Press, 1982), 35–61. ©1982 by the University of Notre Dame. Reprinted with permission.

Curran, *Tradition and Church Reform* (Maryknoll, NY: Orbis Books, 2016), 261–80. ©2016 Orbis Books. Republished with permission.

Curran, *Diverse Voices in U.S. Moral Theology* (Washington, DC: Georgetown University Press, 2018), 249–52. ©2018 by Georgetown University Press. Reprinted with permission. www.press .georgetown.edu.

Curran, "Methodological Approaches in Dealing with Particular Social Issues," in *Building Bridges in Sarajevo: The Plenary Papers from CTEWC 2018*, ed. Kristin E. Heyer, James F. Keenan, and Andrea Vicini (Maryknoll, NY: Orbis Books, 2019). © 2019 Orbis Books. Republished with permission.

Part One

VATICAN II AND ITS AFTERMATH

Introduction and Context

The Second Vatican Council (Vatican II) from 1962 to 1965 was the most important reality in the life of the Catholic Church in hundreds of years. It did not change any core teaching, but Vatican II had a dramatic effect on Catholic life and thought. Think of the one example of liturgy. The language of worship changed from Latin to the vernacular. The presider (formerly called the celebrant) now faced the people and no longer had his back to them. A much greater importance was given to the Scriptures in the Liturgy of the Word. Vatican II recognized many different presences of the risen Jesus in the liturgy and not just at the moment of consecration.

Part 1 will discuss the role of Vatican II with regard to moral theology. However, something should first be said about my relation to Vatican II. In 1955, I was sent as a seminarian of the diocese of Rochester, New York, to study four years of theology at the North American College in Rome, taking classes at the Jesuit Gregorian University. My bishop then told me I was to stay in Rome to obtain a doctorate in moral theology in order to teach that discipline at St. Bernard's Seminary, the major seminary of the diocese of Rochester. I obtained my doctorate at the Gregorian, but the Gregorian required, in addition to the dissertation, only five courses after the licentiate, which I had received in 1959. While still in the seminary in Rome, I read the Italian translation of the first volume of Bernard Häring's *The Law of Christ*, originally written in German in 1954. Here was a new approach to moral theology geared to living the Christian life and not just preparing confessors as judges in the sacrament of penance. I discovered Häring was then teaching at the Redemptorist Alfonsian Academy in Rome with other faculty who also shared the new approach to moral theology. I was very enthusiastic about this biblical, sacramental, and life-centered approach to moral theology.

After receiving another doctorate from the Alfonsian, I started teaching the three-year cycle of moral theology at St. Bernard's Seminary in 1961. The assigned text was the Latin manual of the Austrian

Jesuit Hieronymus Noldin. I began each year with long introductions and handed out notes for the students developing the newer approach to moral theology. Teaching this new approach was exhilarating; most of the students readily accepted it, but some resisted. In my first year of teaching, Paulist Press asked me to contribute a pamphlet on morality and the love of God to their Doctrinal Pamphlet Series. This series of thirty-seven titles published even before Vatican II was the fruit of some very recent developments in biblical, liturgical, historical, and theological writings. In my teaching at St. Bernard's until 1965, I enthusiastically followed the council and incorporated its newer approaches into my classes. The diocesan authorities were upset with some of my teaching and decided I could no longer teach in the seminary. But they gave me permission to accept an earlier offer to teach at the Catholic University of America beginning in September 1965.

Chapter 1 in this section on "Vatican II and Its Aftermath" discusses the approach of Vatican II in comparison with the manuals of moral theology. The first two key issues mentioned in this chapter refer to an emphasis on Scripture and the role of conscience. This essay was the introduction in my first book, *Christian Morality Today: The Renewal of Moral Theology*, published by Fides Publishers of Notre Dame in 1966. The book was a collection of loosely connected essays brought together by illustrations of the new approach to Vatican II, but it went through six printings and a smaller Dome edition in five years. The book was obviously picked up by college teachers, because there was nothing else available dealing with the renewal of Vatican II and its influence on moral theology. This volume sold more than any other book I have written since, though as one of my friends reminded me, it was a nonbook—just a collection of essays.

Chapter 2 in this volume takes up the importance of Scripture by considering the relevancy of the ethical teaching of Jesus in the Christian moral life. This essay was first published in 1967 and became the first chapter in *A New Look at Christian Morality* (Notre Dame, IN: Fides Publishers, 1968). This book was another series of recently published essays.

Chapter 3 deals with conscience. In 1963, Harvard University staged the largest academic ecumenical gathering ever held in the United States. Despite my youth and inexperience, they asked me to give a paper on conscience from the Catholic perspective. With fear and trembling, I delivered this paper to my older and more learned peers on my twenty-ninth birthday. The organizers of the conference at Harvard could find no other Catholic moral theologian who was well acquainted with the repercussions of the newer approach to moral theology. However, for this volume, I have chosen a later, more academic and in-depth discussion of conscience originally published in *Themes in Moral Theology*, a somewhat more unified collection of essays published by the University of Notre Dame Press in 1977.

1. Vatican II and Moral Theology

This chapter was published in my *Christian Morality Today* (Notre Dame, IN: Fides, 1966), 1–12.

Vatican II has issued no decree or constitution on moral theology. Yet the aggiornamento that has characterized the ecumenical council must also renew the science of moral theology. For the most part the present textbooks and manuals of moral theology have now become obsolete—not because they are in error, but because they are not in keeping with the whole spirit of renewal in the Church today. The council has not left us a blueprint for the future textbooks of moral theology, but the spirit of the Vatican Council has established the broad outlines for the further development of moral theology.

THE ORIENTATION OF MORAL THEOLOGY

For the most part, the textbooks of moral theology have pursued the rather limited aim of training confessors; and even then, the textbooks pay little attention to the role of the confessor as father, teacher, and physician. In our contemporary situation, should moral theology have the rather narrow scope of merely training confessors as judges? Whatever the reason might be, most of our people today know what is sinful; and in confession they are looking more for the consolation and advice they need to live better their daily lives as Christians. Even with regard to the narrow purposes of training confessors as judges, the textbooks no longer fulfill their intended function. The real problems for the confessor concern the existence of subjective sin in the particular penitent here and now. Very frequently the confessor can only leave the matter in the merciful hands of God. Contemporary critics, however, should not totally condemn the existing manuals of moral theology. The origin of our present textbooks represents a marvelous aggiornamento, a true accommodation to the needs and spirit of a given time. The renewal of the Christian life and the sacrament of penance in the sixteenth century after the Council of Trent called for priests to be trained as confessors. The *Institutiones Morales*, the forerunners of our present textbooks, represented a successful crash program for the training of confessors. But the same needs and historical circumstances do not exist today.

Moral theology, with such a narrow scope, necessarily concentrated on the minimal, the dividing line between mortal and venial sin. Even such negative considerations reflected the humane and benign attitude of not imposing on Christians anything more than was required. Despite a clumsy and very juridical approach, the older moralists tried to safeguard the freedom of the children of God. Moral theology also reflected the defensive and protective attitude that characterized Catholic life for the last few centuries—the ghetto mentality. If reference is made to the world in any moral treatises, the reference often occurs solely under the heading of "occasions of sin." The good Catholic tried to defend and protect one's faith against the incursions of the world. Catholic thought created a false dichotomy between matter and spirit, body and soul, which is completely foreign to biblical thought. Catholic spirituality implied that Christians recharged their spiritual life through the performance of certain spiritual exercises, but in daily contact with the world, one's spiritual battery wore down. If life in the world was not incompatible with holiness and perfection, at least living in the world was not the perfect or better way of serving God. In such a light one can easily see how the gulf developed between the spiritual life of the Christian and daily existence in our society and world. Emphasis was placed on certain actions (e.g., Friday abstinence) and practices (e.g., novenas, candles) that soon became irrelevant for many people precisely because they bore no real meaning for daily life.

A legalistic and rationalistic attitude, combined with a defensive posture, saw Christian morality in the light of a conformity with pre-existing laws and structures. Every action involved the fear of sin and going against the established order. The passive virtues of loyalty, docility, and obedience became the great Christian attitudes. The closed concept of morality looked down on everything new as suspect and a threat to the existing structures. Perhaps some of the above remarks are overly severe, but such attitudes definitely colored the orientation of moral theology.

The spirit of Vatican II and the needs of our own time must influence the orientation of moral theology today. A life-centered moral theology should replace the confessional-oriented approach of the older textbooks. The Constitution on the Church in chapter 5 boldly proclaims the universal vocation of all Christians to holiness. "Thus it is evident to everyone that all the faithful of Christ of whatever rank or status are called to the fullness of the Christian life and to the perfection of charity" (§40). Moral theology needs to show how the Christian pursues the vocation to holiness in the modern world.

The attitude of moral theology can no longer be minimal and defensive. The Constitution on the Church in the Modern World acknowledges, "The split between the faith which many profess and their daily lives deserves to be counted among the more serious errors of our age" (§43). The Christian life implies a service to humanity and the world— "that we may build a better world based on truth and justice." The council clearly indicates that the moral and spiritual life of the Christian in the world requires a working for the cultural, economic, social, and political good of humanity. The Christian vocation in the world calls for the elimination of all human misery, which is incompatible with the dignity of the human person so frequently mentioned in conciliar documents. The Decree on the Apostolate of the Laity develops the key theme that "the Christian vocation by its very nature is also a vocation to the apostolate" (§2). The Second Vatican Council has sounded the death knell for a moral theology that is primarily confession oriented, minimalistic, and individualistic.

Likewise, moral theology can no longer emphasize conformity to rigid and static laws as if everything were completely spelled out in pre-existing norms. The council insists that the Christian continue the creative and redemptive work of God in the world. The Christian life receives its dynamism from a sharing in the mission and role of Christ: "Clearly then a great promise and a great trust is committed to the disciples: 'All things are yours, and you are Christ's and Christ is God's' (1 Cor 3:23)" (Constitution on the Church 36). The final exhortation in the Decree on the Apostolate of the Laity reads,

> The most holy council then earnestly entreats all the laity
> in the Lord to answer gladly, nobly, and promptly the more
> urgent invitation of Christ...to associate themselves with
> him in his saving mission. Once again he sends them into
> every town and place where he will come so that they may
> show that they are co-workers in the various forms and
> modes of the one apostolate of the Church, which must be
> constantly adapted to the new needs of our times.

The Christian mission and apostolate reflect the dynamic continuing
mission of Christ and remain always open to approaches and structures
that are more adapted to the changing circumstances of our times.

Growth and dynamism characterize not only the Christian mission but the Christian life itself. The call of all to perfection means that
the Christian life is a continual conversion. The conciliar documents
frequently mention the pilgrim Church, but what is said of the Church
also applies to the individual Christian. The Christian continues to grow
closer to that perfect union with God and neighbor that will be achieved
only in the future. Since growth and dynamism characterize both the life
and the mission of the Christian, creativity and not conformity needs to
receive more emphasis. The Christian frequently must assume the risk of
action and growth. Mere passivity or even conformity betrays the meaning of the Christian life. Contemporary moral theology should remind
Christians of the parable of the master who left a sum of money for his
servants. The master richly rewarded the servants who used the money to
make more money, but the master severely condemned the servant who
took the money and buried it in a field because he was afraid of losing it.

KEY EMPHASES IN MORAL THEOLOGY

Sacred Scripture

The Second Vatican Council has tried to renew the central place of
the Scriptures in the life and theology of the Church. Unfortunately, the
present textbooks do not derive their format and inspiration from the
word of God. In treating particular moral questions, the existing textbooks

generally follow a systematization either according to the cardinal and moral virtues or according to the Ten Commandments. The cardinal virtues are not Christian in origin, nor do they represent the more important Christian attitudes. For example, the Scriptures place great stress on humility as the virtue of the poor of God and the necessary disposition to receive the saving love of God; but one very commonly used textbook disposes of humility in one short paragraph. Also the Ten Commandments, especially when wrenched out of the covenant context, do not reflect the meaning of the new life that Christ has brought to us. From the point of view of teaching ethical conduct, the Boy Scout Oath might be better, for the Scout Oath at least uses a positive formulation. Likewise, the considerations of fundamental moral theology or *De Principiis* do not mirror the scriptural approach to the meaning of the Christian life.

The Constitution on Divine Revelation shows the primacy of the gospel as "the source of all saving truth and moral teaching" (§7).

> Sacred theology rests on the written Word of God, together with sacred tradition, as its primary and perpetual foundation. By scrutinizing in the light of faith all truths stored up in the mystery of Christ, theology is most powerfully strengthened and constantly rejuvenated by that word. For the Sacred Scriptures contain the Word of God and, since they are inspired, really are the Word of God; and so the study of the sacred page is, as it were, the soul of sacred theology. (§24)

To think that an exclusively biblical approach would solve all the problems confronting moral theology is a gross oversimplification; but moral theology should receive its inspiration, format, and content primarily from the word of God.

Conscience

Moral theology can no longer be considered especially in the light of conformity of conduct with external norms or laws. In many ways the council teaches that we must find the reason for our moral activity in the depths of our own person, in our conscience. The moral life of the Christian consists in the development of one's own Christian personality. The Declaration on Christian Education states, "For a true education aims at the formation of the human person....This sacred synod likewise declares that children and young people have a right to be motivated to appraise moral values with a right conscience, to embrace them with a personal adherence, together with a deeper knowledge and love of God" (§1).

The Declaration on Religious Liberty teaches that we must respond to the call of God in the depths of our own person. The council does not intend to deny any objectivity, but rather the very objectivity of the human person demands that one freely respond to the call of God in the depths of one's own person. The moral life of the Christian, or any human being, springs from the inner core of personality. The Church never will and never can deny its teaching mission, but the Church's moral teaching always proposes what is the true development and growth of the Christian person. Because we are Christians, we must act in such a manner.

Holy Spirit

Above all, the council has underlined the role of the Holy Spirit as the source of all life and renewal in the Church. The Spirit sanctifies the Church and guides it through the hierarchical and charismatic gifts. Through the life-giving Spirit we receive the very life of God. The Spirit dwells in the hearts of the just and there prays for us and bears witness to the fact that we are the children of God (see Constitution on the Church 4). Chapter 5 of the Constitution on the Church declares that the Holy Spirit produces the holiness of the Church and its members. "Indeed he sent the Holy Spirit upon all men that he might move them inwardly to love God with their whole soul, with all their mind and all their strength (Mark 12:30) and that they might love each other as Christ loves them (see John 3:34; 15:12)" (§40). Moral theology should center on the loving dialogue of the Christian with the Holy Spirit, who unites us in love with the Father and with all God's creatures. The Christian must learn to discover and respond to the true inspiration of the Spirit who dwells in our hearts. The Christian life truly is the spiritual life—for the Spirit becomes both the source and the guiding force of the Christian life. The Spirit makes us the adopted children of the Father, and the Spirit teaches and urges us to act as the children of the Father. In many places the conciliar documents stress love as the primary obligation of the Christian. But Paul reminds us that the Spirit pours out the love of Christ into our hearts (Rom 5:5).

Liturgy

The conciliar emphasis on the liturgy likewise indicates that the moral life of the Christian implies the living out of the new life received in the sacramental encounter with the risen Christ in the Church. Authentic Christian actions are those that are developed from the life we as Christians have received. The importance of conscience, the Holy Spirit, and the liturgy in Christian morality shows that morality is intrinsic and not extrinsic; that is, good actions are those that develop from the very being of the person and not just those actions that are in conformity with external norms.

A more intrinsic approach to morality will also avoid the pitfall of dividing the moral life into isolated actions that are seen merely in their relationship to an external law and not to the total personality. For example, preachers and teachers occasionally mention the one mortal sin that will send a person straight to hell no matter how many other good things one has done in life. But mortal sin can never be just one isolated action. Since mortal sin involves the total orientation of the person, the laws of human psychology remind us that we do not ordinarily make such a drastic change by just one isolated action. Rather the change begins to occur gradually in the person through a number of smaller and less important actions. The theologian must view the moral life with all its continuity and not merely as a collection of individual actions that are judged primarily according to extrinsic norms. Yes, individual actions are important, but such actions have a meaning only insofar as they express and at the same time make more profound the fundamental orientation of the person.

Consequently, a true moral formation does not consist primarily in learning certain rules of moral conduct. Moral formation means that the person learns from experience the authentic demands of being a Christian in the present world. Formation attempts to make the individual a more genuine person, for by living a truly Christian existence, the Christian will know what one is being asked to do in daily life.

Community

The documents on the Church, the liturgy, and the Church in the modern world emphasize the communitarian aspect of the Christian life. Heretofore moral considerations have been primarily individualistic—what must I do to save my soul? The main documents of the council remind us of our corporate personality, the people of God, in pilgrimage toward the new heaven and the new earth. All must work together in truth and love to build up the body of Christ and bring all people and all creation into the unity and holiness of God.

FURTHER ATTITUDES

In keeping with the spirit of the council, moral theology must acquire some further attitudes. The theologian too is always trying to listen to the voice of the Spirit. However, moral theologians can never forget that the Spirit also speaks in the lives of Christians and all people of good will. The Declaration on Religious Liberty calls attention to these manifestations of the Spirit. With regard to religious liberty the document says, "This Vatican Council takes careful note of these desires in the minds of men. It proposes to declare them to be greatly in accord with truth and justice. To this end it searches into the sacred tradition and doctrine of the Church—the treasury out of which the Church continually brings forth new things that are in harmony with the things that are old" (§1). The Constitution on the Church also calls attention to the prophetic office in the Church (§12). The theologian must always listen to the Spirit wherever she speaks.

Too often in the past moral theology, on the one hand, has approached the question of conscience and determining what is right or wrong from too cerebral or rationalistic a viewpoint. Scripture, on the other hand, frequently mentions knowledge of God in conjunction with the love of God as part of an authentic experience of God. How does the Church know, how does the individual Christian know what is right or wrong? The revealed word of God and the Holy Spirit guide both the Church and the Christian. The Church as the community of the saved realizes from the lived experience of its members what is in conformity with the demands of Christian living. The term *conscience* indicates that our knowledge also comes from the lived experience of others. Certainly, the Church and the individual Christian must use their reason to find out the good, but the knowledge of good and evil goes far beyond a mere cerebral and rationalistic approach.

The Constitution on the Church in the Modern World acknowledges the complexity of the modern world. The Church and moral theology do not have all the answers to the problems presented by our contemporary society. The council underscores the need for a true dialogue (not just a one-way conversation as if we had all the answers to tell others) with Protestants, non-Christians, and the world itself. In humble cooperation with all people of good will the Church and theology will better learn what God is doing in this world to bring all creation to its fulfillment. Moral theology needs to enter such a dialogue especially with the important sciences of our day (e.g., sociology, psychology, anthropology), which provide so many helpful insights into the meaning of human existence in our world.

Moral theology does not generally treat the question of punishment and hell. However, in the present circumstances perhaps moralists should give more consideration to the way morality is taught on a popular level. Too often teachers instill morality through fear. The Church can never deny or gloss over the teaching on hell, but all things belong in their proper perspective. The Christian life is above all the loving response to the saving love of God in Christ. Christian teaching always proposes the gospel—the good news of salvation. In regard to the future, moral teachers should follow the example of chapter 7 of the Constitution on the Church, the eschatological nature of the pilgrim Church, which so clearly indicates the only true destiny of the Church and the Christian. The Christian is called to that perfect union of love with God and neighbor that will be ours in heaven.

Pope Paul has stressed that aggiornamento does not mean a break with the true tradition of the past (cf. speech of Pope Paul to the Council on Nov. 18, 1965). To discern the true tradition of the Church is one of the huge tasks confronting moral theology. Only exacting and scholarly historical studies can separate the true tradition of the Church from the historical and cultural overtones of a particular period and society. Moral theology in general has been very slow in investigating the historical backgrounds of the teaching of the Church on particular matters. Unfortunately, many primary texts are still unedited. The work of historical research is slow and tedious but absolutely necessary for a true understanding of the traditional teaching of the Church.

Renewal has become a slogan and even a battle cry in the Church today. However, as the pope and the council have constantly reminded us, renewal must begin especially in our own lives as Christians. A renewed or new moral theology aims above all at forming better Christians. No book or manual can ever make us better Christians, but they can serve to make us more aware of the redeeming love of Christ and more open to cooperate in bringing humankind and all creation to their eschatological fulfillment.

2. The Relevancy of the Ethical Teaching of Jesus

This chapter was published in my *A New Look at Christian Morality* (Notre Dame, IN: Fides, 1968), 1–23.

Contemporary theology has shifted its gaze to include heaven and earth, God and God's creatures, the afterlife and the present life. Human existence and its meaning are the primary problems of contemporary theology. The world today is ageric—the modern person is not a contemplator but a doer. Dogma and speculation for its own sake have very little appeal to us today. Within the Catholic Church some are questioning the primacy attributed to liturgy over life itself. Is liturgy not the celebration of life rather than the font and source of all life? Life is the most important reality.

The Christian Church and the individual Christians are reading the signs of the times. Christians need to speak to the actual life today. What does the ethical teaching of Jesus mean for contemporary human existence? But the Church must carefully avoid just talking. Words without deeds are like the Pauline sounding brass or tinkling cymbal. The credibility gap merely widens when the pious mouthings of the Church are contradicted by its own life and actions.

The Christian trying to realize the meaning of human life naturally turns to the ethic of Jesus. The ethical teaching of Jesus is not a detailed blueprint for human activity, but the follower of Jesus at least begins the quest by examining the ethical teaching of the Scriptures. Many speculative problems arise from a consideration of biblical ethics and modern existence. Theology today is discussing secularity, the relationship between the immanent and the transcendent, the connection between human progress and the coming of the kingdom, the meaning of history. An older theology struggled with the problems of nature and grace or

law and gospel. A thorough consideration of all these issues lies beyond
the scope of the present chapter. This essay will merely attempt to indicate the relevancy of the ethic of Jesus for the contemporary Christian.

AN ETHIC OF LOVE

What is the ethical teaching of Jesus? In general, Jesus calls his
followers to live a life in union with God and neighbor. Many theologians summarize the moral teaching of Jesus under the category of love.
The three Synoptic accounts mention the twofold commandment of love
of God and neighbor as the core of the ethical teaching of Jesus (Mark
12:28–34; Matt 22:34–40; Luke 10:25–37).

Why is the twofold love commandment called a new commandment? Love of God and neighbor was central in the teaching of the Old
Testament and in many other religions. One distinctive characteristic of
the love ethic of Jesus is the insistence on an indissoluble interior bond
between the love of God and the love of neighbor. The follower of Jesus
is recognized by love for others. The judgment scene of Matthew 25
indicates that our relationship to God is known and manifested in our
relationships with others. The follower of Jesus cannot claim to love God
and yet neglect the neighbor who is hungry, thirsty, naked, alone, or in
prison. John says very poignantly that one cannot love the God one does
not see if one does not love the neighbor whom she does see (1 John 4:20).
The ethic of Jesus does not eschew life in this world; rather, the authentic
love of God is found in a loving concern for others. The follower of Jesus
can find no excuse (not even worship at the altar) that takes precedence
over loving concern and forgiveness for the neighbor.

A second characteristic of the love ethic of Jesus centers on the
universality attached to the concept of neighbor. To love friends is easy.
To love when one is loved in return requires no self-giving. But the
Christian love for others is modeled on the love of Jesus for us. Jesus
loved us while we were yet sinners. Jesus' love for us did not depend on
what we could give him in return. The love of Jesus is completely dis-
interested and gratuitous in the sense that his love in no way depends on
our loving qualities or our response. Jesus' love is creative, not responsive; giving, not possessing. Who are the privileged recipients of the

love of Jesus? The strong, the influential, the wealthy, the intelligent, the respected? No, the privileged recipients of Jesus' love are the poor, the children, and even sinners. The nonvalue of the recipients of the good news of salvation is a startling fact.

The Christian is called to love just as Jesus has loved. The greatest example of Christian love is love for enemies. The enemy can give the lover nothing in return. In fact, the enemy returns hatred for love. The enemy might react with vengeance and annoyance, but love of enemies remains the great sign of Christian love. Our love for others does not depend on what they can do for us. Since the love of Jesus does not depend on the loving qualities of others, the object of his love is universal. The parable of the Good Samaritan illustrates the universality of neighbor in the love ethic of Jesus. The neighbor is the person who is in need. The priest and the Levite walk by the person in the road; but the Samaritan, a foreigner and enemy, has compassion on the person in need. Love is not just liking but a loving concern for the neighbor in need.

Perhaps the ethical teaching of Jesus as the complete giving of self to God and neighbor cannot be perfectly expressed in any human formula or concept. There are theological difficulties in reducing the ethic of Jesus even to the twofold commandment of love of God and neighbor. The love of the Christian for God and love for the neighbor are not the same kind of love. Love of God is the adoring gratitude of one who has received all from the giver of life. Love of neighbor is a creative giving and a redemptive forgiving that does not depend on the lovable qualities of the other. The two loves are different. The Scriptures seldom speak of our love for God as *agape* precisely because of the difference between God's love for us and our love for God.

Our relationship to neighbor cannot be adequately explained in terms of *agape*—the loving concern that is a total giving independent of the lovable qualities of the other. The human relationship of love does at times require that I love the other precisely because of loving qualities. A human person does want to be loved for what one is. Bishop Pike has criticized Professor Fletcher for reducing the entire Christian ethic to *agape*. There are times when *eros* as a responsive and possessive love or friendship as a mutual love are absolutely essential for human well-being. The theologian should be cautious in thinking that the ethical teaching of Jesus can be reduced to any neat human formulae. H. Richard Niebuhr claims that no human virtue as such can adequately explain the ethical teaching of Jesus.

However, all can agree that the ethical teaching of Jesus calls for the giving of self to God and neighbor. The neighbor in need, according to many biblical passages, has the first claim on the love of the Christian. We must examine this ethical teaching in more detail. The most prolonged statement of the ethical teaching of Jesus is found in the composite arranged in Matthew around the literary form of the Sermon on the Mount (Matt 5—7). Luke brings together much of the ethical teaching of Jesus in his shorter Sermon on the Plain (Luke 6:20–49). Matthew begins the Sermon on the Mount with the Beatitudes. Although Luke employs the Beatitudes in a sapiential perspective and the more primitive form of the Beatitudes was probably a messianic proclamation, Matthew employs the Beatitudes in a catechizing and moralizing way to outline the characteristics that mark the life of the follower of Jesus. Matthew's spiritualization of the Beatitudes (the poor in spirit and the clean of heart) and the peculiar emphasis on justice or righteousness indicate that Matthew is trying to describe the moral life of the follower of Jesus. The Christian is called to be the light of the world and the salt of the earth through love, meekness, mercy, forgiveness, peacemaking, and the pursuit of righteousness.

Matthew then continues to describe the ethical teaching of Jesus as the completion and fullness of the law. Matthew first contrasts (perhaps by way of completion and not antithesis according to W. D. Davies) the ethical teaching of Jesus with that of the scribes, the theologians of the time. The six antitheses or completions of the ethical teaching of Jesus concern anger, chastity, divorce, oaths, forgiveness, and love of enemies. The section ends with a call to be perfect just as our heavenly Father is perfect. The parallel verse in Luke is a call to be merciful or compassionate as our heavenly Father is merciful (Luke 6:36). Matthew begins chapter 6 by comparing the attitude of the Pharisees and the followers of Jesus on the matters of almsgiving, prayer, and fasting. The follower of Jesus is concerned with a true change of heart and not just a rigid external observance. In the final section of the Sermon on the Mount, Matthew outlines other characteristics of the followers of Jesus. Jesus asks for a complete and loving trust in himself, which leads to the abandonment of all other persons and things. Thus the literary device of the

Sermon on the Mount capsulizes the ethical teaching of Jesus as found throughout the New Testament.

EMBARRASSING QUESTIONS

A meditative reflection on the moral teaching of Jesus raises embarrassing questions. Do the Church and the followers of Jesus really put into practice the ethical teaching of their Lord? Can the Church truly say to Jesus, "When you were hungry, thirsty, naked, lonely, abandoned, and in prison, I was there to comfort you"? Does the average person living today see reflected in the life of the Church the ethical teaching of Jesus? Is the primary concern of the Church the neighbor in need or is the Church more interested in preserving and augmenting its image, status, wealth, and power? Is the Church truly credible when it does raise its voice on particular issues, since so often there is only loud silence on other problems involving the neighbor in need? Has the Church left all to follow Jesus or is it trying to serve two masters? When the hierarchical Church does speak on a particular issue, how often are the words accompanied by appropriate actions even to the giving away of earthly power and possessions? Does the Church really take seriously the ethical teaching of Jesus?

However, one cannot merely point an accusing finger at the Church. How about myself as a Christian? Am I really willing to give all that I possess for my neighbor in need? Am I really willing to forgive my enemies the same way that Jesus did? How difficult it remains to speak well of those who have hurt me in the past. Am I always willing to turn the other cheek or to walk an extra mile? How often do I really go out of my way to help others?

There exists an even more embarrassing question: Can anyone be expected to live the ethical teaching of Jesus? At first glance, all are compelled to admit the beauty and sublimity of the ethical teaching of Jesus. But the moral demands of Jesus are radical and seemingly impossible. The disciple of Jesus leaves all things to follow the master. Luke, who is the evangelist of total renouncement, even goes so far as to call for hatred of father and mother, brother and sister (Luke 15:26–33). Can anyone truly live the ethical teaching of Jesus?

The ethic of Jesus seems totally unreal when applied to the particular problems that so often arise in our lives. How can a Christian not worry about what one is going to eat or drink? What minister of God's word would ever say to an improvident father that he should not worry about food, clothing, and shelter for his family? Can a wife forgive her husband and welcome him with open arms if he constantly beats her and the children? Can I as a Christian stand by and turn the other cheek when other innocent people (e.g., young children) are being attacked? How practical is it not to resist the evildoer? Who can possibly give to everyone who asks? Is the gospel injunction of turning the other cheek an apt solution to the complicated problems of American involvement in Vietnam? In all wars?

Even the Church does not follow the ethical demands of Jesus. Just after speaking about divorce, Matthew reminds the followers of Jesus never to take any oaths but to restrict their speech to yes and no (Matt 5:33–37). However, the Roman Catholic Church has insisted on a number of oaths that must be taken by priests and teachers. Even on such a practical matter as judicial processes and matrimonial courts, Church procedure is practically never willing to accept the word of the Christian. The ethic of Jesus might be sublime and beautiful, but the teaching of Jesus seems impossible and irrelevant for the daily life of Christians.

Proposed Solutions

Conscientious Christians have constantly grappled with the problems created by the ethical teaching of Jesus. A true follower of Jesus cannot dismiss his whole ethical teaching as irrelevant and meaningless for daily human existence. Some explain the difficulty connected with the moral teaching of Jesus as arising from the fondness for imagery and exaggeration, which is associated with the Oriental mentality. The beam in one's eye, the camel and the eye of the needle, forgiveness seventy times seven times, all these expressions embody overstatement and exaggeration. Undoubtedly Jesus reflected the thought patterns of his own culture, but can the entire moral teaching of Jesus be satisfactorily explained in terms of Oriental exaggeration?

Within a Lutheran tradition some want to interpret the Sermon on the Mount as *Moyses Moysissimus*—the Law of Moses in the nth degree. The important function of law is to bring us to acknowledge our own weakness and sinfulness. The Mosaic Law brought believers to Christ not by continuous development, but through discontinuity. The Law makes us aware that we find salvation not in the works of the Law but only through faith in Christ Jesus. The radical and impossible demands of the Sermon on the Mount only intensify the function of law that brings us to realize our sinfulness and need of redemption through faith in Christ. Although such a solution can serve as a partial explanation of the problem, the *Moyses Moysissimus* solution does not really take seriously the ethical teaching of Jesus.

A few have tried to take literally the ethical teaching of Jesus as universal norms for moral conduct that are always and everywhere binding. Such biblical fundamentalism quickly clashes with the problems of everyday human existence. Common sense and experience remind us that we cannot accept the ethical teachings of Jesus as laws of conduct that are always obliging in our circumstances.

The Catholic theological tradition has generally ignored the problem created by the radical ethical demands of Jesus. At least on a popular level, Catholic teaching maintained that only a few people were called to perfection. Such people followed the evangelical counsels and generally entered the religious life. The vast majority of Christians living in the world were content with just observing the commandments that are binding on all. Catholic theology thus ignored the problem created by the radical moral teaching of Jesus. However, the consequences of ignoring the problem have been evident in Catholic life and practice. Only with Vatican II does popular Catholic teaching stress the universal vocation of all Christians to perfection. Catholic theology has not developed a theology and spirituality for life in the world because people outside the religious life were content with just obeying the commandments.

Many serious attempts to come to grips with the radical ethical teaching of Jesus hinge on the question of eschatology. Interestingly, contemporary theologians are also calling for a renewed eschatology. The eschatological views see the ethic of Jesus in connection with his mission in proclaiming the reign of God. The ethic of Jesus is above all a religious ethic, intimately connected with the reign that Jesus proclaimed. The reign of God calls for a complete and radical response from the hearer.

Albert Schweitzer well represents the school that labeled the moral teaching of Jesus an "interim ethic." In reacting against liberal Protestantism, Schweitzer stressed the eschatological dimension of Jesus' mission. Jesus expected the kingdom of God to come even before his disciples returned from their first missionary journey. When the kingdom did not come, Jesus went up to Jerusalem to precipitate the coming of the kingdom by his death. The strenuous ethic proposed by Jesus was for the very short interim that would precede the final coming of the kingdom. The ethical teaching of Jesus cannot be lived and sustained over a long period of time. Jesus' ethic is intimately connected with his own mistaken eschatology. Today, most theologians have rejected the opinion proposed by Schweitzer. The reign of God is not all future; to some extent the kingdom of God in Christ is already present and working in the world. Even many who maintain that Jesus believed in a very quick coming of the final stage of the reign of God do not think that Jesus would have preached a different ethic even if he had realized that the final stage of the kingdom would not arrive for a long period of time.

Perhaps the ethic of Jesus was meant only to describe life in the final stage of the reign of God and has no practical meaning for life here and now. Jesus did not propose a moral teaching for life in this world but was merely describing the life in the final coming of the reign of God. Again there is some truth in such an assertion, but the follower of Jesus cannot conclude that the ethical teaching of the master is completely irrelevant for Christians living in the world of today. Even the conflict and troubling situations described by Jesus seem much more applicable to the situation of our own daily lives than to the description of some future state of blessedness.

Eschatological Tension

The ethic of Jesus is closely aligned with his mission in proclaiming the reign of God. The final stage of the reign of God is coming. The reign is already begun but is now hastening toward its conclusion. The eschatological dimension at least adds a sense of urgency to some of the ethical teachings of Jesus (e.g., anger, lust). But there is also a content to the ethic of Jesus that is influenced by the presence and impending fulfillment of the reign of God. The ethical teaching of Jesus is a constant reminder of the absolute claim that the presence of the reign of God makes on the follower of Jesus. Jesus does not propose universal norms of conduct that are obliging for all Christians under all circumstances. Rather, in a very graphic way Jesus pictures the disciple before the call of the reign of God's love. The reign of God places an all-engaging claim upon the hearer. Nothing else matters or counts when compared to the reign of God proclaimed and inaugurated by Jesus. Many of the ethical sayings of Jesus confront the individual with the inexorable claim of the presence of God's call. Jesus' graphic descriptions prescind from all other circumstances that might enter the picture. The neighbor in need and the follower of Jesus are placed face-to-face in a dramatic fashion.

The complexity of human problems is cast aside. Jesus prescinds from all other circumstances and conditions while showing the claim of the reign of God and the neighbor in need upon the individual follower. No mention is made of the binding obligations that a woman might have to her husband or family. Jesus prescinds from all such realities and simply shows in a very stark and dramatic way the radical claim of the reign of God and the needs of the neighbor upon his followers. The Christian, like Jesus himself, should be willing to sacrifice all for others. One can understand better the sayings about turning the other cheek, walking the extra mile, giving to everyone who asks, imitating the lilies of the field, hating father and mother, plucking out an eye or cutting off a hand that would separate the believer from God, as illustrative of the radical demands of the presence of the reign of God.

The gift of the reign of God puts an unconditional claim on the believer. But what does such a simplistic view of reality mean for the follower of Jesus who lives amid the complexity of modern human existence? Very often the Christian is confronted by many people in need. The Christian has manifold responsibilities that are always on the horizon. Can a Christian so give self and time to the neighbor in need and forget familial obligations? What value is the simplistic evangelical description of the dramatic confrontation between an individual and the call of the kingdom or the neighbor in need?

The radical and seemingly impossible ethical teaching of Jesus is more than rhetoric. Jesus indicates the goal and direction that should characterize the life and actions of his followers. "Give to everyone who asks" is an impossible ethical imperative, but such a demand indicates the constant thrust that characterizes the life of the Christian. I cannot claim everything I have as my own and dispose of it in any way I want. The Christian realizes that one's talents, treasure, and abilities are in the service of the kingdom and the neighbor in need. There are times when the follower of Jesus might not be able to turn the other cheek; but the model of patience and forbearance, coupled with mercy and not vengeance, always remains meaningful. Occasionally the Christian might deem violence necessary to protect innocent human life (e.g., a young child being attacked by a demented person), but the thrust of the radical teaching of Jesus can never be forgotten.

Eschatological considerations introduce an inevitable tension into Christian ethics. The tension results from the fact that the reign of God in Christ is now present and is going forward toward its fullness. We are living in the times in between the two comings of Jesus. The reign of God is present but not yet fully present. The incipient presence of the eschaton calls for a continual growth and development. The followers of Jesus can never rest content with the present. The eschatological future is to some extent now present and urging the Christian forward. The true follower of the New Law can never say, "All these I have kept from my youth." The ethical teaching of Jesus calls for a continual effort to overcome the obstacles and shortcomings of the present moment.

Deficiencies in the Past

Unfortunately, the recent Catholic tradition has forgotten the eschatological tension both in the life of the individual and in the life of the Church. Theology did not insist upon the radical teachings of Jesus. In popular teaching the Christian ethical demands were reduced to a comparatively few, negative, universal norms that were to be observed by all. Such norms not only gave a negative tone to the Christian life, but comparatively easy norms of conduct robbed the Christian life of its inherent dynamism. The Christian could be content with having observed a comparatively few norms of morality. The Christian found a false sense of security in such norms and occasionally succumbed to a pharisaical attitude. On a wider scale the Church itself suffered from the same defect. The charge of triumphalism rang true in the conciliar hall of Vatican II. The Church forgot its pilgrim status and lost the dynamic thrust of continual growth and conversion. The radical ethical teaching of Jesus prevents either his Church or his followers from ever remaining content and smug in the present stage of life.

Specifically in the area of moral theology, Catholic teaching has tried to avoid the tension created by the ethics of Jesus. As a result, Catholic theology very frequently has lost the eschatological dimension of growth; or, less frequently, has required of all a goal that was not always attainable. The loss of the dynamic thrust in moral theology can be seen in the teaching on the right to life. Catholic theologians have not been in the forefront of those who were arguing for the abolition of capital punishment, the suspension of nuclear testing, the cessation of war. Why not? Catholic teaching over the years developed a very intricate system or theory for dealing with problems of life and death. *Direct* killing of the innocent is never permitted; but the state has the right to kill malefactors, and individuals may kill others indirectly or in self-defense. However, such a norm, considered only in itself, lacks the dynamic thrust in favor of human life that should always characterize the Christian life. The principles governing the questions of life and death solve complex problems too easily. The follower of Jesus can never be content when forced to take a life. Every taking of life is a falling short of the radical ethic of Jesus. Perhaps at times it is necessary to take human life; but a Christian can take life with only the greatest remorse and reluctance.

Likewise in the question of war, theologians tend to dismiss too easily the deaths of thousands of people because they are only "indirect" killings. There may be times when the follower of Jesus must act according to the principles of indirect killing, but the Christian can never lose sight of the thrust imposed by the radical ethic of Jesus. Personally, I cannot be a total pacifist in the sense that at times resorting to violence might be necessary to defend innocent people. However, the follower of Jesus always strives in the direction of pacifism. When killing is deemed necessary it can only be as a reluctant accommodation to the needs of the present time.

In many other areas Catholic theology has too easily accommodated itself to the present moment and forgotten the radical ethical demands of Jesus. Problems of slavery and race immediately come to mind. The Church and the theologians too easily acquiesced to predominant social patterns and structures. The Church cannot be altogether proud of its historical record on behalf of the freedom and dignity of the human person. Theologians and Church leaders have also been absent from leadership in the fight for the equality of women. The institutional Church seems to have perpetuated a system of colonization rather than fighting for the rights of people to govern themselves. In the ninth century, Pope Nicholas I condemned physical constraint and torture; but a few centuries later, the Church used torture and violence to further its own dubious goals. Papal teaching on justice and the rights of workers is a comparatively bright chapter in the history of the Church. But history also reminds us that Karl Marx recognized the problem almost half a century before Leo XIII wrote his encyclicals.

The followers of Jesus and his Church can never forget the radical ethical teaching of the Master. However, the imperfections and sinfulness that characterize the present times will mean that the Christian often falls far short of the goal described by Jesus. Accommodation to the present reality is a necessity at times. But the absolute claim of the reign of God and the needs of our neighbor never allow the Christian to be content when it is necessary to fall short of the radical moral teaching of Jesus. The Christian always possesses an uneasy conscience. Compromise and adaptation to present needs can only be accepted reluctantly. Catholic theology has too often forgotten the uneasy conscience of the Christian in confronting the imperfect and sinful situations of the present time. Jesus calls his followers to be the light of the world and the salt of the earth.

IDEAL AND ACCOMMODATION

On the other side of the paradox, there are times when the universal norms in Catholic theology do not sufficiently take into consideration the reluctant but necessary possibility of not fully accomplishing the moral demand of Jesus. Perhaps the universal norm absolutizes what is a radical demand of Jesus that is not always achievable. The biblical teaching on divorce may be an example. (Naturally one cannot settle the teaching of the Catholic Church on divorce merely from biblical evidence, but the solution proposed according to the biblical understanding may very well be applicable to the present understanding of divorce in the Church.) In the Sermon on the Mount in Matthew the two verses on divorce follow the radical maxim of plucking out an eye or cutting off a hand if the eye or the hand lead one astray. The divorce passage is followed by the saying of Jesus that his true followers will never take any oaths but will be content to make their speech a plain yes or no. In Matthew 19 the matter of divorce is approached in the context of the two opposing opinions existing among the rabbis. Jesus definitely upholds the indissolubility of marriage. Jesus explains the permission given by Moses in the Old Testament on the grounds of the hardness of the heart of the people. However, there is in Matthew 19:9 the puzzling exception clause ("except for unchastity"—*porneia*), which also appears in Matthew 5:32.

Within the New Testament times there are accommodations in the teaching of absolute indissolubility. The famous Pauline privilege represents a falling short of the ideal proposed by Jesus. Paul, according to some exegetes, allowed converts to the faith to marry a new wife if their heathen wife wanted a separation (1 Cor 7:12–16). Exegetes have developed many different theories for the famous incisions in the Gospel of Matthew. Although Scripture scholars disagree on the exact meaning of such exceptions, many would agree that the exceptions were probably added to the primitive statements by the early Church. The exceptions may well represent some type of accommodation within the early Church to the radical ethical demands of Jesus. The accommodations made in New Testament times, whatever they may have been, are not the only possible accommodations that the Church and Christians might have to make in the course of time.

The radical ethic of Jesus, although seemingly impossible, is relevant precisely because the presence of the reign of God tending toward its eschatological fulfillment places an absolute claim upon the follower of Jesus. Even when the Christian must fall short of the radical demand of Jesus, one cannot rest content with the accommodation to the needs and imperfections of present reality. The dangers in any ethic of pure accommodation are manifold. The collaboration of citizens with the war aims and activities of their governments is perhaps the most painful and obvious example for the modern Christian. The conscience of the Christian can never rest content with any type of accommodation, but always seeks new ways to pursue the direction and goal pointed out in the radical ethics of

Jesus. The ethic of Jesus for the contemporary Christian involves a creative tension between the present and the final stage of the reign of God.

Unfortunately, we find such tension difficult to live with. Some eliminate the tension by forgetting about the future and the continual call to growth and development. Others overthrow the tension by naively forgetting the present reality. Until very recently Catholic theology and life dissolved the tension and the frustration by forgetting about the radical ethics of Jesus and the consequent call for continual growth and even revolution. Absolute norms capable of being observed to the letter provided us with a false sense of security. Catholics acted as if they had all the answers to the problems confronting humankind. The certitude and the security of the Church were a rock against the shifting sands of human existence. Various types of security were built into the system in addition to the watered-down ethical demands that gave a reassuring sense of security to those who obeyed them. Indulgences, First Fridays, and First Saturdays were all means of providing assurance of eternal salvation. The Church had all the answers to the problems that confronted individuals and society. The Church itself did not know doubt, confusion, growth, pain, and tension.

Catholic life and theology in the post–Vatican II era no longer claim to have the security and certitude that characterized Catholic life and teaching just a few short years ago. However, there is still a tendency to avoid the doubts, growing pains, and frustrations of a pilgrim people and a pilgrim Church. For Catholic life today the older securities and certitudes are gone forever; but many still look, somewhat naively, for a false sense of security. In opening up the Church to the world, in opening up ourselves to others, we reveal our own uncertainties, frustrations, and weaknesses. In the midst of such frustration we easily seek a false sense of security. Postconciliar life in the Church has seen a number of new messiahs appear on the horizon with great expectations, but the hopes of their followers are quickly dashed against the realities of human existence in the times in between. Many pinned their hopes on the liturgy in English or lately on an entirely new liturgy, but experience shows that the liturgy will never become the new messiah. Many other messiahs have appeared—ranging from Martin Buber to Harvey Cox to the scriptural renewal. But the eschaton has not yet come. Perhaps the pessimism of Sartre serves as an excellent reminder to the naive personalism and optimism of many today.

Some Catholics have abandoned a triumphalism in the Church only to embrace a triumphalism of the world or the secular city. I firmly believe that the mission of the Christian and the Church is in service of the world, but the present state of the world is not entirely salvific. There is too much suffering and inequality in our own country, let alone in a world blighted by injustice, ignorance, and hunger, for the Christian to be content with the present situation. Professor Charles West of Princeton Theological Seminary, in describing the meeting on Church and Society sponsored by the World Council of Churches in Geneva in the summer of 1966, remarked about the opposition to the theological advocates of the secular city. West claims that the majority of theologians from the underdeveloped countries were "theological guerrillas" who saw revolution as the only way of shaking off the shackles of contemporary political and social structures. The "theological technocrats" of the secular city were amazed at the vehemence of the revolutionaries.

To live with the eschatological tension is difficult. The Christian too experiences doubt, frustration, opposition, and resistance to any growth. One who realizes the difficulties in breaking away from his own selfishness and sinfulness also understands the slowness of growth in the structures of human existence. To become resigned to the present is just as inadequate a solution as to expect miraculous progress without opposition or frustration. The virtue of hope allows the Christian to live the eschatological tension. Hope constantly beckons in the direction of the final stage of the kingdom of God. The follower of Jesus can never rest content with the present situation of one's own change of heart or the present situation of humanity. But hope also strengthens the follower of Jesus against the frustrations and opposition that accompany any growth. Hope makes the Paschal Mystery of Christ a reality. Only by dying does the Christian rise in the newness of life.

Despair looms all too easily on the horizon for one who expects the eschaton to come too easily or too quickly. The greatness of God's gift to us is the fact that we have a role to play in bringing about the new heaven and the new earth. The radical ethic of Jesus could very easily bring one to despair because of the impossibility that it entails. However, the ethic of Jesus is both gift and demand. Our inability to live according to the strenuous moral teaching of Jesus is a constant reminder of the need for God's mercy and forgiveness. At the same time the radical ethical demand serves as a constant reminder to the Christian to open self ever more to the call of God and neighbor. All the old securities and certitudes are gone. There are no false props that the Christian can use. Christian maturity demands that the follower of Jesus stand on one's own feet and carve out human existence despite all the frustrations and doubts of life. The Christian as a pilgrim traveling to the new heaven and the new earth never has the luxury and the security of one who has already arrived at the final destination. In the insecurity of the journey only hope in the word and work of God gives the pilgrim Christian the courage to continue. Hope is the virtue that allows the Christian to live the tension of the reign of God present but not yet fully here.

There are tendencies in the evangelical ethic to abandon entirely life in this world. However, the contemporary Christian realizes that the needs of the neighbor can and must be met at the present time. The Christian's hope in the final coming of the reign of God does not furnish us with any blueprint for human development and growth. Only a naive biblicism would expect to find in the Scriptures the solutions to the problems confronting individuals and society today. The ethical teaching of Jesus urges his followers to creatively find solutions to come to the aid of the neighbor in need.

Like the individual Christian, the Church too must take seriously the moral teaching of Jesus and the virtue of hope. The primary concern of the Church should be the neighbor in need. The Church constantly needs to rethink the ways in which it tries to accomplish its primary purposes. The tendency to seek security in the means that were helpful in the past is all too tempting. There is also the temptation to seek security in other things and not in the word of God in Christ. For a long time the Church tried to find its security in the protection of the state. Now the temptation seems to be for the Church to find its security in brick and mortar institutions. Structures and institutions will always be necessary, but they only serve to help the Church be faithful to the mission and teaching of Jesus that puts primary emphasis on the neighbor in need. The Church should not seek false security in status, wealth, or power. The pilgrim Church finds its only security in the promise of its founder.

The relevancy of the gospel ethic of Jesus is the challenge and vocation given to the followers of Jesus and his Church.

BIBLIOGRAPHY

W. D. Davies, *The Sermon on the Mount* (Cambridge University Press, 1966). Davies answers both yes and no, with more emphasis on the yes, to the question: Has Matthew departed from the mind of Jesus by making the words of Jesus in the Sermon on the Mount into "the new law"?

C. H. Dodd, *Gospel and Law* (Cambridge University Press, 1951). Four essays originally given as the Bampton Lectures at Columbia University in 1950. The radical ethical sayings of Jesus are interpreted in the third essay as showing the goal and direction toward which the Christian strives and also serving as a reminder of our constant need for forgiveness.

Bernard Haring, CSsR, "The Normative Value of the Sermon on the Mount," *Catholic Biblical Quarterly* 29 (July 1967): 365–85. The article merely summarizes the main points in the already existing literature. Haring argues that the saving message and the moral imperative are one and that the ethical sayings of the Sermon are "goal commandments."

John Knox, *The Ethic of Jesus in the Teaching of the Church* (Abingdon Press, 1961). A somewhat popular and very readable summary of the different solutions to the problem of the radical ethic of Jesus.

Noel Lazure, OMI, *Les Valeurs Morales de la Théologie Johannique* (J. Gabalda, 1965). The latest and one of the few studies devoted exclusively to the moral teaching of John.

Norman Perrin, *The Kingdom of God in the Teaching of Jesus* (Westminster Press, 1963). A fine, scholarly summary of the discussion about the nature of the kingdom and its relationship to ethics from Schleiermacher to the present.

Paul Ramsey, *Basic Christian Ethics* (Charles Scribner's Sons, 1950). A text in Christian ethics with a long introductory section on the love ethic of Jesus. However, the later works of Ramsey show, at least, a different emphasis in his moral methodology.

Rudolf Schnackenburg, *The Moral Teaching of the New Testament* (Herder and Herder, 1964). A one-volume summary and synthesis of the moral teaching of the entire New Testament.

Ceslaus Spicq, OP, *Agape in the New Testament*, 3 vols. (B. Herder, 1963, 1965, 1966). An exegetical and scriptural study of *agape* in the New Testament without the very complete footnotes found in the original French volumes.

Ceslaus Spicq, OP, *Theologie Morale du Nouveau Testament*, 2 vols. (J. Gabalda, Paris, 1965). A comparatively complete and analytical treatment (there is no attempt made at a synthesis of the teaching) of the different moral themes and teachings in the New Testament. The footnotes with very complete bibliographies are most valuable.

3. Conscience

This chapter was published in my *Themes in Fundamental Moral Theology* (Notre Dame, IN: University of Notre Dame Press, 1977), 202–32.

In my judgment there are significant deficiencies in the manualistic understanding of conscience, which will be briefly mentioned. In the first place the basic approach is too legalistic with the resulting problems of minimalism and an extrinsic understanding of morality and the moral life. Second, conscience viewed as a faculty tends to give too little importance to the person as a whole—the subject of the action. Third, the understanding of conscience is too one-sidedly rationalistic—there is little or no mention of affectivity. Fourth, the emphasis is on a deductive reasoning process that bespeaks a classicist approach.

Now it is time to propose a more adequate understanding of conscience that will avoid the criticisms briefly mentioned above. These criticisms of the manuals do not imply that there is nothing of value in the past Catholic tradition. It will be pointed out that the manuals, perhaps because of some aspects of the historical development, do not necessarily represent the best of the Catholic tradition. On the other hand, there are changes called for in the light of contemporary understandings.

As a preliminary consideration it is important to establish the different theological context within which the question of conscience is to be situated. The manuals operated almost exclusively within the realm of the natural as differentiated from and distinct from the supernatural. The natural, rather than being considered as existing apart from the supernatural, must be incorporated into the total Christian vision or stance. Such a theological context is a very necessary prerequisite for a proper understanding of conscience.

ETHICAL MODEL

The first and primary consideration involves the ethical model within which one situates the reality of conscience. There is no doubt that the manuals understand morality primarily in terms of deontology. The objective norm is God's law as this is mediated in and through other laws—divine positive, natural, and positive law. The impression is readily given that the law spells out all one's moral obligations and conscience passively conforms to the existing law.

There are three possible models that can be employed for understanding the moral life—deontology, teleology, and relationality-responsibility. The legalistic theology of the manuals, which sees the moral life primarily in terms of law, seems totally inadequate and accentuates the negative characteristics of minimalism and juridicism that so often characterized this morality. Interestingly, the manuals of Catholic moral theology do not follow the approach of Thomas Aquinas. They continually quote Aquinas in their discussion of law and appear to be following him, but in reality they do not.

Thomas Aquinas properly belongs under the category of teleology—morality is based on the ultimate end and acts are good or bad depending on whether or not they bring us to the ultimate end or impede this progress.[1] Thomas's first consideration is the ultimate end of human beings, followed by his discussion of the human acts by which we achieve the ultimate end. His next major treatise concerns the principles of human actions. The intrinsic principles are the various powers or potencies from which our acts come—such as the intellect, the appetites; but these powers can be modified by habits that are stable ways of acting, inclining us either to the good or to evil. Among the good habits affecting our powers or faculties, Aquinas considers at great length the virtues and also mentions the gifts of the Holy Spirit, the Beatitudes, and the fruits of the Holy Spirit. Only then does Thomas consider the external principles of actions, which are both law and grace.[2] The manuals unfortunately do not follow either the whole of the Thomistic teaching or the tone of that moral teaching.

However, I choose a relationality-responsibility model as the basic ethical model. There are a number of important theological and ethical considerations arguing for the acceptance of a relationality-responsibility model for moral theology. The first important impetus has come from biblical ethics. In Roman Catholic theology the renewal associated with the Second Vatican Council first appeared in the area of Scripture and then grew as scriptural insights were incorporated more and more into the whole of theology so that Scripture truly became the soul of theology.[3] In biblical ethics it became clear that relationality-responsibility was a very significant ethical theme. The primary ethical category even in the Old Testament is not law but covenant, which is the loving relationship that God has made with the people.[4] The gospel ethic with its call to perfection fits much better in relational categories than in deontological terms.

The understanding of the Scriptures also played a significant role in leading Protestant scholars to a relationality model. Protestant ethics had always been firmly based on the Scriptures. The more critical approach to the Scriptures made theologians realize that the Scriptures could no longer be used as a source of laws or norms universally binding in the Christian life. In the Scriptures God revealed God's self in loving acts so that the concept of propositional revelation was no longer accepted. Especially in Barthian ethics the God of the Scriptures is the God who acts with mighty deeds. In relationship to the God who acts and saves, the Christian is a responder.[5] A theological actualism can easily develop in the light of this approach, but such an abuse does not destroy the valid understanding of the moral life in terms of relationality and responsibility.

Theological emphasis on eschatology also influences the selection of the relationality model. Contemporary eschatology no longer sees its subject as the last things but rather the kingdom of God is already somewhat present and trying to become more present in history. The Christian then has a responsibility to make the kingdom more present and to overcome the evils of social, economic, political, and sexual oppression that too often continue to imprison many human beings. Such a theme is particularly central in the theology of liberation, which in the Roman Catholic context has been developing especially in South America.[6]

Theological anthropology today understands the individual person as called to creatively make the kingdom more present in the struggle against the reality of sin in the world. Such an anthropology, highlighting the powers and capabilities of human beings, does not view the individual primarily in terms of conformity to a minutely spelled-out law or plan. Here again there is a danger of overestimating human creativity. The true realization that the individual creates one's own meaning and value can be distorted to deny the limitations that continually exist for human beings.

From a more philosophical-anthropological perspective the relationality-responsibility model fits in better with the emphasis on historicity. The tone of the manuals of moral theology with their insistence on all embracing laws characterized by universality and immutability is the product of a classicist worldview. This is not to deny that there is a place for law or for considerations of universality in ethics and the moral life of the Christian, but primary emphasis does not belong here. Historicity favors the stress on growth and development, which is also much better incorporated in a relationality-responsibility model. A proper understanding of our multiple relationships with God, neighbor, self, and the world does justice to all the aspects of human existence including the political and social dimensions.

The emphasis on the person and personalism rather than the natural has also influenced the shift toward a model of relationality-responsibility. The individual as person is seen as a subject interacting with other persons. This approach rejects an understanding of natural law as based on physical and biological processes or the innate teleologies of particular faculties seen apart from the person.

The adoption of a relationality-responsibility model rests on convincing theological and ethical arguments. Naturally it is necessary to develop at great detail what precisely is meant by relationality-responsibility. In many ways I accept the basic approach of H. Richard Niebuhr to the model of relationality-responsibility. Niebuhr understands responsibility as embracing four elements—response, interpretation, accountability, and social solidarity.[7] My approach differs from Niebuhr in two important aspects. First, my understanding of relationality has a more metaphysical basis to it. Second, I want to give a greater emphasis to the subject as agent and incorporate here some of the findings of transcendental philosophical approaches. This emphasis will now be developed at much greater length in the subsequent steps of this chapter within the context of a relationality-responsibility model.

THE PERSON AS SUBJECT AND AGENT

The second step in developing a more adequate concept of conscience in the Catholic theological tradition concerns giving greater importance to the subject or the person as agent. The legalistic and extrinsicist view of the manuals saw the moral life primarily as actions in obedience to the law. The law was recognized as an objective norm of morality to which the individual conformed one's acts. In this perspective, conscience formation consisted primarily in instructing people about what is in the law. To this in practice was often added a motivational aspect emphasizing the fear of sin and hell.

In general an emphasis on the person as subject or agent accepts the fact that the acts of the individual must be seen not in relation to an extrinsic norm but in relation to the person acting. An older axiom in Catholic thought understood this reality very well—*agere sequitur esse*—action follows from being—in other words, what we do follows from who we are. Actions are expressive and revelatory of the person. The person expresses oneself and extends oneself in and through one's actions. The biblical metaphor expresses the reality very well—the good tree brings forth good fruit while the bad tree brings forth bad fruit. Loving and compassionate actions come from a loving and compassionate person.

But there is also another important aspect to the emphasis on the person as agent. Not only are actions expressive and revelatory of the person, but by one's actions the individual shapes and constitutes the self as subject and as moral agent. By our actions we make ourselves the moral agents we are. Truly the individual human person has the opportunity and the destiny to create one's own moral self.

In more technical ethical terminology, emphasis is placed on an ethics of character or of the virtues. How often we talk about the character of the person coming through in one's action. Character, as distinguished from particular character traits, emphasizes that the person is more than what happens to the self. One can determine oneself and one's character, recognizing that there are some factors over which we have no control. James Gustafson has emphasized the role of the self, virtues, and character in Christian ethics.[8] Stanley Hauerwas, influenced by Gustafson, has recently developed an ethics of character, understanding character as the qualification of self-agency that is an orientation of the self.[9] Obviously there would be many ways in which one could develop an ethics of character.

An ethics of the virtues also rests on the recognition of the importance of the subject as agent. This emphasis was present to a degree in Aquinas, who saw the virtues as good habits or stable ways of acting modifying the faculties or powers and inclining them to the good.[10] Contemporary Christian ethicists are speaking again about an ethic of the virtues and some even want to develop an independent ethic of virtues with no place for an ethic of obligation.[11] An ethic of the virtues could be developed in many different ways, but all such approaches stress the importance of the person as subject and agent.

Unfortunately this emphasis is missing in the approach of the manuals and much of contemporary moral thought, which often reduces ethical considerations to the moment of decision, forgetting about the self who continues from decision through decision and who actually affirms and creates one's moral self in and through those decisions. Again the Catholic tradition with the understanding of the virtues tried in some way to do justice to the importance of the subject and the person, but the manuals tended to neglect this aspect in their development. Even when treating of the virtues the manuals primarily discuss only the acts of the virtues and the obligations to place such actions.

From a theological perspective Catholic ethics possessed a strong basis for developing an ethic of the person as subject. The Catholic theory of grace maintains that grace produces an ontological change in the person. By freely responding to the gracious gift of God's love in Jesus Christ, one truly now becomes intrinsically changed, a different person mystically and really united with Jesus in the family of God. The Christian should then live in accord with the new life that has been received in Christ Jesus and grow in that life. The teaching of Aquinas can readily be understood in the light of the agent transformed by grace.[12] Some Protestant theology with its teaching on justification and the lesser emphasis on sanctification would have a greater difficulty in developing an ethic stressing the fact that the moral subject constitutes oneself as subject in and through one's actions and that the subject grows and progresses in the moral life.[13] However, Hauerwas develops an ethic of character judged to be in accord with some Protestant theories of justification.[14]

In the light of the importance of the person as agent and subject, the centrality of continual conversion in the moral life of the Christian emerges. Continual conversion has strong roots in the scriptural notion of *metanoia* and well illustrates the dynamism and call to perfection that characterizes a gospel-inspired ethic. Bernard Häring has made conversion a central concept in moral theology.[15]

The Christian through responding to and accepting the gift of God's love in Jesus Christ becomes a new person, a new creature sharing in the life of Jesus. But one must continue to grow and deepen this new life. There is a true sense in which the individual remains *simul justus et peccator*—at the same time justified and a sinner. The reality of venial sin understood as the continuing sinfulness of the redeemed takes on added importance in this view, for the Christian constantly strives to overcome the sinfulness that is still present in the individual as well as in the world. The Christian continues both to express in actions the new life received in baptism and to constitute the self as a person ever more united with Jesus through the Spirit. Spiritual theology in the Catholic tradition, which unfortunately became separated from moral theology, has often insisted on the injunction to put on the Lord Jesus, to imitate Jesus, and to live in union with the risen Lord. All of these notions, when made more dynamic in the light of continual conversion, underscore the personal growth of the subject who not only expresses this reality in one's actions but also constitutes one's moral self through these choices.

The biblical concept of conversion seen as the change of heart in response to the gracious gift of God in Jesus also avoids some of the dangers of Pelagianism that lurked in older approaches to morality in the Catholic tradition. With the insistence on works there was always the danger of thinking that one is saved by one's own efforts. Conversion as the opposite of sin has personal, social, and cosmic dimensions and thereby views the Christian subject in the context of an ethical model of relationality-responsibility.

The virtues can be readily integrated into a theology of conversion and continual conversion. Virtues refer to the attributes and dispositions that characterize the Christian life. In the Thomistic presentation of the virtues some problems arose because of the faculty psychology on which they were based—virtues are habits modifying the individual faculties or powers of the soul. Likewise, there exist some dangers of Pelagianism in the Scholastic understanding of the virtues. However, the basic concept of the virtues as the attitudes, dispositions, and inclinations characterizing the Christian person as subject must be seen as very important in the moral life of the Christian. One could develop the important virtues of the Christian on the basis of the Beatitudes or the list of virtues in Paul or those characteristics such as hope, humility, mercy, and forgiveness that so often appear in the New Testament.

The understanding of conscience must give central importance to the self—the person who acts and the characteristics of the person. Formation of conscience in this context can never settle merely for instruction in the law but rather must spur the individual to grow in wisdom, age, and grace as a follower of Jesus. What has been developed in this second step is a general emphasis on the subject and the person. The level of generality at which it was presented needs to be specified. The third and especially the fourth steps involve this process of specifying exactly how to understand the person as subject in deciding and acting.

Conscience Is More than Cognitive

The third step in a more adequate understanding of conscience is to overcome the one-sidedly cognitive aspect in the manuals of moral theology. Conscience should also have an affective dimension as well as a cognitive aspect. The affective dimension has taken on increased importance in light of work done in depth psychology and psychiatry. There were different traditions even within Roman Catholicism that saw conscience as either connected with the intellect as in the Thomistic approach or connected with the will as in the Franciscan approach.

In my judgment one of the sources for the problem in the Catholic tradition stems from an anthropology accepting a faculty-psychology approach. If conscience is viewed in terms of a particular faculty or power, then there lurks the danger of not giving enough importance to all the aspects of conscience.[16] It seems better to identify conscience with the moral consciousness of the subject as such. Bernard Lonergan shows how his intentionality analysis of the subject differs from the older faculty approach.

The study of the subject is quite different, for it is the study of oneself inasmuch as one is conscious. It prescinds from the soul, its essence, its potencies, its habits, for none of these are given in consciousness. It attends to operations and to their center and source, which is the self. It discerns the different levels of consciousness, the consciousness of the dream, of the waking subject, of the intelligently inquiring subject, of the rationally reflecting subject. It examines the different operations on the several levels and their relations to one another.[17]

A transcendental methodology that begins with the subject as conscious provides one way of overcoming the problems connected with the one-sided view of conscience as related to only one faculty or power and not to the whole subject. However, one must avoid any simplistic reduction and carefully distinguish the different levels of consciousness and operations in the subject—the levels of experiencing, understanding, judging, and deciding.

The recognition of the importance of the affective aspects and feelings in the formation of conscience have important practical ramifications. Much can be learned from all branches of psychology. Appeal must be made not only to the intellect but to the imagination and the affectivity of the person. In this connection one can mention an element that unfortunately has been lost in recent Catholic life—emphasis on the lives of the saints.[18] The saints furnished inspiration and supplied heroes and heroines for many younger Catholics in the past. These stories in their own way fired the imagination, triggered the feelings, and inflamed the hearts of those who strove to follow in the footsteps of the saints. With the passing of this emphasis on the lives of the saints, Catholic life has lost an important element in conscience formation.

THE JUDGMENT OF CONSCIENCE

A fourth step in arriving at a better understanding of conscience calls for a deeper understanding of the subject and how the subject arrives at its judgments and decisions. What do we mean by the self knowing, feeling, deciding, and how does the self do these things? Our inquiry starts with the traditionally accepted notion that a good conscience indicates that a good decision has been made. The precise question concerns what is a good conscience. When has the subject judged rightly and decided well? This question raises very fundamental issues about our understanding of human knowing, judging, and deciding. The approach developed here will differ from the considerations of the manuals, which propose a heavily deductive reasoning process going from the universal to the particular and which see a correct judgment in terms of the correspondence of the mind to the objective reality existing "out there" or outside the subject.

As a preliminary note it can be pointed out that the neo-Thomist Jacques Maritain rejected the deductive reasoning process often proposed in the definitions of conscience. According to Maritain's interpretation, the manner or mode in which human reason knows natural law is not rational knowledge but knowledge through inclination. Such knowledge is not clear knowledge through concepts and conceptual judgments. It is obscure, unsystematic, vital knowledge by connaturality or congeniality in which the individual in making judgments consults and listens to the inner melody that the vibrating strings of abiding tendencies make present in the subject.[19]

More radical solutions have been proposed in the context of transcendental method, which sees objectivity not in conformity to the object out there but rather in terms of the human knowing, deciding, loving subject itself. Both Karl Rahner and Bernard Lonergan have made significant contributions to the understanding of conscience in this area.

Rahner has developed his approach in the context of discussions of the discernment of spirits and of a formal existential ethic.[20] The discernment of spirits has been a traditional part of Catholic spirituality.[21] There are three types of phenomena that the individual can experience—revelations and visions; internal enlightenment or impulses concerning some determinate object; general states of consolation or desolation. The discernment of spirits tries to determine the causes of these as either God and the good angels or the bad angels or human nature.[22]

Rahner develops his thought in commenting on the spiritual exercises of St. Ignatius. The whole purpose of the exercises is to bring the individual to make a vital decision—the election. According to Ignatius there are three times or occasions for making such an election. The first time arises when God moves the soul without any hesitation, as in private revelation. The second time occurs when light and understanding are derived through the experience of desolation and consolation in the discernment of spirits. The third time arises in tranquility when the soul is not agitated by different spirits and has the free and natural use of its powers. Rahner maintains that most commentators mistakenly interpret Ignatius as choosing the third time as the time for making the election. But Rahner argues, convincingly in the eyes of many,[23] that the second time is the usual time for making an election.[24]

Rahner attempts to explain the reality of discernment in the second time in light of his transcendental metaphysics. Knowledge does not mean only the conceptual knowledge of an object. In all human knowing there is also the concomitant awareness of the knowing self as the subject. This is not the knowledge of an object or even of the self as an object but is the subject's awareness as subject. Rahner interprets the Ignatian expression of consolation without previous cause as consolation without an object of that consolation. In all conscious acts the human being has an indistinct awareness of God as transcendent horizon, but this awareness does not ordinarily emerge into explicit consciousness. Just as the individual is conscious to oneself as subject, so God as transcendent horizon but not as an object is present in consciousness. Now, however, in this second time the soul explicitly feels oneself totally drawn to the love of God and thus experiences this consolation, peace, and joy that is coming from God's presence. This consolation is the nonconceptual experience of God as the individual is drawn totally into God's love. If this consolation perdures when the person places oneself in accord with the projection of the election to be made, the individual rightly concludes that the prospective choice harmonizes with one's own human, Godward subjectivity. Obviously, this requires that the person as subject be truly open to the call of God. This experience by which the soul is wholly drawn to the love of God as God, unlike discursive or conceptual knowledge, possesses intrinsically an irreducibly self-evident, self-sufficient character.[25]

In an earlier essay Rahner proposes a formal existential ethic in addition to and in no way opposed to an essential ethic resulting in the general principles of natural law. Rahner agrees that in addition to one's essence each individual also has a positive individual reality. This positive individuality cannot be the object of reflective, objective knowledge that can be articulated in propositions. How does conscience perceive this individual moral obligation? Rahner again appeals to nonreflective, nonpropositional self-presence of the person to self in one's positive uniqueness.[26]

Rahner in this way tries to develop a theory of conscience that corresponds with the traditionally accepted idea of the peace and joy of a good conscience when a good decision has been made or is to be made.[27] Obviously, there are questions that can and should be put to Rahner. One problem is that his transcendental method, while handling quite well questions primarily of a personal and individual nature such as vocation, does not even try to say anything to questions of social ethics. Perhaps this is just the appearance in the realm of moral theology of the reality that Metz criticized in Rahner's systematics for not giving enough importance to the social and political aspects of reality.[28] Likewise, in my judgment Rahner's approach does not seem to give enough importance to empirical reality.

Bernard Lonergan in his work on theological method and elsewhere has outlined a transcendental approach to ethics that seems to overcome the problems mentioned above with the theory of Karl Rahner.[29] Lonergan is opposed to deductive reasoning. He always begins with the concrete. Lonergan understands consciousness as the presence of the subject to oneself—not the presence of an object. In the following paragraphs Lonergan's approach to conscience or moral consciousness will be sketched although it is impossible to give a full and complete understanding of his complex thought.[30]

Conscience for Lonergan is seen in the context of the thrust of the personal subject for the authenticity of self-transcendence. The person shares sensitivity with the other animals, but the human individual can go beyond (transcend) this level of consciousness. In addition to the empirical level of consciousness and intentionalities, in which one perceives, senses, and so on, human beings go beyond this to the intellectual level of understanding and to the rational level of judgment, which not only goes beyond the subject but also affirms that which is so. On the next level self-transcendence becomes moral—in the order of deciding and doing, not just knowing. By responding to questions about value we can effect in our being a moral transcendence. This moral transcendence is the possibility of becoming a person in human society. Our capacity for self-transcendence becomes fully actual when we fall in love. Being in love is of different kinds but being in love with God is the basic fulfillment of our conscious intentionality. This brings a joy and a peace that can remain despite failure, pain, betrayal, and so on. The transcendental subjectivity of the person stretches forth toward the intelligible, the unconditioned, and the good of value. The reach of this intending is unrestricted.[31]

Within the context of self-transcendence Lonergan develops the three conversions that modify the horizon of the subject. Intellectual conversion denies the myth of the object out there as the criterion of objectivity and reality. This is a naive, comic-book realism. Lonergan strives for a critical realism. The real world for Lonergan is mediated by meaning and is not the world of immediate experience. The real world mediated by meaning is known by the cognitional process of experiencing, understanding, and judging, which is based on the thrust of cognitional self-transcendence. Moral conversion consists in opting for the truly good, for values against satisfactions when they conflict. Here we are no longer cajoled as children, but we freely opt for value. Thus we affect not only the object of choice but we decide for ourselves what to make of ourselves.

Religious conversion, the third conversion, is being grasped by ultimate concern. It is the total and permanent self-surrender of other-worldly falling in love.[32] Lonergan himself succinctly summarizes his understanding of the three conversions.

> As intellectual and moral conversion, so also religious conversion is a modality of self-transcendence: Intellectual conversion is to truth attained by cognitional self-transcendence. Moral conversion is to values apprehended, affirmed and realized by a real self-transcendence. Religious conversion is to a total being-in-love as the efficacious ground of all self-transcendence, whether in the pursuit of truth, or in the realization of human values, or in the orientation man (*sic*) adopts to the universe, its ground and its goals.[33]

How do we know our judgments have attained the true and our decisions have achieved the value? In other words, what are the criteria by which we know our judging and deciding have been good and proper? In the manuals of moral theology the criterion of judgment is conformity to the objective truth out there. Lonergan firmly rejects that criterion. In a judgment one arrives at truth when there are no more pertinent questions to ask. The self-transcending thrust toward truth is satisfied. The judgment for Lonergan is thus described as virtually unconditioned because the subject seeking the truth can now rest content. Thus we have established the radical identity between genuine objectivity and authentic subjectivity.[34]

Likewise, the criterion of value judgments is not the value or reality out there; rather, it is the satisfaction of the moral subject as a self-transcending thrust toward value. A rounded moral judgment is ever the work of a fully developed self-transcending subject or, as Aristotle would put it, of a virtuous person.[35] The drive to value rewards success in self-transcendence with a happy conscience and saddens failure with an unhappy conscience.[36] Thus once again the peaceful and joyful conscience of the authentic subject understood in terms of self-transcendence becomes the criterion of objective value. One might truly say that for Lonergan the norms for the proper formation of conscience are the transcendental precepts, which correspond to the basic levels of consciousness of the subject and the basic operations—be attentive, be intelligent, be reasonable, be responsible.[37]

Lonergan is well aware of the dangers and difficulties in achieving authenticity and self-transcendence. Development is not inevitable; there are many failures. In moral conversion one must overcome enticing but misleading satisfactions and fears of discomfort, pain, and privation. Lonergan speaks of bias as affecting authentic transcendence on all levels and going against the transcendental precepts.[38] He applies to all levels of self-transcendence what was said about intellectual conversion in *Insight*. Bias as a block or a distortion appears in four principal matters: the bias of unconscious motivation brought to light in depth psychology; the bias of individual egoism; the bias of group egoism; and the bias of common sense.[39] The recognition of such obstacles in the way of authentic self-transcendence continually reminds the individual to be self-critical. Human authenticity has no room for complacency and self-satisfaction. One must continually question, inquire, and be open to learn.

Again, one should critique and discuss the theory proposed by Lonergan. One set of problems arises from the nature of conversion, the order of conversion (according to Lonergan there is usually, first, religious, followed by moral, and then, and only rarely, intellectual conversion),[40] and the frequency of conversion (Lonergan admits intellectual conversion is rare and describes the other conversions, especially religious, in such a way that they would seem to be very rare in practice).

I would make two suggestions. First, I do not think there is that great a difference or distinction between moral and religious conversion. The strictly theological data (love of God and neighbor) and existential experience seem to see the two conversions as basically one.[41] Second, Lonergan could introduce a variant of the notion of continual conversion to indicate that both conversions involve a continual growth and that these conversions might take place on a fundamental and beginning level even though the radical description of conversion has not yet been fully achieved.[42]

I have tried to develop through various steps a basic understanding of the reality of conscience and how it functions in the Christian life. First, conscience must be understood in the context of a relationality-responsibility model of the Christian life—never forgetting the multiple relationships within which one lives. The second step affirmed the importance of the self as agent and subject who expresses oneself in actions and also by those very actions constitutes oneself as subject. The third step insisted on seeing conscience as more than merely cognitive and strove to bring together the cognitive, the affective, and the moral aspects of conscience. Finally, the fourth step proposed specific metaphysical theories explaining the reality of conscience and how one arrives at good judgments and decisions. Lonergan's basic theory has advantages over Rahner's for three reasons: (1) it deals more adequately with the empirical; (2) it can handle better the social aspect as well as the personal aspect of moral existence; (3) it is a unified theory explaining all knowing and deciding and does not distinguish between the essential and the existential aspects of conscience formation. This theory attempts to explain in a more systematic and reflective way the traditionally accepted notion that joy and peace mark the good conscience, which is the adequate criterion of good moral judgment and decision.

One further point deserves mention. This understanding of conscience recognizes the importance of the development of conscience. The approach proposed here calls for and readily incorporates within its philosophical context the work of developmental psychologists in describing the way in which conscience itself develops and grows.[43]

What has to be remembered is that development occurs not only in childhood, although it is obviously more dramatic in childhood, but continues to occur throughout adult life. Theologians must take the biblical concept of continual conversion and see how this can be psychologically understood in terms of the development of conscience.

PRACTICAL CONCLUSIONS

The first practical conclusion of the discussion on conscience reaffirms the traditionally accepted teaching that conscience is the norm of personal action. Yes, the conscience judgment and decision might be wrong, but the individual must be true to one's own self. Authentic subjectivity excludes the possibility of error, but authentic subjectivity is not always present. Many abuses have existed in the past in the name of conscience, and there will continue to be many abuses in the future. But this does not take away the basic realization that the individual must decide and act in accord with conscience. Christians and the Church should learn from the divine wisdom both to accept the freedom and responsibility of the individual to decide in conscience despite all the abuses of that freedom and to challenge the individual to achieve authenticity. God's loving gift of self to human beings respects human freedom and the choices made by human beings, even though God's gift is often spurned.

Second, however, one must be well aware of the dangers involved in judgments and decisions of conscience. Yes, the ultimate decision and judgment rest with the individual, but the individual must recognize the limitations and dangers involved in trying to achieve subjective authenticity, which is synonymous with objectivity. In a practical way human experience reminds us of the many horrendous realities that have been done in the name of conscience—slavery, torture, atrocities, and deprival of basic human rights. The realization of the dangers involved becomes even more acute when recognizing how seemingly even good people can disagree over such basic issues as the use of force in the service of justice, abortion, or the just ordering of the economic system for the good of all. The authentic development of self-transcendence is threatened on every level.

The Christian can and should recognize the two basic sources of this danger as human finitude and sinfulness. Finitude is different from sinfulness. As a result of our finitude we are limited; we see only a partial aspect of reality; we cannot achieve all possible goods or values. Human sinfulness, on the other hand, stems not from creation itself but from the actions of ourselves or others and can be seen in the sinfulness both of the individual and of the society in which we live.

Although the basic sources of the dangers in a theological perspective are easy to identify, the actual dangers can take many different forms. Again, these dangers exist in the cognitive, affective, and moral levels and operations. Bias and prejudice can easily affect our judgments and decisions. Why is it that those who espouse the just war theory generally judge wars of their own country to be just while rejecting the justice of the wars of their opponents? An examination of conscience reveals the lack of courage that prevents us from acting upon what we believe to be right or the lack of ardor that weakens our pursuit of value.

One example will well illustrate the complexity of the problem of how limitation and sinfulness can affect our judgments and decisions of conscience. Will better conscience decisions result if a person is involved in the problem or if a person is an "objective" observer? Frankly, there are pluses and minuses to both approaches. The one who is intimately involved in the struggle knows and appreciates the problem. One must honestly admit that white, male, middle-class theologians have not been as aware as we should be of the problems of racism, poverty, and sexism in our society. On the other hand, personal involvement in an issue might prejudice one's judgments and decisions. Do the heads of powerful governments or people desperately fighting for the rights of the poor and oppressed tend to resort too quickly to violence? Do people involved in equal rights and opportunities for women tend to overlook the fetus? Yes, it is not too difficult to become aware of the difficulties and dangers in making judgments and decisions of conscience.

Third, one must not only be aware of the dangers but strive to overcome them. This is what it means to live out a theory of critical self-transcendence. From the Christian perspective the basic disposition that we all need to cultivate is openness to the gift of God and the needs of our neighbor. The Christian should try to put aside all prejudice, bias, and egoism. There is much talk today about openness, but to be truly open is not easy. The fundamental importance of openness stems from the theory of conscience proposed on the basis of critical self-transcendence, which sees the individual person in terms of an unrestricted thrust toward truth, value, love, and the unconditioned. The proof of a good conscience is had when one affirms the true and embraces the value. A false conscience arises from a lack of authenticity on the cognitive, affective, and moral levels of our existence. Openness therefore keeps one truly open to the truth, value, and love that alone can satisfy the unrestricted thrust toward the unconditioned. Openness also seems to be a very good understanding of the biblical attitude of humility of spirit. The humble in spirit are truly those who are open to the gift of God and the needs of neighbor. Openness aptly describes the primary disposition in conscience formation.

The individual should be critically alert to the many different ways of trying to guarantee that openness characterizes our existence in the quest for truth, value, and love. Many ways have been proposed but one must remember that they are usually only prudential specifications of the basic disposition of openness. The gospel gives us a very significant way of trying to overcome our finitude and sinfulness—love your neighbor as yourself. To put ourselves in the position of the other person remains an excellent way to overcome our own finitude and sinfulness. This same wisdom is found in the golden rule—do unto others as you would have them do unto you. Some contemporary philosophers speak of the veil of ignorance. In choosing what social system should be in existence, all individuals must choose from behind the veil of ignorance—that is, not knowing which of the various positions in society might be theirs.[44] Other philosophers speak of the ideal observer as the way of overcoming the prejudice and bias of any one individual.[45] The philosophical principle of universalization, based on the understanding that one must always be willing to see all others act in a similar way in similar circumstances, also serves as a strong antidote to individual bias, prejudice, and sinfulness.

Above all openness for the Christian calls for one to be an authentic self with all those attitudes and dispositions that should characterize a human and Christian person. In this way the person develops the feeling for the true and the good as well as the yearning and inclination to affirm and embrace them. The good conscience remains the work of a virtuous person.[46]

Fourth, community and especially the Christian community of the Church are very important in the formation of conscience. The discussion thus far has concerned only the individual, but the insistence on multiple relations and on the social aspects of morality recalls that the individual judges and decides in dialogue with other individuals and as members of various communities in which one lives. The various communities to which we belong play a very important role in personal conscience formation.

These considerations will be limited to what for the Christian must be the most important community—that of the Church. The Church as the people of God, called together to live in the risen Lord and to bear witness to that life, has a very significant role to play in the formation of the conscience of the individual Christian. The Church as the mediator and sign of the gospel strives to have its own people become signs of that gospel to others. From an ethical perspective, the Church is a great help in the formation of conscience precisely because it can overcome the two basic dangers of finitude and sinfulness that always threaten the individual. Because of our finitude we are limited historically, spatially, and temporally. The Church as a universal community existing in different cultures, in different times, and in different places is thus able to help overcome the limitations of finitude. The Church as the community of gospel and grace also tries to overcome human sinfulness and egoism. Although the Church remains a sinful Church still in need of continual redemption, the believer sees in the Church the presence of redeeming grace and a power to overcome sin and its ramifications.

Take a particular example of how the Church is able to help conscience. In my judgment some Protestant clergy deserve great credit for the leadership role they played through early opposition to the recent American involvement in the war in Vietnam. Many of these people suffered greatly because their stand was far from popular when they first took it. Some of these clergy admitted that at the very beginning they favored American participation in the war, but their early opposition was greatly influenced by the questions posed to them by Christians from other countries. These other Christians in the light of a broader perspective could overcome the narrowness, limitations, and group egoism of Americans.

The Church by every means possible—challenging, accusing, approving, questioning, supporting, teaching—helps in the formation of the conscience of the individual Christian. There are myriad ways in which this formation can and should take place in the Christian community. The Roman Catholic believer also recognizes the God-given function of the hierarchical magisterium as one mode in which the Church teaches and forms consciences. One way in which the whole Church and the hierarchical magisterium can inform conscience is by giving specific directions for specific actions, but the hierarchical magisterium must go through a proper discernment process to understand just what these specific directives are. Likewise, as also pointed out earlier, the Roman Catholic Church has recognized that this teaching of the hierarchical magisterium on specific moral matters cannot claim the certitude that excludes the possibility of error. At times the individual Christian, conscious of all the dangers, can rightly dissent from such teaching in theory and practice. Here again in making that decision one must carefully follow all the available approaches to conscience formation mentioned above. Here again, too, the ultimate criterion is the peace and joy of a good conscience.

This rather lengthy, but still unfortunately sketchy, consideration of conscience attempts to understand conscience in the light of recent developments in fundamental moral theology. The concept of conscience proposed here overcomes the criticisms proposed against the theory of conscience found in the manuals of moral theology. Above all this, theory of conscience incorporates an understanding of the Christian life that highlights its gospel, personal, dynamic, historical, and social characteristics.

Notes

1. For a categorization of Aquinas as belonging to a deliberative rather than a prescriptive motif, see Edward LeRoy Long Jr., *A Survey of Christian Ethics* (New York: Oxford University Press, 1967), 45–49.

2. This paragraph merely summarizes the outline of the *prima pars* of the *Summa theologiae.*

3. Dogmatic Constitution on Divine Revelation 24; Decree on Priestly Formation 16.

4. Robert Koch, "Vers une morale de l'alliance," *Studia Moralia* 6 (1968): 7–58.

5. James M. Gustafson, "Christian Ethics," in *Religion*, ed. Paul Ramsey (Englewood Cliffs, NJ: Prentice Hall, 1965), 309–20.

6. For the best theological explanation of liberation theology stressing especially the changed understanding of eschatology, see Gustavo Gutierrez, *A Theology of Liberation: History, Politics and Liberation* (Maryknoll, NY: Orbis Books, 1973).

7. H. Richard Niebuhr, *The Responsible Self* (New York: Harper and Row, 1963), 55–68.

8. James M. Gustafson, *Christ and the Moral Life* (New York: Harper and Row, 1968), 1–5 and throughout the book; James M. Gustafson, *Christian Ethics and the Community* (Philadelphia: Pilgrim Press, 1971), 151–216.

9. Stanley Hauerwas, *Character and the Christian Life: A Study in Theological Ethics* (San Antonio, TX: Trinity University Press, 1975).

10. For a development of the Thomistic concept of the virtues, see George P. Klubertanz, *Habits and Virtues* (New York: Appleton-Century-Crofts, 1965). In the next step I will express my disagreement with the faculty psychology on which the Thomistic approach is based.

11. E.g., see the following articles in the first issue (1973) of *The Journal of Religious Ethics*: Frederick Carney, "The Virtue-Obligation Controversy," 5–19; William K. Frankena, "The Ethics of Love Conceived as an Ethics of Virtue," 21–36; Arthur J. Dyck, "A Unified Theory of Virtue and Obligation," 37–52.

12. Yves Congar, "Le saint Ésprit dans la théologie thomiste de l'agir morale," in *Tommaso D'Aquino nel suo VII Centenario, Congresso Internazionole, Roma-Napoli, 17–24 aprile, 1974* (Naples: Edizioni Deomenicane Italiene, 1974), 175–87.

13. As an illustration of an unwillingness to accept such an approach, see Victor Paul Furnish, *Theology and Ethics in Paul* (Nashville: Abingdon Press, 1968), 176, 239, 240.

14. Hauerwas, *Character and the Christian Life*, 183–95.

15. Bernard Häring, *The Law of Christ* (Westminster, MD: Newman Press, 1961) 1:287–481; Bernard Häring, *Pastoral Treatment of Sin*, ed. P. Delhaye et al. (New York: Desclée, 1968), 87–176.

16. For an illustration of the faculty-psychology approach to conscience, see Ralph McInerny, "Prudence and Conscience," *The Thomist* 38 (1974): 291–305. McInerny restricts conscience to the cognitive, but he recognizes other important affective aspects in the moral life.

17. Bernard Lonergan, *The Subject* (Milwaukee: Marquette University Press, 1968), 7, 8.

18. Berard L. Marthaler, "A Traditional and Necessary Ingredient in Religious Education: Hagiography," *The Living Light* 11 (1974): 580–91.

19. Jacques Maritain, *Man and the State* (Chicago: University of Chicago Press, 1951), 91, 92.

20. Karl Rahner, "The Logic of Concrete Individual Knowledge," in *The Dynamic Element in the Church* (New York: Herder and Herder, 1964), 84–170; Karl Rahner, "On the Question of a Formal Existential Ethic," in *Theological Investigations*, vol. 2 (Baltimore: Helicon Press, 1963), 217–34.

21. For an overall view of this question, see Jacques Guillet, et al., *Discernment of Spirits* (Collegeville, MN: Liturgical Press, 1970). This book is the authorized English translation of the article in the *Dictionnaire de spiritualité*. For a contemporary theological discussion, see Philip S. Keane, "Discernment of Spirits: A Theological Reflection," *American Ecclesiastical Review* 168 (1974): 43–61.

22. Joseph de Guibert, *The Theology of the Spiritual Life* (London: Sheed and Ward, 1956), 130ff.

23. See, e.g., the special issue of *The Way Supplement* 24 (1975), which is devoted to the spiritual exercises of Ignatius.

24. Rahner, *Dynamic Element in the Church*, 89–106.

25. Rahner, *Dynamic Element in the Church*, 129–70.

26. Rahner, *Theological Investigations*, 2:217–34.

27. For an interpretation of Rahner's entire ethical theory, see James F. Bresnahan, "Rahner's Ethic: Critical Natural Law in Relation to Contemporary Ethical Methodology," *The Journal of Religion* 56 (1976): 36–60. For a fuller development, see James F. Bresnahan, "The Methodology of Natural Law: Ethical Reasoning in the Theology of Karl Rahner and Its Supplementary Development Using the Legal Philosophy of Lon L. Fuller" (PhD diss., Yale University [Ann Arbor, MI: University Microfilms, 1972, no. 72–29520]).

28. Johannes B. Metz, "Foreword: An Essay on Karl Rahner," in Karl Rahner, *Spirit in the World* (New York: Herder and Herder, 1968), xvi–xviii.

29. The two major works of Bernard Lonergan are: *Insight: A Study of Human Understanding* (New York: Philosophical Library, 1957); *Method in Theology* (New York: Herder and Herder, 1972).

30. Of great value are two, unfortunately unpublished, dissertations: Walter Eugene Conn, "Conscience and Self-Transcendence" (PhD diss., Columbia University [Ann Arbor, MI: University Microfilms, 1973, no. 73–26600]); John P. Boyle, "Faith and Community in the Ethical Theory of Karl Rahner and Bernard Lonergan" (PhD diss., Fordham University [Ann Arbor, MI: University Microfilms, 1972, no. 72–20554]).

31. Lonergan, *Method in Theology*, 103–5.

32. Lonergan, *Method in Theology*, 239–41.

33. Lonergan, *Method in Theology*, 241.

34. Lonergan, *Insight*, 279–316.

35. Lonergan, *Method in Theology*, 41.

36. Lonergan, *Method in Theology*, 35.

37. Lonergan, *Method in Theology*, 53, 231.

38. Lonergan, *Method in Theology*, 51–55.

39. Lonergan, *Method in Theology*, 231.

40. Lonergan, *Method in Theology*, 243, 267.

41. Charles E. Curran, "Christian Conversion in the Writings of Bernard Lonergan," in *Foundations of Theology: Papers from the International Lonergan Congress 1970*, ed. Philip McShane (Notre Dame, IN: University of Notre Dame Press, 1972), 41–59.

42. For different criticisms of the questions involving conversion in Lonergan's approach, see Conn, "Conscience and Self-Transcendence," 526ff.

43. Conn develops at great length the theories of Piaget, Erikson, and Kohlberg, incorporating their findings in a critical way into his understanding of conscience.

44. E.g., John Rawls, *A Theory of Justice* (Cambridge, MA: Harvard University Press, 1971), 136–42.

45. E.g., F. C. Sharp, *Good and Ill Will* (Chicago: University of Chicago Press, 1950), 156–62.

46. For a discussion of discernment from the viewpoint of a Protestant ethician who approaches the question in a nonmetaphysical way, see James M. Gustafson, "Moral Discernment in the Christian Life," in *Norm and Context in Christian Ethics*, ed. Gene Outka and Paul Ramsey (New York: Charles Scribner's Sons, 1968), 17–36.

Subsequent Developments

Until the present day, Catholic theologians in general frequently cite Vatican II documents and claim they are carrying out the proposals of the council. But there is no general agreement about what Vatican II means even today. The documents of Vatican II reflect the times in which they were written. In addition, the documents by their very nature sought as much consensus as possible, thus compromising language came through in many places. Historical consciousness explains even more why there are different and sometimes quite opposing interpretations today. Interpreters look at the documents through their own different lenses and thus come to different conclusions. An excellent practical example of these differences is the stark contrast between two international journals published after the council. *Concilium* began publishing in 1965 and aimed to keep alive the spirit of Vatican II. Its founders included Hans Küng, Edward Schillebeeckx, and Yves Congar. *Communio* was started in 1972 by Joseph Ratzinger, Hans Urs von Balthasar, and Henri de Lubac, all of whom had been a part of the original *Concilium* but emphasized a hermeneutic of continuity with what went before Vatican II. This is not the place to explore in depth the different interpretations of Vatican II, but simply to point out that different and even opposing interpretations exist today. In my *The Development of Moral Theology: Five Strands* (Washington, DC: Georgetown University Press, 2013), I recently developed further my understanding of how Vatican II shaped moral theology.

Part Two

HUMANAE VITAE AND ITS AFTERMATH

Introduction and Context

Humanae vitae, the 1968 encyclical of Pope Paul VI reaffirming the condemnation of artificial contraception for spouses, was the second reality that had a major and lasting effect on Catholic moral theology. Artificial contraception became a burning issue in the Catholic Church in the middle of the 1960s. The first article in a theological journal calling for a change in the teaching only appeared in late 1963. Then other articles began to appear, and the discussion continued and grew. In June of 1964, Pope Paul VI announced that a special commission had been appointed (originally by Pope John XXIII) to study the question, but in the meantime the existing norm was in effect. Expectations for change grew when the *National Catholic Reporter* in April 1967 published papers from the commission showing that the majority of the commission favored a change in the teaching. But the encyclical *Humanae vitae* issued in July 1968 reaffirmed the existing teaching. This set off a strenuous debate and discussion in Catholicism.

I was quite involved in the birth control issue. In a 1965 article, I maintained that the Church should change its teaching on birth control. In September 1965, I became an assistant professor in the School of Theology at the Catholic University of America (CUA), thus moving from the pastoral ethos of the seminary to the more academic ethos of the university. My position on changing the birth control position occasioned some tensions at CUA. In June 1966, I delivered a paper at the meeting of the Catholic Theological Society of America disagreeing with the unanimous position of the manuals of moral theology that masturbation always involved a grave matter, which in the popular mentality meant that it was always a mortal sin. Early in 1967, the School of Theology and the Academic Senate of the University approved my promotion to associate professor as of September 1967.

On April 17 the rector (president) of CUA, Bishop William J. McDonald, informed me that the board of trustees, apparently because of my position on birth control, had voted not to renew my contract. When this became known on campus, a very strong negative reaction came from faculty and students alike. The faculty of the School of Theology unanimously voted to go on strike unless and until I was reinstated. The full faculty of the university voted four hundred to eighteen to join the strike. Student demonstrations and picketing replaced the usual classes. The strike made front-page news in newspapers around the country. Finally, on Monday evening, April 24, after a number of meetings, the administration caved in. Archbishop Patrick O'Boyle, the chancellor of the university, and Bishop McDonald announced to a huge crowd of faculty and students that the trustees had rescinded their action, and I was promoted to associate professor.

The successful strike brought me into a prominent and leadership role. Within the Church the debate about birth control continued. On the morning of July 29, 1968, the Vatican released the encyclical *Humanae vitae* reiterating the condemnation of birth control. I arranged a meeting of about ten theologians (the majority from CUA) to meet that night at CUA to study the encyclical and decide what steps to take. We agreed on a ten-paragraph statement concluding that Catholics could responsibly decide in conscience to use birth control to preserve and foster the values of marriage. That night we called around the country and eighty-seven theologians agreed to sign the statement. Ultimately, more than six hundred professors signed our statement. At a press conference on Tuesday morning, July 30, I was the spokesperson for the group who presented the document to the press and the public. Our statement made front-page news all over the country the next day. I acted as organizer, leader, and spokesperson for the group. In my estimation our quick, responsible, measured, and respectful dissent was necessary to assure Catholics they did not have to leave the Church if they disagreed with the condemnation of birth control.

This introduction helps to explain the four chapters that appear in this part 2: "*Humanae Vitae* and Its Aftermath." Chapter 4 is the statement of dissent, which was originally published in the *New York Times* on July 31, 1968, and afterward in many other places. As the statement indicates, the two major issues involved in the discussion concern the natural law methodology used by the encyclical to reach its conclusions and the possibility of dissent from noninfallible teaching. Chapter 5 examines the understanding of natural law found in the encyclical. This chapter, originally entitled "Natural Law and Contemporary Moral Theology," appeared in *Contraception: Authority and Dissent* (New York: Herder and Herder, 1969). Immediately after the encyclical and the dissent, I edited this volume of nine essays from various scholars dealing with the issues raised by *Humanae vitae.*

Chapter 6 examines the legitimacy of dissent from the encyclical in the light of Catholic ecclesiology and moral theology. This chapter was originally published in my *Catholic Moral Theology in the United States: A History* (Washington, DC: Georgetown University Press, 2008). Chapter 7, written in the mid-1980s, points out the differences in moral methodology in official Catholic sexual teaching and official social teaching. This chapter shows why those who dissent from hierarchical sexual teaching often agree quite strongly with hierarchical social teaching. The chapter was published in my *Tensions in Moral Theology* (Notre Dame, IN: Notre Dame University Press, 1988).

4. Statement of Catholic Theologians

This statement was first published in the *New York Times*, July 31, 1968.

As Roman Catholic theologians we respectfully acknowledge a distinct role of hierarchical magisterium (teaching authority) in the Church of Christ. At the same time Christian tradition assigns theologians the special responsibility of evaluating and interpreting pronouncements of the magisterium in the light of the total theological data operative in each question or statement. We offer these initial comments on Pope Paul VI's Encyclical on the Regulation of Birth.

The encyclical is not an infallible teaching. History shows that a number of statements of similar or even greater authoritative weight have subsequently been proven inadequate or even erroneous. Past authoritative statements on religious liberty, interest-taking, the right to silence, and the ends of marriage have all been corrected at a later date.

Many positive values concerning marriage are expressed in Paul VI's encyclical. However, we take exception to the ecclesiology implied and the methodology used by Paul VI in the writing and promulgation of the document: they are incompatible with the Church's authentic self-awareness as expressed in and suggested by the acts of the Second Vatican Council itself. The encyclical consistently assumes that the Church is identical with the hierarchical office. No real importance is afforded the witness of the life of the Church in its totality; the special witness of many Catholic couples is neglected; it fails to acknowledge the witness of the separated Christian Churches and Ecclesial Communities; it is insensitive to the witness of many men of good will; it pays insufficient attention to the ethical import of modern science.

Furthermore, the encyclical betrays a narrow and positivistic notion of papal authority, as illustrated by the rejection of the majority view presented by the commission established to consider the question, as well as by the rejection of the conclusions of a large part of the international Catholic theological community.

Likewise, we take exception to some of the specific ethical conclusions contained in the encyclical. They are based on an inadequate concept of natural law: the multiple forms of natural law theory are ignored and the fact that competent philosophers come to different conclusions on this very question is disregarded. Even the minority report of the papal commission noted grave difficulty in attempting to present conclusive proof of the immorality of artificial contraception based on natural law.

Other defects include: overemphasis on the biological aspects of conjugal relations as ethically normative; undue stress on sexual acts and on the faculty of sex viewed in itself apart from the person and the couple; a static worldview that downplays the historical and evolutionary character of humanity in its finite existence, as described in Vatican II's Pastoral Constitution on the Church in the Modern World; unfounded assumptions about "the evil consequences of methods of artificial birth control"; indifference to Vatican II's assertion that prolonged sexual abstinence may cause "faithfulness to be imperiled and its quality of fruitfulness to be ruined"; an almost total disregard for the dignity of millions of human beings brought into the world without the slightest possibility of being fed and educated decently.

In actual fact, the encyclical demonstrates no development over the teaching of Pius XI's *Casti connubii*, whose conclusions have been called into question for grave and serious reasons. These reasons, given a muffled voice at Vatican II, have not been adequately handled by a mere repetition of past teaching.

It is common teaching in the Church that Catholics may dissent from authoritative, noninfallible teachings of the magisterium when sufficient reasons for doing so exist.

Therefore, as Roman Catholic theologians, conscious of our duty and our limitations, we conclude that spouses may responsibly decide according to their conscience that artificial contraception in some circumstances is permissible and indeed necessary to preserve and foster the values and sacredness of marriage.

It is our conviction also that true commitment to the mystery of Christ and the Church requires a candid statement of mind at this time by all Catholic theologians.

5. Natural Law and *Humanae Vitae*

This chapter was published in *Contraception: Authority and Dissent*, ed. Charles E. Curran (New York: Herder and Herder, 1969), 151–75; the final section of this chapter was published in my *Catholic Moral Theology in the United States: A History* (Washington DC: Georgetown University Press, 2008), 106–11.

Pope Paul's encyclical *Humanae vitae* (HV) explicitly employs a natural law methodology to arrive at its particular moral conclusions on the licit means of regulating births. The encyclical admits that the teaching on marriage is a "teaching founded on natural law, illuminated and enriched by divine revelation" (HV 4). The papal letter then reaffirms that "the teaching authority of the Church is competent to interpret even the natural moral law" (HV 4). Recently, Catholic moral theologians have been reappraising the notion of natural law.[1] The sharp response to the papal letter indicates there is a great divergence between the natural law methodology employed in the encyclical and the methodology suggested by recent studies in moral theology. The natural law approach employed in the encyclical raises two important questions for moral theology: (1) the place of natural law in the total understanding of Christian ethics, (2) the concept of natural law itself.

NATURAL LAW IN THE TOTAL CHRISTIAN PERSPECTIVE

The recent papal pronouncement realizes that natural law forms only a part of the total horizon of moral theology. The apostles and their successors have been constituted "as guardians and authentic interpreters of all the moral law, not only, that is, of the law of the Gospel, but also of the natural law, which is also an expression of the will of God" (HV 4).

The encyclical admits, however, there is a source of ethical wisdom and knowledge for the Christian apart from the explicit revelation of the Scriptures.

There have been some theologians especially in the more strict Protestant tradition who would tend to deny any source of ethical wisdom and knowledge that Christians share with all humankind.[2] Such theologians based their position on the uniqueness and self-sufficiency of the scriptural revelation, the doctrine of justification, and an emphasis on sin as corrupting whatever exists outside the unique revelation of Jesus Christ.[3] However, Protestant theologians today generally maintain the existence of some ethical wisdom apart from the explicit revelation of God in the Scriptures and in Christ Jesus, even though they may avoid the term "natural law."[4] Protestant theologians have employed such concepts as the orders of creation (Brunner), the divine mandates (Bonhoeffer), love and justice (Reinhold Niebuhr), love transforming justice (Ramsey), common ground morality (Bennett), and other similar approaches.

The natural law theory as implied in the encyclical has the theological merit of recognizing a source of ethical wisdom for the Christian apart from the explicit revelation of God in Christ Jesus. The difficult question for Christian theology centers on the relationship between the natural law and the distinctively Christian element in the understanding of the moral life of the Christian. The same basic question has been proposed in other terms. H. Richard Niebuhr describes five different models of the relationship between Christ and culture.[5] An older Catholic theology spoke about the relationship between nature and grace, between the natural and the supernatural. Niebuhr has described the typical Catholic solution to the question of Christ and culture in terms of "both-and"— both culture and Christ.[6] Such an approach corresponds with an unnuanced understanding of the relationship between nature and grace. The two are neither opposed nor identical; but they exist side by side. Grace adds something to nature without in any way destroying it. A simplistic view of the supernatural sees it as something added to the natural. But the natural retains its own finality and integrity as the substratum to which the supernatural is added.[7]

In such a perspective the natural tends to be seen as something absolute and sufficient in itself to which the supernatural is added. The natural law thus exists as a self-contained entity to which the law of the gospel or revelation is then added. *Humanae vitae* seems to accept such a "both-and" understanding of the relationship between natural law and the gospel or revelation. "All the moral law" is explained as "not only, that is, of the law of the Gospel, but also of the natural law, which is also an expression of the will of God…" (HV 4). The papal letter calls for an anthropology based on "an integral vision of man and his vocation, not only his natural and earthly, but also his supernatural and eternal vocation" (HV 7). The "both-and" relationship appears again in paragraph 8, which refers to "the entire moral law, both natural and evangelical."

Not only the wording of the encyclical but the methodology presupposed in the argumentation employs a "both-and" understanding of the relationship of natural law and evangelical law. Monsignor Lambruschini, who explained the encyclical at a press conference, said that purposely no mention was made of scriptural arguments, but the entire reasoning was based on natural law.[8] Bernard Häring has criticized the encyclical because it does not even mention the admonition of St. Paul that husband and wife should "not refuse each other except by mutual consent, and then only for an agreed time, to leave yourselves free for prayer; then come together again in case Satan should take advantage of your weakness to tempt you" (1 Cor 7:5).[9] The Pastoral Constitution on the Church in the Modern World did take heed of Paul's admonition. "But where the intimacy of married life is broken off, it is not rare for its faithfulness to be imperiled and its quality of fruitfulness ruined" (§51). However, the primary criticism is not the fact that there is no reference to any particular scriptural text, but the underlying understanding that the natural law is something totally integral in itself to which the evangelical or supernatural law is added.

Christian ethics cannot absolutize the realm of the natural as something completely self-contained and unaffected by any relationships to the evangelical or supernatural. Christian theology derives its perspective from the Christian faith commitment. The Christian views reality in the light of the total horizon of the Christian faith commitment—creation, sin, incarnation, redemption, and parousia. Natural law itself is thus christocentric.[10] The doctrine of creation forms the theological basis for natural law, and Christ as Logos is the one in whom all things are created and through whom all things are to be returned to the Father.

Natural law theory has taken seriously the implications of the incarnation through which God has joined God's self to the human, the worldly, and the historical. However, nature and creation form only a part of the total Christian view. The reality of "the natural" must always be seen in the light of sin, redemption, and the parousia. Nature and creation are relativized by the transforming Christian themes of redemption and final resurrection destiny of all creation. The natural law theory is theologically based on the Christian truths of creation and incarnation, but these aspects are not independent and unrelated to the full horizon of the Christian view of reality. The Christian situates natural law in the context of the total history of salvation, which transforms and criticizes what is only "the natural." Thus in the total Christian perspective there is a place for the "natural," but the natural remains provisional and relativized by the entire history of salvation.

The full Christian view of reality also takes account of the existence of sin and its effects on human existence. However, the natural law theory as illustrated in *Humanae vitae* does not seem to give sufficient importance to the reality and the effect of human sinfulness. In section III under "Pastoral Directives," the papal letter speaks about the compassion of Christ and the Church for sinners. "But she [the Church] cannot renounce the teaching of the law which is, in reality, that law proper to a human life restored to its original truth and conducted by the Spirit of God" (HV 19). The implication remains that the disruptive force of sin has already been overcome by the grace of God. Such an approach has definite affinities with a simplistic view of sin as depriving the human person of the supernatural gift of grace, but not affecting the substratum of nature. However, in the total Christian horizon, the disrupting influence of sin colors all human reality.

Humanae vitae does recognize some effects of sin in human creatures. Sin affects the human will, but the help of God will strengthen human good will (HV 20). Sin affects human instincts, but ascetical practices will enable human reason and will to achieve self-mastery (HV 21). Sinfulness also makes itself felt in some aspects of the social environment, "which leads to sense excitation and unbridled customs, as well as every form of pornography and licentious performances" (HV 22). But no mention is made of the fact that sin affects reason itself and the very nature on which natural law theory is based. Sin relativizes and affects all reality. How often has reason been used to justify human prejudice and arrogance! Natural law has been appealed to in the denial of human dignity and of religious liberty. The just war theory has been employed to justify wars in which one's own nation was involved.[11] History shows the effect of sin in the very abuses that have accompanied natural law thinking.

Recently, I have proposed the need for a theory of compromise in moral theology precisely because of the existence of sin in the world.[12] The surd brought about by human sinfulness is so oppressive that occasionally we humans cannot overcome it immediately. The presence of sin may force a person to do something she would not do if there were no sin present. Thus in sin-filled situations (notice all the examples of such situations in the current literature) the Christian may be forced to adopt a line of action that one would abhor if sin were not present. A theory of compromise does not give a blank check to shirk Christian responsibilities. However, there are situations in which the value sacrificed is not proportionate to the demand asked of the Christian. Protestant theology has often adopted a similar approach by saying that in some circumstances the Christian is forced to do something sinful. The sinner reluctantly performs the deed and asks God for mercy and forgiveness.[13] At times Protestant theology has overemphasized the reality of sin, but Catholic theology at times has not paid enough attention to the reality of sin.

The recent papal encyclical presupposes a natural law concept that fails to indicate the relative and provisional character of natural law in the total Christian perspective. Critics have rightly objected to a theory that tends to absolutize what is only relative and provisional. Take, for example, the teaching in Catholic theology on the right of private property. The modern popes have approached the question of private property in a much more absolute way than Thomas Aquinas. The differences of approach are instructive for the moral theologian. The popes, especially Leo XIII, stressed private property as the right of every person stemming from the dignity of the human person, rational nature, labor, the need to provide for oneself and family, and the need to overcome the uncertainties of life.[14] Thomas gave greater importance to the social function of all property and the reality of human sinfulness. Perhaps Thomas was influenced by the often-cited opinion of Isidore of Seville that according to the natural law all things should be held in common.[15] Thomas ultimately sees human sin as the reason for the existence of private property. Society would not have peace and order unless everyone possessed one's own goods. Likewise, Thomas pointed out that earthly goods are not properly cared for if they are held in common.[16] Thomas maintained there would be no need for private property in the world of original justice.

There are other indications that private property is not as absolute a right as proposed in some papal encyclicals. With his understanding of a more absolute right of private property, Leo XIII spoke of the obligation of the rich to share their goods with the poor as an obligation of charity and not justice.[17] However, a very respectable and long tradition in the medieval Church maintained that the rich had an obligation in justice to share their goods with the poor.[18] Even in our own day one can ask if private property is the best way to protect the dignity and freedom of the human person. The great inequalities existing in society today at the very least must modify and limit the concept of the right of private property. In our historical circumstances we are much more conscious of the social aspect of property than was Leo XIII.[19] The teaching on private property well illustrates the dangers of a natural law approach that is not relativized by the whole reality of salvation history.

The natural law theory suggested in, and employed by, the encyclical *Humanae vitae* has the advantage of affirming the existence of a source of ethical wisdom apart from the explicit revelation of God in Christ in the Scriptures. However, such a concept of natural law tends to absolutize what the full Christian vision sees as relative and provisional in the light of the entire history of salvation.

"PHYSICALISM" IN THE ENCYCLICAL

The encyclical on the regulation of birth employs a natural law methodology that tends to identify the moral action with the physical and biological structure of the act. (Note that I am not denying the fact that the moral aspect of the act may correspond with the physical structure of the act.) The core practical conclusion of the letter states, "We must once again declare that the direct interruption of the generative process already begun, and above all directly willed and procured abortion, even if for therapeutic reasons, are to be absolutely excluded as licit means of regulating birth" (HV 14). "Equally to be excluded...is direct sterilization....Similarly excluded is every action which, either in anticipation of the conjugal act, or in its accomplishment, or in the development of its natural consequences, proposes, whether as an end or as a means, to render procreation impossible" (HV 14). The footnotes in this particular paragraph refer to the Roman Catechism and the utterances of more recent popes. Reference is made to the Address of Pius XII to the Italian Catholic Union of Midwives in which direct sterilization is defined as "that which aims at making procreation impossible as both means and end" (13; AAS 43 [1951], 838). The concept of direct sterilization is thus described in terms of the physical structure and causality of the act itself.

The moral conclusion of the encyclical forbidding any interference with the conjugal act is based on the intimate structure of the conjugal act (HV 12). The "design of God" is written into the very nature of the conjugal act; the human person is merely "the minister of the design established by the Creator" (HV 13). The encyclical acknowledges that "it is licit to take into account the natural rhythms immanent in the generative functions." Recourse to the infecund periods is licit, whereas artificial contraception "as the use of means directly contrary to fecundation" is condemned as being always illicit (HV 16). "In reality there are essential differences between the two cases; in the former, the married couple make legitimate use of a natural disposition; in the latter, they impede the development of natural processes" (HV 16). The natural law theory employed in the encyclical thus identifies the moral and human action with the physical structure of the conjugal act itself.

CRITIQUES OF NATURAL LAW EXISTING IN 1968

In the context of the contemporary scene in moral theology, Catholic thinkers have been analyzing and criticizing the concept of natural law, especially understood as it is in *Humanae vitae*. The next few paragraphs will summarize some of the recent considerations.[20] The natural law does not refer to a coherent philosophical theory with an agreed-upon body of ethical content in existence from the beginning of time. Many thinkers in the course of history have employed the term *natural law*, but frequently they defined natural law in different ways. Thinkers employing different natural law approaches have arrived at different conclusions on particular moral topics. Natural law in the history of thought does not refer to a monolithic theory, but tends to be a more generic term that includes a number of different approaches to moral problems.

Many erroneously believe that Catholic theology is committed to a particular natural law approach to moral problems. In practice, however, the vast majority of Catholic teaching on particular moral questions came into existence even before Thomas Aquinas enunciated his theory. Likewise, contemporary Catholic theology recognizes the need for a pluralism of philosophical approaches in the Christian's quest for a better understanding of human existence. There is no longer "one Catholic philosophy."

In particular there has been much criticism of a natural law approach that defines the moral action in terms of the physical structure of the act itself. If the natural law is human reason, then reason should be able to interfere in physical and biological processes. Thomas's own understanding of the absolute character of moral law is much less rigid than the exposition of the absolute character of the natural law found in many theology manuals.[21] The identification of the total human act with its physical and biological structure logically comes from the theory of the Roman lawyer Ulpian. Ulpian distinguished the natural law from the *ius gentium*. The natural law is that which is common to humans and all the animals; whereas the *ius gentium* is that which is proper to humans because of their reason.[22] The natural law thus was equated with physical, biological processes that we share with all the animals. In general, Catholic theology avoids the identification of the human act with the physical structure of the act. Not every killing is murder; not every taking of something is theft; not every falsehood is a lie. However, in the case of contraception, Catholic moral theology describes the moral act in physical terms.

Such a theory of natural law seems conditioned by the prescientific circumstances in which it arose. In a pretechnological civilization, people found happiness by conforming themselves to the rhythms of nature. But through science and technology, contemporary people can interfere with the laws of nature to make human life more human.

Perhaps the greatest reason for the insufficiency in the natural law theory found in the papal encyclical stems from the shift in horizon from a classicist worldview to a more historically minded worldview.[23] In a more historically conscious methodology things have a tendency to become "unstuck."[24] A classicist approach emphasizes the eternal, the immutable, and the unchanging. A more historically minded approach stresses the individual, the particular, the temporal, and the changing. The classicist view gives great importance to rationality, objectivity, order, and substances viewed in themselves. The historically conscious view sees rationality as only a part of the human and appreciates the importance of the subjective and the intersubjective in its understanding of human existence. A classicist methodology tends to be more a priori and deductive; whereas the historically conscious methodology employs a more a posteriori and inductive approach. The different methodologies also have different understandings of truth and certitude that, of necessity, color one's understanding of the moral life.

Humanae vitae in its methodology well illustrates a classicist approach. The papal letter admits that "changes which have taken place are in fact noteworthy and of varied kinds" (HV 2). These changes give rise to new questions. However, the changing historical circumstances have not affected the answer or the method employed in arriving at concrete conclusions on implementing responsible parenthood. The primary reason for rejecting the majority report of the papal commission was "because certain criteria of solutions had emerged which departed from the moral teaching on marriage proposed with constant firmness by the teaching authority of the Church" (HV 6).

The encyclical specifically acknowledges the fact that there are new signs of the times, but one wonders if sufficient attention has really been paid to such changes. The footnotes to the encyclical are significant even if the footnote references alone do not constitute a conclusive argument. The references are only to random scriptural texts, one citation of Thomas Aquinas, and references to earlier pronouncements of the hierarchical magisterium. A more inductive approach would have been inclined to give more importance and documentation to the signs of the times. The footnote references contain no indication of any type of dialogue with other Christians, non-Christians, and the modern sciences. When the letter does mention social consequences of the use of contraception, no documentation is given for what appear to be unproven assumptions. Since the methodology describes the human act in physical terms, the practical moral conclusion is the absolute condemnation of means of artificial birth control. The encyclical thus betrays an epistomology that has been rejected by many Catholic theologians and philosophers today.

DIFFERENT APPROACHES WITH DIFFERENT CONCLUSIONS

Natural law theory has traditionally upheld two values that are of great importance for moral theology: (1) the existence of a source of ethical wisdom and knowledge that the Christian shares with all humankind; (2) the fact that morality cannot be merely the subjective whim of an individual or group of individuals. However, one can defend these important values for moral theology without necessarily endorsing the particular understanding of natural law presupposed in the encyclical. In the last few years Catholic thinkers have been developing and employing different philosophical approaches to an understanding of morality. One could claim that such approaches are modifications of natural law theory because they retain the two important values mentioned above. Others would prefer to abandon the term *natural law* since such a concept is very ambiguous. As mentioned, there is no monolithic philosophical system throughout history called the natural law, and also the term has been somewhat discredited because of the tendency among some to understand natural in terms of the physical structure of acts. We can briefly describe three of the alternative approaches that have been advanced in the last few years—personalism, a more relational and communitarian approach, and a transcendental methodology. All these approaches would deny the absolute conclusion of the papal encyclical in condemning all means of artificial birth control.

A more personalist approach has characterized much of contemporary ethics. For the Christian, the biblical revelation contributes to such an understanding of reality. A personalist approach cannot be something merely added on to another theory. A personalist perspective will definitely affect moral conclusions, especially when such conclusions have been based on the physical structure of the act itself. Personalism always sees the act in terms of the person placing the act. The Pastoral Constitution on the Church in the Modern World realized that objective standards in the matter of sexual morality are "based on the nature of the human person and his acts" (§51). For the good of the person, one can interfere with the physical and biological processes.

Classical ethical theory embraces two types or models of ethical method: the teleological and the deontological. H. Richard Niebuhr has added a third ethical model—the model of responsibility. There are various relationships within which the responsible self exists. "The responsible self is driven as it were by the movement of the social process to respond and be accountable in nothing less than a universal community."[25] Robert Johann in developing his understanding of the human person acknowledges a great debt to Niebuhr.[26]

The natural law approach as found in the manuals of theology views nature as a principle of operation within every existing thing. The human being thus should act according to the design of God inscribed in human nature that should be unfolded in one's life and actions. Note that the encyclical adopts such a view. However, many thinkers today view the human person not as a substantial entity existing with its own nature as the guiding principle of one's life, but rather as a person existing as a being with others in a network of relationships. The person is not a being totally programmed by the nature one has. Rather, the person is characterized by openness, freedom, and the challenge to make self and the world more human in and through many relationships. The human person is actually constituted in and through these relationships. Relationality thus characterizes human existence. A philosophy of process is somewhat further along the same line of a more relational and historical approach to reality.

In the particular question of contraception, a more relational approach would not view the person or a particular faculty as something existing in itself. Each faculty or power such as sexuality exists in relationship with the total person and other persons within a universal community. Morality cannot merely be determined by examining a particular faculty and its physical structure or a particular act in itself. The changed ethical evaluation of lying illustrates the point. Manuals of moral theology have generally accepted the Augustinian definition of lying as speech against what is in the mind (*locutio contra mentem*). The malice of lying thus consists in violating the purpose of the faculty or power of speech. Recently Catholic theologians have proposed a different understanding of lying that actually corresponds more with the thinking of the earlier Augustine before he arrived at his famous definition of *locutio contra mentem*.[27] The malice of lying consists in the violation of my neighbor's right to truth. Falsehood is the physical act of speech that is contrary to what is in the mind; but lying as a moral act consists in the violation of my relationships with my neighbor and the community. Both Robert Johann and William van der Marck have employed a more relational approach to argue for the liceity of contraception in certain circumstances.[28]

A third philosophical theory espoused by a growing number of Catholic thinkers today is a theory of transcendental method. Transcendental methodology owes much to Joseph Maréchal and is espoused today in different forms by Bernard Lonergan, Karl Rahner, and Emerich Coreth.[29]

In general, transcendental method goes beyond the object known to the structures of the human knowing process itself. According to Lonergan, "the intrinsic objectivity of human cognitional activity is its intentionality."[30] Lonergan's ethics is an extension of his theory of knowing. Moral value is not an intrinsic property of external acts or objects; it is an aspect of certain consciously free acts in relation to my knowledge of the world. Humans must come to examine the structures of their knowing and deciding process.[31]

Lonergan uses as a tool the notion of horizon analysis. Basic horizon is the maximum field of vision from a determined standpoint. This basic horizon is open to development and even conversion. Lonergan posits four conversions that should transpire from the understanding of the structures of human knowing and deciding—the intellectual, the moral, the religious, and the Christian. Ethics must bring people to this Christian conversion so that they can become aware of their knowing and doing and flee from inauthenticity, unreasonableness, and the surd of sin. Thus Christian ethics is primarily concerned with the manner in which an authentic Christian person makes ethical decisions and carries them out. However, such a meta-ethics must then enter into the realm of the normative, all the time realizing the provisional value of its precepts, which are limited by the data at hand.[32] One commentator has said of Lonergan's ethic as applied to moral theology, "The distinct contribution of the moral theologian to philosophical ethics would consist in clarifying the attitudes which are involved in man's responding in faith to the initiative of a loving God who has redeemed man in Christ."[33] Thus a transcendental method would put greater stress on the knowing and deciding structures of the authentic Christian subject. Such a theory would also tend to reject the encyclical's view of morality based on the finality of the faculty or power.

DEVELOPMENTS IN THE YEARS AFTER *HUMANAE VITAE*

The two criticisms of the natural law theory as found in the manuals and in papal documents—the identification of the human moral act with the physical structure and aspect of the act and the criterion of the nature and purpose of the faculty rather than the good of the person and the person's relationships—help to explain the questioning by revisionist theologians of almost all the disputed specific issues that have arisen in moral theology in the past fifty years. This short section does not try to prove or support a dissenting position on these issues but only to explain why these are the issues that are being debated in Catholic moral theology. The problem of physicalism and the finality of the faculty explain why questions have been raised about sterilization, masturbation, artificial insemination, and homosexual acts between two committed persons with a homosexual orientation. The most important condition of the famous principle of the double effect is based on the physical causality of the act. The good effect cannot be achieved by means of the bad effect, which explains why many have questioned this condition. There has been a discussion about the beginning of truly individual human life because some do not want to identify truly individual human life with only the physical and biological union of the ovum and sperm. The manualist approach talked about the existence of the bond of marriage that comes into effect when two people make their commitment to each other. But does a bond truly exist when the relationship of love has ceased to exist? A few have questioned why euthanasia, as the physical act of bringing about death, is always wrong. But a word of caution is also in order. The physical, the biological, and the body are a part of the human and, in general, can never be totally dismissed. The generally accepted understanding of the death of the human person is based on the physical realities of the breakdown of the circulatory or respiratory systems or the lack of total brain function.

The debate over these issues has also raised the question about the existence of absolute moral norms and intrinsically evil acts. Revisionist moral theologians are not opposed to either. They maintain that torture, rape, and lying (understood as the violation of my neighbor's right to truth) are intrinsically wrong and constitute absolute norms that have no exception. But revisionists hold that actions that are described only in terms of the physical aspect or structure are neither necessarily always wrong nor intrinsically evil.

The traditional Catholic natural law approach maintained that the morality of an act is determined by its object, the end, and the circumstances. Some acts are intrinsically wrong by reason of the object. Revisionists can accept such an approach if the object is defined in terms of the moral reality of the object and not just the physical aspect of the object.

Revisionist theories arose as an attempt to explain systematically and coherently the positions often taken by revisionist theologians, especially in the area of sexuality and the principle of double effect. Individual moral judgments and positions came into being first; the theory came later to explain the existing positions. At a very minimum, there will always be a two-way relationship between theory and individual moral judgments. Individuals and the Church community often make their individual moral judgments based on the broadest possible moral experience, including more theoretical aspects, but individual judgments influence and sometimes even call for a change in the theory.

Proportionalism

The proponents of revisionism involved many Catholic moral theologians from Europe: Peter Knauer, Josef Fuchs, Bruno Schüller, and Louis Janssens were the primary European voices. Richard McCormick and I were the leading revisionists in the United States.[34] In his "Notes on Moral Theology" in *Theological Studies*, McCormick chronicled the debate and also developed and defended his own understanding of proportionalism. One can do premoral evil if there is a proportionate reason for so doing.[35] The development and defense of proportionalism took place in two overlapping contexts: the dissatisfaction with the manualistic and hierarchical Church teaching on sexual issues and its natural law basis, and the contemporary debate among Christian ethicists and philosophical ethicists over teleology and deontology. Utilitarianism or consequentialism, one form of teleology, makes the net good of the consequences of the act the moral criterion. In other words, the end justifies the means. The deontological position in general maintains that some actions are always wrong, no matter what the consequences. McCormick recognizes his own position as avoiding the two extremes of absolute deontology, as found in the Catholic manualist tradition and in German Grisez, and absolute consequentialism, as identified with Joseph Fletcher and some utilitarians. His moderate teleology sees the role of consequences as necessary but not sufficient for determining the morality of actions.[36]

McCormick maintains that proportionate reason is the criterion used even in the manuals themselves and in the Catholic hierarchical teaching in most areas, except in the areas of sexuality and the principle of double effect. For example, the Catholic tradition justifies breaking promises or killing people if there is a proportionate reason for doing so. In reality the objection to the manualist teaching on sexual issues such as masturbation, contraception, sterilization, and homosexual relations does not in any way imply the danger of accepting absolute consequentialism or utilitarianism. Many theologians and philosophers accept such positions and strongly oppose utilitarianism. The specter of absolute consequentialism arises especially in issues of justice and the direct killing of noncombatants in war. One case that illustrates the justice issue is the framing of an innocent person in order to avoid very great evils. A Southern sheriff framed and handed over to the white mob an innocent person in order to prevent the mob from killing, raping, and pillaging in the African American section of the city, even though he knew that the mob would kill the innocent person. McCormick will not accept the framing of an innocent person, or the direct killing of noncombatants to end a war quickly and save more lives in the long run.

McCormick's final understanding of proportionate reason indicates how he differs from the absolute consequentialists. The very fact that he speaks of premoral values shows that he recognizes that these values have some moral meaning apart from consequences. He does not want to base morality on aggregating all the consequences of the action. There has to be a proportionate reason for choosing a premoral evil in order to achieve this particular end or value.

Another way to avoid consequentialism is to bring in the concept of associated goods. McCormick holds that there are basic human goods grounded in our natural inclinations and tendencies. His theory of the association of basic goods implies some indirect way to make them commensurate. The sheriff should not hand over the innocent prisoner to the mob to avoid the horrendous consequences to the black community in the town. The good life, the end of the sheriff's action, would be undercut in the long run by serious injury to the associated good of human freedom. The mob should recognize its moral obligation not to participate in such violence.[37]

In addition to associated goods, McCormick insists that a proportionate reason is present when the means are in a necessary causal relationship to the end.[38] There is no necessary connection between killing innocent people and ending a war, thereby avoiding greater evil. But there is a necessary connection between aborting a fetus to save the life of the mother. McCormick refers to such prohibitions as virtually without exception, but James Walter points out that the requirement of a necessary connection between the premoral evil committed and the good consequences means that these prohibitions are intrinsically evil.[39]

In the process of defending his theory of proportionalism, McCormick responds to three criticisms of his approach: once one knows that there is a proportionate reason to justify the act, one cannot choose a wrong option; the basic goods are themselves incommensurate; and one cannot establish a hierarchy or order among the basic goods.[40]

By the latter part of the twentieth century the defense of proportionalism was no longer a major topic in moral theology. James Keenan claims that proportionalism was a temporary attempt to deal with particular issues, because it shared the basic focus of avoiding evil rather than the pursuit of the good. Basically, it followed the logical approach of the manuals without their concept of intrinsic evil.[41] Aline Kalbian makes basically the same point by showing that newer approaches, such as feminism, virtue ethics, and casuistry, have taken over the concerns of proportionalism.[42]

New Natural Law Theory

Proponents of the natural law approach of the manuals strongly object to revisionism and its dissent from official Catholic teachings. But the most creative and innovative defense of the negative moral absolutes proposed by the hierarchical magisterium comes from the theory often called the "new natural law theory" or the "basic human goods theory" proposed by Germain Grisez, frequently writing with Joseph Boyle and others.[43] Later, John Finnis, an Australian teaching legal jurisprudence at Oxford and now also teaching at Notre Dame, proposed and defended the same basic approach.[44]

Grisez strongly disagrees with the manualistic approach to natural law. He accepts the basic insight of David Hume that one cannot go from an "is" to an "ought." This approach is the naturalistic fallacy. Nature itself has no normative character. The argument against contraception as violating the God-given purpose of the sexual faculty—the perverted-faculty argument—is not valid. Many times we go against the purpose of a faculty, as in holding our noses to avoid a repugnant smell.[45] Thus, Grisez, in a certain way, joins the revisionists in objecting to the physicalism of the manualistic approach. But Grisez strongly opposes revisionism and proportionalism. It is impossible to make a judgment about the greater good because diverse basic values or goods cannot be compared. Moral situations are complex and without fixed borders, and so we can never know all that is involved in a situation and its consequences. Basic human goods (e.g., justice and truth) are incommensurate. There is no common denominator for judging what is the greater good.[46]

Grisez and others have recognized that their approach is not Thomistic and that their theory is neither teleological nor deontological. Aquinas begins with the teleology of the ultimate end and recognizes inclinations in nature that have moral content. For Grisez, Aquinas's first principle of practical reason—good is to be done and pursued and evil is to be avoided—is not itself a moral precept.[47] For Grisez, the first principle of morality is this: "In voluntarily acting for human goods and avoiding what is opposed to them, one ought to choose and otherwise will those and only those possibilities whose willing is compatible with the will toward integral human fulfillment."[48]

Modes of responsibility are intermediate principles that are somewhat formal in nature and involve not moral actions but ways of choosing and acting that spell out the first general principle. The first mode of responsibility, for example, maintains that one should not be deterred by inertia from acting for intelligible goods. The most significant of the modes of responsibility for the defense of the absolute moral norms taught by the hierarchical magisterium is the eighth and final mode: one should not be so moved by desire for one instance of an intelligible good that one chooses to destroy, damage, or impede some other instance of an intelligible good to obtain it. In other words, one cannot go against a basic human good in trying to achieve some other human good.[49]

What are these basic human goods? Grisez maintains that there are eight self-evident basic human goods. They are not deduced from any first principle or derived from our understanding of human nature. We know them just by knowing the meaning of their terms. Four are existential goods—integration; practical reasonableness or authenticity; friendship and justice; and religion or holiness. Three are substantive goods—life and bodily well-being; knowledge of truth and appreciation of beauty; and skill for performance and play. The eighth good is the complex good of marriage and family The permanent union of man and woman, which normally unfolds in parenthood and family life, is both substantive and reflexive. This is a substantive good insofar as it fulfills the natural capacity of men and women to complement one another, have children, and bring them up; but it is also a reflexive good insofar as it includes the free choices of a couple marrying and committing themselves to fulfill all the responsibilities of marriage.[50] Contraception is the choice to prevent the passing on of human life. But this is a choice to impede a basic human good (life) in a particular instance. Such a choice against an instance of the basic human good of life violates the eighth mode of responsibility. William E. May has also written extensively to explain and defend the Grisez approach in areas of general moral theology, sexual ethics, and bioethics.[51]

With many, I disagree with the theoretical and practical aspects of this theory. On the basis of a relational ethical model, one easily recognizes that many basic human goods, such as justice and truth, might come into conflict.[52] In fact, from a different perspective, Pope Pius XII, in his defense of using only ordinary means to preserve life, recognized that life and health are subordinated to spiritual ends.[53] Grisez in reply points out the incommensurability of basic goods, but it seems that the Catholic tradition has recognized the existence of these conflicts and has tried to deal with them. On the practical issue of contraception, contraception itself does not have a very close connection with the basic good of human life. In fact, there is no human life present when contraception occurs. Would someone who did not hold that contraception and masturbation are intrinsically grave evils ever come to the conclusion that these acts go against the basic good of life itself?

Notes

1. E.g., *Light on the Natural Law*, ed. Illtud Evans (Baltimore: Helicon, 1965); *Das Naturrecht im Disput*, ed. Franz Böckle (Dusseldorf: Patmos-Verlag, 1966); "La Nature fondement de la morale?" *Supplement de la Vie Spirituelle* 81 (May 1967): 187–324; *Absolutes in Moral Theology?*, ed. Charles E. Curran (Washington, DC: Corpus Books, 1968).

2. Edward LeRoy Long Jr., *A Survey of Christian Ethics* (New York: Oxford University Press, 1967); Thomas G. Sanders, *Protestant Concepts of Church and State* (Garden City, NY: Doubleday, 1965).

3. Such emphases can still be found, although not in an absolute sense, in the writings of Niels H. Söe. See Söe, "Natural Law and Social Ethics," in *Christian Social Ethics in a Changing World*, ed. John C. Bennett (New York: Association Press, 1966), 289–309. The same article with a response by Paul Ramsey appeared in *Zeitschrift fur Evangelische Ethik* 12 (March 1968): 65–98.

4. John C. Bennett, "Issues for the Ecumenical Dialogue," in Bennett, *Christian Social Ethics in a Changing World*, 377, 378.

5. H. Richard Niebuhr, *Christ and Culture* (New York: Harper & Row, 1956).

6. Niebuhr actually describes the Thomistic approach as "Christ above culture." He goes on to explain that "Thomas also answers the question about Christ and culture with a 'both-and'; yet his Christ is far above culture, and he does not try to disguise the gulf that lies between them" (129).

7. One cannot simplistically condemn the nature-grace and natural-supernatural distinctions. In their original historical contexts such distinctions

tried with considerable success to describe and synthesize this complex reality. Although such distinctions do have some meaning today, many Catholic theologians realize the need to reinterpret such distinctions in the light of different metaphysical approaches. See the three articles by Bernard Lonergan, which appeared in *Theological Studies* 2 (1941): 307–24; 3 (1942): 69–88, 375–402. For an exposition of the thought of Karl Rahner on this subject, see Carl J. Peter, "The Position of Karl Rahner Regarding the Supernatural," *Proceedings of the Catholic Theological Society of America* 20 (1965): 81–94.

8. A wire release of N. C. News Service with a Vatican City dateline published in Catholic papers in this country during the week of August 4.

9. Bernard Häring, "The Encyclical Crisis," *Commonweal* 88 (September 6, 1968): 588–94.

10. Joseph Fuchs, *Natural Law*, trans. Helmut Reckter and John Dowling (New York: Sheed & Ward, 1965).

11. Christian Duquoc, *L'Église et le progrès* (Paris: Éditions du Cerf, 1964), 68–117. The author considers the past teaching in the Church on slavery, the freedom of nations, the dignity of women, church and state, torture, and questions of war and peace.

12. Charles E. Curran, "Dialogue with Joseph Fletcher," *Homiletic and Pastoral Review* 67 (1967): 828, 829.

13. Helmet Thielicke, *Theological Ethics*, vol. 1, *Foundations*, ed. William Lazerath (Philadelphia: Fortress Press, 1966), 622ff.

14. Pope Leo XIII, *Rerum novarum* 7–14; Pope Pius XI, *Quadragesimo anno* 44–52.

15. Thomas explicitly cites Isidore in I–II, q. 94, a. 2, ob. 1. In II–II, q. 66, a. 2, Thomas gives the opinion proposed by Isidore without a direct reference. Thomas explains that reason has called for the right of private property not as something against natural law, but as something added to natural law.

16. The reasons adduced by Thomas in II–II, q. 66, a. 2, indicate that human sinfulness is a very important factor in the argument for the right of private property.

17. *Rerum novarum* 22.

18. Hermenegildus Lio, "Estne obligatio justitiae subvenire pauperibus?" *Apollinaris* 29 (1956): 124–231; 30 (1957): 99–201.

19. Leo XIII was conscious of the social aspect of property (*Rerum novarum* 22), but he did not emphasize it. The subsequent popes down to Paul VI have put increasingly more emphasis on the social aspects of property. The concentration on such social aspects explains the many discussions about the notion of socialization in the encyclicals of Pope John XXIII.

20. See above, n. 1; also essays by Curran, Häring, McCormick, and

Milhaven in *Norm and Context in Christian Ethics*, ed. Gene H. Outka and Paul Ramsey (New York: Scribners,1968).

21. John G. Milhaven, "Moral Absolutes and Thomas Aquinas," in Curran, *Absolutes in Moral Theology?*, 154–58.

22. *The Digest* or *Pandects of Justinian*, Book I, t. 1, n. 1–4.

23. Bernard Lonergan, "The Transition from a Classicist World View to Historical Mindedness," in *Law for Liberty*, ed. James E. Biechler (Baltimore: Helicon, 1967), 126–33; John Courtney Murray, "The Declaration on Religious Freedom," *Concilium* 2 (May 1966): 3–10.

24. The phrase comes from Robert O. Johann, *Building the Human* (New York: Herder and Herder, 1968), 62. In this one volume Johann has gathered many of his articles expounding his relational approach to morality.

25. H. Richard Niebuhr, *The Responsible Self* (New York: Harper & Row, 1963), 88.

26. Johann, *Building the Human*, 7–10.

27. J. A. Dorszynski, *Catholic Teaching about the Morality of Falsehood* (Washington, DC: Catholic University of America Press, 1949).

28. Robert O. Johann, "Responsible Parenthood: A Philosophical View," *Proceedings of the Catholic Theological Society of America* 20 (1965): 115–28; William H. van der Marck, *Toward a Christian Ethic* (Westminster, MD: Newman Press, 1967), 48–60. Note that Germain G. Grisez, in his *Contraception and the Natural Law* (Milwaukee: Bruce, 1964), argues against artificial contraception although he explicitly denies the "perverted faculty" argument. However, Grisez seems to accept too uncritically his basic premise that the malice of contraception "is in the will's direct violation of the procreative good as a value in itself, as an ideal which never may be submerged."

29. For a succinct exposition of transcendental philosophy, see Kenneth Baker, *A Synopsis of the Transcendental Philosophy of Emerich Coreth and Karl Rahner* (Spokane, WA: Gonzaga University, 1965).

30. Bernard Lonergan, *Collection* (New York: Herder and Herder, 1967), 278.

31. In addition to the bibliography of Lonergan's that has already been mentioned, see Bernard Lonergan, *Insight* (New York: Longmans, Green, 1964); also Donald H. Johnson, "Lonergan and the Redoing of Ethics," *Continuum* 5 (1967): 211–20.

32. David W. Tracy, "Horizon Analysis and Eschatology," *Continuum* 6 (1968): 166–79.

33. Johnson, "Lonergan and the Redoing of Ethics," 219, 220.

34. For a systematic study of proportionalism, see Bernard Hoose, *Proportionalism: The American Debate and Its European Roots* (Washington, DC: Georgetown University Press, 1987); Garth L. Hallett, *Greater Good: A Case*

for Proportionalism (Washington, DC: Georgetown University Press, 1996). For a negative evaluation of proportionalism, see Christopher Kaczor, *Proportionalism and the Natural Law Tradition* (Washington, DC: Catholic University of America Press, 2002). For the critical debate occasioned by John Paul II's encyclical *Veritatis splendor*, see Michael E. Allsopp and John J. O'Keefe, eds., Veritatis Splendor: *American Responses* (Kansas City, MO: Sheed & Ward, 1995); John Wilkins, ed., *Understanding* Veritatis Splendor (London: SPCK, 1994).

35. For an overview of McCormick's position, see Paulinus Ikechukwu Odozor, *Richard A. McCormick and the Renewal of Moral Theology* (Notre Dame, IN: University of Notre Dame Press, 1995), 91–118. For critical but basically favorable analyses of McCormick's position, see John Langan, "Direct and Indirect—Some Recent Exchanges between Paul Ramsey and Richard A. McCormick," *Religious Studies Review* 5 (1979): 95–101; James J. Walter, "The Foundation and Formulation of Norms," in *Moral Theology: Challenges for the Future; Essays in Honor of Richard A. McCormick*, ed. Charles E. Curran (New York: Paulist Press, 1990), 125–54.

36. Richard A. McCormick, "A Commentary on the Commentaries," in *Doing Evil to Achieve Good: Moral Choice in Conflict Situations*, ed. Richard A. McCormick and Paul Ramsey (Chicago: Loyola University Press, 1978), 245.

37. Richard A. McCormick, *Notes on Moral Theology, 1965–1980* (Washington, DC: University Press of America, 1981), 720–21.

38. McCormick, "Commentary on the Commentaries," 210; McCormick, *Notes on Moral Theology, 1980–1984*, 63–64.

39. Walter, "Foundation and the Formulation of Norms," 143.

40. Todd A., Salzman, *What Are They Saying about Catholic Ethical Method?* (New York: Paulist Press, 2003), 36–44. In this book Salzman gives a good overview of the discussion between revisionism and the new natural law theory.

41. James F. Keenan, "The Moral Agent: Actions and Normative Decision Making," in *A Call to Fidelity: On the Moral Theology of Charles E. Curran*, ed. James J. Walter, Timothy E. O'Connell, and Thomas A. Shannon (Washington, DC: Georgetown University Press, 2002), 39.

42. Aline H. Kalbian, "Where Have All the Proportionalists Gone?" in *Journal of Religious Ethics* 30 (2002): 3–22.

43. Germain Grisez, a prolific scholar, has written a three-volume systematic moral theology: *The Way of the Lord Jesus*, vol. 1, *Christian Moral Principles* (Chicago: Franciscan Herald, 1983); vol. 2, *Living a Christian Life* (Quincy, IL: Franciscan Herald, 1993); and vol. 3, *Difficult Moral Questions* (Quincy, IL: Franciscan Herald, 1997). For a very readable, succinct, and accurate summary of his basic theory, see Germain Grisez and Russell Shaw, *Fulfillment in Christ: A Summary of Christian Moral Principles* (Notre Dame, IN: University of Notre

Dame Press, 1991). For a personal and intellectual overview of Grisez's life and work, see Russell Shaw, "The Making of a Moral Theologian," in *Catholic World Report*, March 1996, at https://www.ewtn.com/catholicism/library/making-of-a-moral-theologian-10811.

44. Among Finnis's most significant works are John Finnis, *Natural Law and Natural Rights* (Oxford: Clarendon Press, 1980); *Fundamentals of Ethics* (Washington, DC: Georgetown University Press, 1983); and *Moral Absolutes, Tradition, Revision, and Truth* (Washington, DC: Catholic University of America Press, 1991).

45. Grisez and Shaw, *Fulfillment in Christ*, 44–48.

46. Grisez and Shaw, *Fulfillment in Christ*, 56–71.

47. German Grisez, John M. Finnis, and Joseph M. Boyle Jr., "Practical Principles, Moral Truth, and Ultimate Ends," in *American Journal of Jurisprudence* 32 (1987): 99–151 provides a good summary of the development of this theory.

48. Grisez and Shaw, *Fulfillment in Christ*, 80.

49. Grisez and Shaw, *Fulfillment in Christ*, 305–14.

50. Grisez and Shaw, *Fulfillment in Christ*, 54–56.

51. For William E. May's many publications, see his home page at http://www.christendom-awake.org/pages/may/may.html.

52. Charles E. Curran, *Catholic Moral Tradition Today: A Synthesis* (Washington, DC: Georgetown University Press, 1999), 158–60.

53. Pope Pius XII, "The Prolongation of Life," in *Medical Ethics: Sources of Catholic Teaching*, ed. Kevin D. O'Rourke and Philip J. Boyle (St. Louis: Catholic Health Association of the United States, 1989), 207.

6. Dissent

This chapter was published in my *Catholic Moral Theology in the United States: A History* (Washington, DC: Georgetown University Press, 2008), 111–24.

Theological dissent from noninfallible teaching became a burning issue in response to Pope Paul VI's encyclical *Humanae vitae* in July 1968 condemning artificial contraception for Catholic spouses. The whole Catholic world knew that in the previous years a special papal commission had been studying the issue and that a majority of the commission was in favor of change. The encyclical created a greater furor than any other Church document since it directly affected so many people and great publicity surrounded its issuance and the reactions to it.[1]

The questioning of some absolute norms taught in the Catholic Church coincided with this related issue of the binding force of the teaching of the papal magisterium on moral issues. Revisionist theologians challenged some of these norms, while the new natural law theorists and proponents of the neo-Scholastic natural law approach staunchly defended these norms. A significant factor in the discussion about dissent from the teaching of *Humanae vitae* on artificial contraception for spouses was the practice of many married Catholics, and today the vast majority of Catholic married people do not follow the condemnation of artificial contraception. Chapter 3 treated the Catholic teaching that one must follow one's conscience but conscience can be wrong. This section will support that understanding of the role of conscience by emphasizing the importance of the reception of hierarchical teaching in the Church and the *sensus fidelium*—the sense and practice of the faithful—as a true source of wisdom for the Church community. In light of these factors, revisionist theologians point out that the hierarchical teaching on a number of issues in the past has changed precisely because of the practice of the Christian people who did not go along with the former teaching.

Many theologians contributed to the debate supporting the legitimacy of dissent from the teaching on contraception and the possibility of dissent from authoritative noninfallible Church teaching. This section will synthesize the primary reasons proposed in this debate and concentrate heavily on the work of two moral theologians—Charles E. Curran and Richard A. McCormick, singled out by Germain Grisez, a strong opponent of such dissent, as the primary representatives in favor of what he calls radical dissent.[2]

The Constitution on the Church of Vatican II addressed the issue of the hierarchical magisterium or teaching office in the Church. To infallible teachings, a Catholic owes the assent of faith. The religious submission (*obsequium*) of will and intellect is due to authoritative noninfallible papal teaching.[3] Proponents of theological dissent from the papal teaching on artificial contraception and the possibility of dissent from other noninfallible Church teachings proposed three generic types of reasons—reasons from history, ecclesiology, and moral theology—to justify such dissent.

HISTORICAL REASONS

The first historical reason concerns the proper meaning and understanding of Vatican II's teaching on the religious *obsequium* of intellect and will that is owed to authoritative noninfallible teaching. This terminology came into existence only in the nineteenth century when the First Vatican Council proclaimed the infallibility of the pope. One had to distinguish from this infallible teaching the category of noninfallible teaching. Objections were raised against papal infallibility at the time of the council on the basis of the historical teachings of Pope Liberius (352–66), Pope Vigilius (540–55), and Pope Honorius (625–38). These three were cited as teaching erroneous doctrines in the course of the debate over papal infallibility.[4] A threefold answer responded to the objection that these erroneous statements argued against papal infallibility. First, some of these events and statements might not be historically certain. Second, they do not pertain to the subject of infallibility that involves only *ex cathedra* statements. Third, they do not pertain to the object of infallibility that is a doctrine about faith and morals.[5] Such discussions at Vatican I recognized the need to realize the existence of a category of teaching—noninfallible teaching—that might be wrong or erroneous.

An early and important study by Joseph Komonchak analyzed the teaching of the accepted manuals of dogmatic theology—the textbooks used in the seminaries throughout the world. These authors were often called in Latin the *auctores probati*—the approved authors. The manualists maintained that one owes an internal religious assent to authoritative noninfallible teaching that differs from the assent of faith owed to infallible teaching. Divine faith is absolutely certain and firm, whereas internal religious assent is not absolutely or metaphysically certain. Most authors speak of a morally certain teaching excluding the likelihood of error but not the possibility of error.[6]

According to many of these approved authors, internal religious assent is conditional. Different authors propose the condition differently—unless an equal or superior Church authority should decree otherwise; unless the Church changes its teaching or the contrary becomes evident; unless a grave suspicion arises that the presumption is not verified; so long as it does not become positively clear that they are wrong; unless there is something that could prudently persuade one to suspend assent. But there is a presumption in favor of the teaching so that assent cannot be suspended rashly, casually, or out of pride. Generally these authors thought it highly unlikely that error would ever be taught by the authoritative magisterium. Some of the manualists explain more fully than others the possibility of error and its correction. Ludwig Lercher maintained that ordinarily the Holy Spirit preserves the Church from error through the assistance given to the pope. But it is not out of the question that the Holy Spirit might overcome error by the subjects' detecting the error and not giving their internal assent. Thus the manuals, which were the official textbooks of theology in Catholic seminaries throughout the world, recognized that some noninfallible teaching might be erroneous and Catholics could, at times, suspend their internal assent from such teaching.[7]

This understanding seems to be behind some events that occurred at Vatican II. The first schema on the Church proposed to the council fathers was rejected. This schema cited Pope Pius XII's 1950 encyclical *Humani generis* maintaining that when the Roman pontiff goes out of his way to pronounce on a heretofore controverted subject, the subject can no longer be regarded as a matter for free debate among theologians. Subsequent schemas and the finally approved Constitution on the Church no longer included that statement that was found in the first draft or schema.[8]

During the conciliar debate three bishops proposed an emendation (modus 159) about an educated person who for serious reasons cannot give internal assent to a noninfallible teaching. The Doctrinal Commission responded that approved theological explanations should be consulted.[9] The obvious reference is to the authors of the manuals mentioned above. In the conciliar debate on religious liberty, one emendation wanted to change the statement that in the formation of their consciences, "the Christian faithful ought carefully attend to the sacred and certain doctrine of the Church." The emendation wanted to substitute, "ought to form their consciences according to" rather than "ought carefully attend to." The commission in charge of the text responded that the proposed emendation was too restrictive. The obligation was sufficiently expressed in the text as it stands.[10]

There is much discussion about the actual meaning and translation of the Latin word *obsequium*, which is frequently translated as *assent*. Francis Sullivan, for example, finds *submission* to be an adequate translation.[11] Bishop Christopher Butler of England prefers *due respect*.[12] John Boyle points out the confusion resulting from the fact that *obsequium* originally was limited to describe the response to definitive Church teaching of revelation but has now been extended to matters that are not definitive and not based on revelation—the category of noninfallible teaching.[13] Ladislas Örsy recognizes the various usages of *obsequium* that basically signify communion or being one with the Church. *Obesequium fidei* is being one with the believing Church, whereas *obsequium religiousum* is being one with the searching Church. The duty to offer *obsequium* calls for respect or submission or to any other attitude in-between.[14]

What then is the meaning of the religious *obsequium* of intellect and will? Among the many theologians recognizing the possible legitimacy of dissent from noninfallible teaching, general agreement exists that such a religious *obsequium* calls for a docile and honest attempt to assimilate and accept the proposed teaching, but such an attempt can result in the inability to give such an assent, in other words, dissent.[15]

The second historical reason supporting dissent from authoritative noninfallible Church teaching comes from the change that has occurred in specific moral teachings in history. John T. Noonan has analyzed the changes that have occurred in Catholic moral teaching on slavery, usury, religious liberty, and divorce. For over 1,900 years the Catholic Church did not condemn slavery.[16] In addition, change took place on the right of the defendant to remain silent, the ends of marriage, human rights.[17] Some want to refer to development and not change, but in all these cases the specific norm changed. With regard to usury, Noonan points out that within thirty years three papal bulls, *Cum onus*, *In eam*, and *Debilitatis avaritia* were deprived of force to influence anyone's behavior. "Acts of papal authority, isolated from theological support and contrary to the conviction of Christians familiar with the practices condemned, could not prevail, however accurately they reflected the assumptions and traditions of an earlier age." The theologians were to have the last word because those who cared consulted them, because they taught the next generation, and because acts of papal authority are inert unless supported by theologians.[18]

Avery Dulles once pointed out that Vatican II indirectly worked in a powerful way to undermine the authoritative theory of the hierarchical magisterium with its emphasis on blind obedience and to legitimate dissent in the Church. Vatican II quietly reversed the positions of the Roman magisterium on a number of important issues—the critical approach to the Bible, the acceptance of the ecumenical movement, the acceptance of religious freedom, and an evolutionary view of history. "By its actual practice of revision, the Council implicitly taught the legitimacy and even the value of dissent. In effect the Council said that the ordinary magisterium of the Roman Pontiff had fallen into error and had unjustly harmed the careers of loyal and able scholars."[19]

ECCLESIOLOGICAL REASONS

From the perspective of the theology of the Church (ecclesiology), a number of reasons support the possibility of such dissent. The first theological argument is linguistic. The very word *noninfallible* means that the teaching is fallible. If the teaching is fallible, it can be wrong.

The most fundamental ecclesiological reason for the possibility of dissent from noninfallible teaching is the recognition that the teaching function of the Church is broader than the hierarchical teaching function. The primary teacher in the Church is the Holy Spirit. Through baptism all Christians share in the threefold office of Jesus as priest, king, and teacher. Catholic theology has recognized the importance of the *sensus fidelium*.[20] Cardinal John Henry Newman's *On Consulting the Faithful in Matters of Doctrine* is a good example of recognizing the teaching role of all the faithful.[21] The Constitution on the Church of Vatican II speaks of the *sensus fidei*. The whole people of God share in the prophetic role of Christ. The universal body of the faithful who have received the anointing of the Spirit cannot be mistaken in belief. Vatican II recognizes the supernatural sense of faith in all the people of God. The Spirit distributes charismatic gifts among the faithful of every rank.[22] The Spirit bestows various gifts both hierarchical and charismatic.

Canonists and theologians today recognize the significant role of reception by the whole Church of hierarchical teaching.[23] The neo-Scholastic notion of the Church as a hierarchical pyramid forgot about the role of reception. An ecclesiology of communion now recognizes the important role of reception of Church teaching by the whole Church. Such communion ecclesiology sees a two-way street between the hierarchical teaching office and all the people of God.[24]

In addition to a role of the *sensus fidelium* and the entire people of God, theologians also have a teaching role in the Church. In the medieval period the triad that provided leadership and direction for the life of society was the *sacerdotium*, the *studium*, and the *imperium*. With the development of universities beginning in the twelfth century, theologians played an important teaching role in the Church. University schools of theology regularly presented judgments on the orthodoxy of various theological opinions. Theologians participated in even larger numbers than bishops in the Council of Constance (1414–18) and the Council of Basel (1431). By the time of the Council of Trent (1545–63) theologians were clearly only involved in a consultative manner, but they still had a great influence.[25] The experience of Vatican II illustrates the significant role played there by theologians even though they had no voting powers in the council itself. In talking about Vatican II, most commentators give much more importance to the role played by theologians than the role played by individual bishops. In a 1980 article from which he later distanced himself, Avery Dulles discussed the two magisteria in the Church—the hierarchical magisterium and the theological magisterium.[26]

The word *magisterium* itself, until the nineteenth century, referred to the activity of an authority in a particular area such as in military endeavors or in teaching. Before the nineteenth century the term *magisterium* did not refer to what we call the magisterium today—the authoritative teaching role of pope and bishops—although this reality itself certainly existed. One of the reasons contributing to the overcentralization of the hierarchical magisterium in the teaching office of pope and bishops was the fact that the university faculties of theology no longer existed after the French Revolution.[27]

In a groundbreaking and perceptive article, Daniel Maguire in 1968, even before *Humanae vitae*, insisted that the word *magisterium* has a plural. There are many magisteria in the Church—papal and episcopal magisteria, the authentic magisterium of the laity, and the magisterium of theologians. Each of these provides a creative service and contributes to the search for the understanding of faith in the life of the community of Jesus.[28] As the years after Vatican II and *Humanae vitae* passed, Catholic theologians in the United States came to a greater awareness that the hierarchical magisterium does not involve the total teaching activity of the Church.

The changes that have occurred in specific Catholic moral teachings well illustrate the teaching role of the *sensus fidelium* and of theologians. The Declaration of Religious Freedom of Vatican II also recognizes the limits of the teaching role of the hierarchical magisterium. The declaration begins by noting the desires in society for the free exercise of religion. The document takes careful note of these desires and declares them to be greatly in accord with truth and justice.[29] Thus the declaration recognizes that the truth of religious liberty existed before the council adopted this newer teaching.

These overlapping teaching roles are necessary for the life of the Church, but inevitably some tensions will always be present. Too often the tension has been expressed as a contest between authority and conscience. But that is too simple. Actually there are three terms involved—truth, the magisterial teaching authority, and conscience. Both the hierarchical magisterium and the individual conscience are seeking the truth. Both can be wrong and have made mistakes in the area of noninfallible teaching.[30]

A third theological argument justifying the possibility of such dissent comes from the shifting understanding at Vatican II of the nature of the Church and the corresponding shift in the understanding of what it means to be an authoritative teacher in the Church. In the pyramid model of the Church in the pre–Vatican II period, all authority and truth came from the top down. In such an understanding the teaching role of the hierarchical magisterium was often seen as an exercise of the power of jurisdiction. As a result the global response of the faithful to this teaching was obedience. The magisterium had the truth and imparted it to the faithful.[31]

In an illiterate society the teacher is the answer person who provides solutions for those who are ignorant. Anyone who teaches today in a college or university knows that the ideal teacher is also the one who inspires students to think for themselves. A great problem arises when the concept of teacher becomes closely identified with the concept of jurisdiction or ruling. The concept of "authoritative teaching" tends to tie the teaching and ruling functions in the Church too closely together. The proper response to ruling is obedience, but this should not be the proper response to teaching. One does not obey the teacher. For this reason, *obsequium*, the response to noninfallible teaching, should not be called *obedience*.

Any teacher realizes that she has to learn the truth before she can teach it. This applies also to the hierarchical magisterium. Vatican II pointed out that the hierarchical magisterium is subject to the word of God and must conform itself to the word of God. As mentioned above, the hierarchical magisterium, like the conscience of the individual believer, strives to know the truth. The history of the Church illustrates this important reality. In the fourth and fifth centuries the early Church struggled with a better understanding of the basic beliefs of the Catholic faith—there are three persons in one God and two natures, human and divine, in the one person of Jesus. But these concepts of person and nature are not found in the New Testament but rather come from Greek philosophy. Only after a long discernment process could the hierarchical Church teach that there are three persons in one God and two natures in

Jesus. The hierarchical magisterium learned this truth from others before it could teach it.

The need to learn the truth before teaching it is even more essential in moral matters. Specific moral teachings arise in a particular historical context. In addition, the Catholic tradition has insisted that much of the moral teaching in the Catholic Church is based on the natural law or human reason. Over the centuries, as mentioned above, the hierarchical magisterium changed some of its specific moral teachings. The hierarchical magisterium with the help of the Holy Spirit learned much of this development from the experience of Christian people. Since specific Catholic moral teachings are often based on human sources of moral wisdom and knowledge, the hierarchical magisterium has to use these sources of reason and experience to learn moral truth.

REASONS FROM MORAL THEOLOGY

In addition to historical and ecclesiological reasons justifying the possibility of dissent, moral theology itself indicates why some specific norms cannot be absolutely certain. As a general rule the greater the specificity and complexity, the less certitude one can have about a specific norm. Recall that in the Thomistic tradition the secondary principles of the natural law generally oblige but can and do admit of exceptions precisely because of the complexity of the human situation. For example, the hierarchical magisterium has taught that direct killing and direct abortion are always wrong. But the distinction between direct and indirect cannot claim absolute certitude. This distinction is based on one philosophical approach and has been questioned by many others. Conflict situations by their very nature are very complex, and it is hard to imagine that one proposed way of solving them can claim absolute certitude.

In addition, Catholic moral theology, to its great credit, has insisted on an intrinsic morality—something is commanded because it is good. The will of the legislator or the teacher does not make something good. Rather the teacher or legislator has to conform to the good as known through human reason. Law for Aquinas is not an act of the will of the legislator but rather an ordering of reason for the common good made by the one who has charge of the community. Such an approach also grounds the possibility of civil disobedience. For Aquinas, the justification of civil disobedience is simple, maybe too simple—an unjust law is no law and is not obliging in conscience.[32] In moral matters the will of the teacher does not make something right or wrong, but the teacher must conform to right reason.

OTHER ASPECTS OF DISSENT

What about the assistance of the Holy Spirit given to the hierarchical magisterium? The Catholic Church is characterized by its acceptance of mediation—the divine is mediated in and through the human. The gift of the Holy Spirit does not substitute for the normal way of human knowing but rather assists and helps the two human processes of evidence gathering and evidence assessing.[33] The assistance of the Holy Spirit gives a special and distinct importance to the hierarchical teaching office. The hierarchical teaching office is not just another voice in the Church like that of any Catholic theologian or reflective believer. The assistance of the Holy Spirit grounds the special nature of the hierarchical magisterium and is the basis for the presumption in favor of its teaching, but that presumption always cedes to the truth.

The presumption in favor of the hierarchical teaching explains a primary grounding for the use of the word *dissent* when there is disagreement from such teaching. The hierarchical teaching is in place and presumed true unless and until reason and experience convince one to overturn this presumption. Charles Curran, more than any other American moral theologian, has been identified in theory and in practice with dissent from noninfallible Church teaching. But some people in basic agreement with Curran's positions disagree with his use of the term *dissent*. Kevin Kelly, and later Linda Hogan and Lisa Cahill, have objected to using the term *dissent* because it is negative and associated with opposition and confrontation. Also, the term *dissent* does not recognize all that is positive about what is involved in this reality—concern for truth, love of the Church, respect for tradition, and a commitment to shared responsibility in the Church.[34] Curran recognizes there are some pejorative aspects connected with dissent although in our society dissent does not necessarily have only a pejorative connotation. Dissent, which is in the ecclesial order, is analogous to civil disobedience in the civil order and does not involve rebellion and revolution. But the word *dissent* clearly recognizes the presumption in favor of the teaching of the hierarchical magisterium.

Some have maintained that in light of the presumption in favor of authoritative hierarchical teaching, dissent should be a rare phenomenon. But dissent has now become somewhat widespread in moral matters in the Church. Yes, dissent does extend to a number of significant areas, but the same basic factors are involved in all these issues—a questionable natural law understanding, an unwillingness to accept contemporary experience of the Christian faithful, a failure to dialogue with theologians, and the claim for too great a certitude. The presumption itself is weakened when the hierarchical magisterium fails to carry out the required human activities of amassing the evidence and assessing it.[35]

Proponents of the possibility of dissent from noninfallible Church teachings frequently point out the danger of creeping infallibility on the part of the hierarchical Church. Noninfallible teachings by their very nature are fallible. The hierarchical Church should not claim absolute certitude for these teachings. The West German bishops in a 1967 letter gave the following description of noninfallible teaching: "In order to maintain the true and ultimate substance of faith it must, even at the risk of error in points of detail, give expression to doctrinal directives which have a certain degree of binding force and yet, since they are not *de fide* definitions, involve a certain element of the provisional even to the point of being capable of including error."[36] In this context Margaret Farley has recently called for the need for the grace of self-doubt in light of the attempts by the hierarchical magisterium to claim too great a certitude for some of its teachings.[37]

In the 1968 dissent from *Humanae vitae*, the dissenting Catholic University theologians and others so clearly made the point about the possibility of dissent from noninfallible Church teachings that the United States bishops themselves publicly recognized the legitimacy of such dissent under certain conditions. "The expression of theological dissent from the magisterium is in order only if the reasons are serious and well-founded, if the manner of the dissent does not question or impugn the teaching authority of the Church, and is such as not to give scandal."[38]

Some Catholic theologians put strict limits on dissent. William E. May recognizes that theologians can propose hypotheses but they can never suggest that their views are to be preferred to the authoritative teaching of the magisterium. Theologians cannot take over the role of bishops.[39] Michael Novak insists that the Church needs dissenters, but theologians only propose. The pope and the bishops dispose.[40] The positions developed earlier in favor of dissent refute these objections.

Public Dissent

Some, including bishops, recognize the legitimacy of private dissent but oppose public dissent. Daniel Pilarczyk refers to those who oppose the Church's teaching openly.[41] William Levada accepts private dissent but not public dissent that places the theological judgment on a par with the magisterium's judgments.[42] Roger Mahony sees dissent existing between the two extremes of private dissent and organized dissent. Church teaching authority must responsibly intervene when theologians propose their personal theory as pastoral practice.[43] In my judgment this is why it is important for theologians to call their position dissent and thereby recognize that they are not authoritative teachers in the Church.

Without doubt the opposition to public organized dissent referred especially to the dissent from *Humanae vitae* led by Charles Curran in 1968 in which over six hundred Catholic scholars signed a statement maintaining that in theory and practice one could disagree with the encyclical's condemnation of artificial contraception and still be a loyal Roman Catholic. Some historians have referred to "three Curran affairs."[44] The first Curran affair occurred at Catholic University in 1967. After a university-wide strike of faculty and students, the board of trustees at the national Catholic university who were mostly bishops rescinded their previous decision to fire Curran. The underlying, but never explicitly mentioned, reasons were Curran's liberal positions on a number of issues, especially his disagreement with official Church teaching on contraception.

The second Curran affair was the dissent from *Humanae vitae* in 1968 and its aftermath. The board of trustees of Catholic University called for an academic hearing to determine if the dissenting professors had violated their various commitments as Catholic theologians teaching at Catholic University by their dissent from the encyclical and by the manner and mode of their dissent. The faculty inquiry board concluded that the professors had acted responsibly, and the trustees of Catholic University took no action against them.

The third Curran affair occurred in the 1980s. In 1986, after a seven-year investigation, the Congregation for the Doctrine of the Faith, with the approval of the pope, declared about Curran, "that one who dissents from the magisterium as you do is not suitable nor eligible to teach Catholic theology." The Congregation objected to Curran's generic defense of the possibility of dissent from authoritative noninfallible Church teaching and from his nuanced dissent on such issues as contraception, masturbation, premarital sexuality, divorce, homosexual acts, and abortion. Correspondence between Curran and the Congregation never stated precisely what the Congregation's position was on dissent despite Curran's repeatedly asking them to do so. Curran continued to defend his dissent on the basis of its conformity with what the U.S. bishops said in 1968—serious reasons exist to support dissent, there is no impugning of the teaching authority of the Church, and no scandal.[45] The Curran affair caused a great stir in the United States Church.[46]

The procedures of the Congregation for the Doctrine of the Faith deal only with one's writings and thus the issue of public and/or organized dissent did not explicitly come up in the investigation of Curran by the Vatican. But the 1990 "Instruction on the Ecclesial Vocation of the Theologian" from the Congregation for the Doctrine of the Faith condemns dissent understood as public opposition to the magisterium of the Church that causes the Church severe harm.[47] *Veritatis splendor*, the 1993 encyclical of Pope John Paul II, condemns dissent "in the form of carefully orchestrated protests and polemics carried on in the media."[48]

The CUA professors who dissented from *Humanae vitae* defended such public dissent at their academic hearing in 1968–69.[49] Academic practice in the United States at the time fully recognized such public statements signed by professors. Church documents including the Decree on the Media of Social Communications of Vatican II insisted on the right of human beings to information about matters concerning individuals and the community. Theologians have a responsibility to communicate with many people—the pope and bishops, fellow theologians, individuals particularly affected by a specific issue, other members of the academic community, priests and pastoral ministers, and to the public communications media as a whole. The public media invariably contact Catholic theologians to comment on events and happenings in the Church. The CUA professors feared that many Catholics would think they had to leave the Church if they did not agree with the condemnation of artificial contraception in *Humanae vitae*. This public dissent from *Humanae vitae* fulfilled the three conditions laid down by the United States bishops in their 1968 letter. Such public dissent was for the good of the Church and not in opposition to the Church.

Public dissent can take many forms—an individual theologian writing in a theological journal, publishing in a more popular journal, or being quoted in the public media. Organized public dissent involves groups of theologians making public statements. The important public role given to faculties of theology in the medieval period provides strong historical precedent for the public and even organized role of theologians today.

Opposition to Dissent

The strongest theological opposition to the somewhat widespread dissent by many U.S. Catholic moral theologians and ecclesiologists came from Germain Grisez. In his estimation the present situation is truly a crisis because this widespread dissent is a cancer growing in the Church's organs and interfering with her vital functions.[50]

To overcome this crisis, Grisez proposed his own understanding of how in practice the roles of theologians and the hierarchical magisterium should function in the Church. Grisez is quite critical of the way Pope Paul VI used theologians and laypeople in the so-called birth control commission. When there is an issue of debate, the pope and other bishops should fully listen to the theological opinions coming from all sides, then dismiss the theologians and engage in their own teaching efforts in light of the authority given them by the Holy Spirit. The pope should actively engage in this dialogue with all the bishops before the final judgment is given.[51] Revisionists reject such a proposal as based on a very juridical model that can never replace the ongoing dialogue that is always required between bishops and theologians.[52]

But Grisez has proposed another position—the condemnation of artificial contraception has been taught infallibly by the ordinary universal magisterium. The Constitution on the Church of Vatican II recognizes this ordinary universal magisterium. Bishops can proclaim Christ's doctrine infallibly even when dispersed throughout the world "provided that while maintaining the bond of unity among themselves and with Peter's successor, and while teaching authentically on a matter of faith or morals, they concur in a single viewpoint as that to be held definitively (*tamquam definitive tenendam*)."[53] Grisez maintains that the teaching condemning artificial contraception has been taught infallibly by the ordinary magisterium.[54] The vast majority of U.S. theologians have strongly disagreed with Grisez's contention.[55] Two major issues come to the fore in this discussion—can a natural law teaching such as the condemnation of artificial contraception be an object of infallible teaching and how does one verify when the conditions necessary for an infallible teaching by the ordinary universal magisterium have been fulfilled?

With regard to the object of infallibility, Catholic scholars after Vatican II (and even before) recognized the primary object of infallibility is what has been revealed for our salvation whether explicitly or implicitly, whether written or handed on. The secondary object of infallibility is what is necessary to adequately safeguard and faithfully expound the deposit of faith or that which has been revealed. Grisez maintains that, if the norm against contraception is not contained in revelation, it is at least connected with it as a truth required to guard and faithfully expound the deposit of faith and thereby belongs to the secondary object of infallibility. This teaching has been constantly proposed by the bishops together with the pope as something to be held definitively by the faithful.

The vast majority of Catholic moral theologians and ecclesiologists maintain that teachings based on the natural law do not and cannot belong to the secondary object of infallibility. The determinations of the natural law with regard to specific and complex moral issues are neither formally nor virtually revealed nor are they so necessarily connected with revealed truth that the magisterium could not defend revelation if it could not teach infallibly in these areas.[56] Here it seems that Grisez has an unnecessarily and unacceptably broad interpretation of what is necessarily or strictly and intimately connected with revealed truth. Among the many theologians holding the majority position is William Levada, now the prefect of the Congregation for the Doctrine of the Faith, in his 1970 doctoral dissertation at the Gregorian University written under the direction of Francis Sullivan.[57]

The other question concerns what is required to verify that something has been taught infallibly by the ordinary universal magisterium. The most significant issue in discussion concerns the condition that all the bishops must have taught that this matter is to be held definitively by all the faithful. Grisez gives a very broad understanding of the need for something to be taught as held definitively by all the faithful. This means that the point in question is not proposed as merely probable but as certain, not as something optional but as something that bishops are obliged to teach and Catholics are obliged to accept.[58] Francis Sullivan, who taught for many years at the Gregorian University in Rome, and others insist that to be held definitively does not mean just to teach something as a serious moral obligation but to maintain that this position is to be held definitely and with an irrevocable assent by the faithful.[59] It is very difficult if not impossible to prove the consensus of all the bishops that something is to be held definitely and irrevocably and not just as a serious obligation.[60]

Notes

1. For the history of the contemporary debate over contraception, see Robert Blair Kaiser, *The Politics of Sex and Religion: A Case History in the Development of Doctrine, 1962–1984* (Kansas City, MO: Leaven, 1985).

2. Germain Grisez and Russell Shaw, *Fulfillment in Christ: A Summary of Christian Moral Principles* (Notre Dame, IN: University of Notre Dame Press, 1991), 421. For the position of Curran and McCormick, see, among other sources, Charles E. Curran and Richard A. McCormick, eds., *Readings in Moral Theology No. 3: The Magisterium and Morality* (New York: Paulist Press, 1982); Charles E. Curran and Richard A. McCormick, eds., *Readings in Moral Theology No. 6: Dissent in the Church* (New York: Paulist Press, 1988).

3. Constitution on the Church 25, in *Documents of Vatican II*, ed. Walter M. Abbott (New York: Guild, 1966), 47–49.

4. Karl Bihlmeyer and Hermann Tüchle, *Church History*, vol. 1, *Christian Antiquity* (Westerminster, MD: Newman, 1958), 250–56, 292–95, 295–99.

5. Joachim Salaverri, *Sacrae Theologiae Summa*, vol. 1, *Theologia Fundamentalis*, 3rd ed. (Madrid: Biblioteca de Autores Cristianos, 1955), n. 650, p. 710.

6. Joseph A. Komonchak, "Ordinary Papal Magisterium and Religious Assent," in *Contraception: Authority and Dissent*, ed. Charles E. Curran (New York: Herder and Herder, 1969), 105–8.

7. Komonchak, "Ordinary Papal Magisterium," 108–14.

8. Komonchak, "Ordinary Papal Magisterium," 102–3.

9. Komonchak, "Ordinary Papal Magisterium," 104.

10. Francis A. Sullivan, *Magisterium: Teaching Authority in the Catholic Church* (New York: Paulist Press, 1983), 169.

11. Sullivan, *Magisterium*, 158–68.

12. Christopher Butler, "Authority and the Christian Conscience," in Curran and McCormick, *Readings in Moral Theology No. 3*, 86.

13. John P. Boyle, *Church Teaching Authority: Historical and Theological Studies* (Notre Dame, IN: University of Notre Dame Press, 1995), 63–78.

14. Ladislas Örsy, *The Church Learning and Teaching: Magisterium, Assent, Dissent, Academic Freedom* (Collegeville, MN: Liturgical, 1991), 85–89.

15. Richard Gaillardetz, *Teaching with Authority: A Theology of the Magisterium in the Church* (Collegeville, MN: Liturgical, 1997), 268.

16. John T. Noonan Jr., *A Church That Can and Cannot Change* (Notre Dame, IN: University of Notre Dame Press, 2005); John T. Noonan Jr., "Development in Moral Doctrine," *Theological Studies* 54 (1993): 662–77.

17. Charles E. Curran, ed., *Change in Official Catholic Moral Teachings: Readings in Moral Theology No. 13* (New York: Paulist Press, 2003).

18. John T. Noonan Jr., "The Amendment of Papal Teaching by Theologians," in Curran, *Contraception: Authority and Dissent*, 75.

19. Avery Dulles, "Doctrinal Authority for a Pilgrim Church," in Curran and McCormick, *Readings in Moral Theology No. 3*, 264–65.

20. For a bibliography of the abundant literature on this subject in the post–Vatican II Church, see Daniel J. Finucane, Sensus Fidelium: *The Use of a Concept in the Post–Vatican II Era* (San Francisco: International Scholars, 1996), 655–89.

21. John Henry Newman, *On Consulting the Faithful in Matters of Doctrine*, ed. John Coulson (London: Collins Liturgical, 1986).

22. Constitution on the Church 12, in Abbott, *Documents of Vatican II*, 29–30. See also Ormond Rush, "*Sensus Fidei*: Faith 'Making Sense' of Revelation," *Theological Studies* 62 (2001): 231–61.

23. The entire *Jurist* 57 (1997) is devoted to "Reception and Communion among Churches." See also Hermann J. Pottmeyer, "Reception and Submission,"

Jurist 51 (1991): 262–92; James A. Coriden, "The Canonical Doctrine of Reception," *Jurist* 50 (1990): 58–82.

24. Gaillardetz, *Teaching with Authority*, 227–54.

25. Boyle, *Church Teaching Authority*, 174.

26. Avery Dulles, "The Two Magisteria: An Interim Reflection," *Proceedings of the Catholic Theological Society of America* 35 (1980): 155–69. For his later moving away from this approach, see Avery Dulles, "Criteria of Catholic Theology," *Communio* 20 (1995): 303–15.

27. Yves Congar, "A Brief History of the Forms of the Magisterium and Its Relations with Scholars," in Curran and McCormick, *Readings in Moral Theology No. 3*, 318–22.

28. Daniel C. Maguire, "Moral Absolutes and the Magisterium," in *Absolutes in Moral Theology?*, ed. Charles E. Curran (Washington, DC: Corpus, 1968), 57–107.

29. Declaration on Religious Liberty 1, in Abbott, *Documents of Vatican II*, 675.

30. Congar, "A Brief History of the Forms of Magisterium," 328.

31. Gaillardetz, *Teaching with Authority*, 3–30.

32. Aquinas, Ia IIae, qq. 90–97; IIa IIae, q. 120.

33. McCormick, *Notes on Moral Theology 1965–1980*, 262–66.

34. Kevin Kelly, "Serving the Truth," in Curran and McCormick, *Readings in Moral Theology No. 6*, 479–80; Linda Hogan, *Confronting the Truth: Conscience and the Catholic Tradition* (New York: Paulist, 2000), 176–79; Lisa Sowle Cahill, "Sexual Ethics," in *A Call to Fidelity: On the Moral Theology of Charles E. Curran*, ed. James J. Walter, Timothy E. O'Connell, and Thomas A. Shannon (Washington, DC: Georgetown University Press, 2002), 113–14.

35. Richard A. McCormick, "The Search for Truth in the Catholic Context," in Curran and McCormick, *Readings in Moral Theology No. 6*, 425.

36. This letter is cited at length by Karl Rahner, "The Dispute Concerning the Teaching Office of the Church," in Curran and McCormick, *Readings in Moral Theology No. 3*, 115.

37. Margaret A. Farley, "Ethics, Ecclesiology, and the Grace of Self-Doubt," in Walter, O'Connell, and Shannon, *A Call to Fidelity*, 55–75.

38. Collective Pastoral Letter of the American Hierarchy, *Human Life in Our Day* (Washington, DC: U.S. Catholic Conference, 1968), 18.

39. William E. May, "Catholic Moral Teachings and the Limits of Dissent," in *Vatican Authority and American Catholic Dissent: The Curran Case and Its Consequences*, ed. William W. May (New York: Crossroad, 1987), 100.

40. Michael Novak, "Dissent in the Church," in Curran and McCormick, *Readings in Moral Theology No. 6*, 124–26.

41. Daniel Pilarczyk, "Dissent in the Church," in Curran and McCormick, *Readings in Moral Theology No. 6*, 157–59.

42. William Levada, "Dissent and the Catholic Religion Teacher," in Curran and McCormick, *Readings in Moral Theology No. 6*, 146–47.

43. Roger Mahony, "The Magisterium and Theological Dissent," in Curran and McCormick, *Readings in Moral Theology No. 6*, 171–73.

44. Robert J. Wister, "The Curran (Charles) Controversy," in *The Encyclopedia of American Catholic History*, ed. Michael Glazier and Thomas J. Shelley (Collegeville, MN: Liturgical, 1997), 400–402; Samuel J. Thomas, "A 'Final Disposition...One Way or Another': The Real End of the First Curran Affair," *Catholic Historical Review* 91 (2005): 714–42. For Curran's memoir, see Charles E. Curran, *Loyal Dissent: Memoir of a Catholic Theologian* (Washington, DC: Georgetown University Press, 2006).

45. For the correspondence between Curran and the Congregation, see Charles E. Curran, *Faithful Dissent* (Kansas City, MO: Sheed & Ward, 1986), 113–287.

46. Kenneth A. Briggs, *Holy Siege: The Year That Shook Catholic America* (San Francisco: HarperSanFrancisco, 1992).

47. Congregation for the Doctrine of the Faith, "Instruction on the Ecclesial Vocation of the Theologian (*Donum Veritatis*)," nn. 30–33, in *Origins* 20 (1990): 123–24.

48. Pope John Paul II, *Veritatis splendor* 113, in *The Encyclicals of Pope John Paul II*, ed. J. Michael Miller (Huntington, IN: Our Sunday Visitor, 2001), 56.

49. Charles E. Curran, Robert E. Hunt, et al., *Dissent in and for the Church: Theologians and* Humanae Vitae (New York: Sheed & Ward, 1971), 133–53.

50. Germain Grisez, "How to Deal with Theological Dissent," in Curran and McCormick, *Readings in Moral Theology No. 6*, 456.

51. Grisez, "How to Deal with Theological Dissent," 465–66.

52. Todd A. Salzman, *What Are They Saying about Catholic Ethical Method?* (New York: Paulist Press, 2003), 118–24.

53. Constitution on the Church 25, in Abbott, *Documents of Vatican II*, 48. The last six words are the translations given by Grisez and Shaw, *Fulfillment in Christ*, 412.

54. Grisez and Shaw, *Fulfillment in Christ*, 412–16; Grisez, *The Way of the Lord Jesus*, vol. 1, *Christian Moral Principles* (Chicago: Franciscan Herald, 1983), 839–49.

55. For an overview of the discussion about infallibility and natural law teachings, see Salzman, *What Are They Saying?*, 124–39. For the protracted debate between Grisez and Francis Sullivan on this issue, see Germain Grisez, "Infallibility and Specific Moral Norms: A Review Discussion," *Thomist* 49

(1985): 248–87; Francis A. Sullivan, "The 'Secondary Object' of Infallibility," *Theological Studies* 54 (1993): 536–50; Germain Grisez, "*Quaestio Disputata*: The Ordinary Magisterium's Infallibility; A Reply to Some New Arguments," *Theological Studies* 55 (1994): 720–32, 737–38; Francis A. Sullivan, "Reply to Germain Grisez," *Theological Studies* 55 (1994): 732–37.

56. Sullivan, *Magisterium*, 138–52.

57. William Levada, "Infallible Church Magisterium and the Natural Moral Law," (STD diss., Pontifical Gregorian University, 1970).

58. Grisez and Shaw, *Fulfillment in Christ*, 413.

59. Sullivan, *Magisterium*, 147.

60. The discussion in the United States preceded the documents from the papal magisterium on the understanding of the infallible magisterium, but these have not affected the substance of the arguments. For a discussion and analysis of these recent hierarchical statements, see Richard Gaillardetz, "The Ordinary Universal Magisterium: Unresolved Questions," *Theological Studies* 63 (2002): 447–71.

7. Methodological Comparison of Sexual and Social Papal Teaching

This chapter was published in my *Tensions in Moral Theology* (Notre Dame, IN: University of Notre Dame Press, 1988), 87–109.

The official hierarchical teaching of the Roman Catholic Church in moral matters has importance not only for the Church members themselves but also for others in society at large. The attention given to this moral teaching in the popular press illustrates the newsworthiness attached to it. Thanks to the popular media, people in the United States were widely alerted to the stance taken by the United States Roman Catholic bishops on war and the economy as well as the position of the Vatican on test-tube babies.

A general impression is in evidence both within and outside the Catholic Church that Catholic moral teaching in social and sexual areas appears to be somewhat different. From the perspective of the general public, contemporary Catholic social teaching with its criticism of the United States economic system and of our nuclear war and deterrence policy falls into what is often called the "liberal camp." However, Catholic teaching in sexual matters is definitely in the more "conservative camp."

The impression of differences between official Catholic social and sexual teaching also exists within the Catholic Church itself. Many conservative and neoconservative Roman Catholics have objected strenuously to the recent social teachings of the United States bishops but seem to have no problems with the official Church teaching on sexual ethics. On the other hand, liberal Catholics have applauded the recent social teachings while often dissenting from the sexual teachings.

The purpose of this chapter is not to discuss the relationship between social and sexual ethics; nor will I take sides in the dispute between "liberal" and "conservative" Catholics, even though my own position is well known. My purpose is to examine the ethical methodology employed in each of these two aspects of official Catholic moral teachings and to point out the clear differences between the methodologies.

CATHOLIC SOCIAL TEACHING

Today a body of official Catholic social teaching exists going back to Pope Leo XIII's encyclical *Rerum novarum* in 1891.[1] Subsequent encyclicals and official documents were often issued on anniversaries of *Rerum novarum*, such as Pope Pius XI's *Quadragesimo anno*[2] in 1931, Pope John XXIII's *Mater et magistra*[3] in 1961, Pope Paul VI's *Octogesima adveniens*[4] in 1971, and Pope John Paul II's *Laborem exercens*[5] in 1981. In addition there are other papal documents as well as documents from the Second Vatican Council and the synods of bishops that constitute this body of official Catholic social teaching.

One significant question about these documents and other hierarchical social teaching concerns the authoritative nature of such teaching and the response that is due to such teaching on the part of Roman Catholic believers. To discuss the nature, extent, and limits of authoritative teaching in the Catholic Church lies beyond the scope of the present considerations. However, one point should be made. There are many other hierarchical church teachings from Pope Leo XIII and later that are no longer remembered today. Leo's teaching on the political order is seldom read or even mentioned on the contemporary scene. Leo's political writings generally insist on at best a paternalistic or at worst an authoritarian view of society.[6] The unofficial canon of Catholic social teaching today has been brought about by the reception of the Church itself—the voices of subsequent popes but also the response of the total Church. The whole Church has played a role in what is viewed today as constituting the body of official Catholic social teaching.

Within the documents themselves the popes and the episcopal bodies explicitly stress the continuity with what went before. Popes are very fond of quoting their predecessors of happy memory. However, in reality much change and development have occurred within this body of social teaching. This section will study three important methodological issues that have experienced a very significant change in the less than hundred-year historical span covered by this body of official Catholic social teaching. These methodological changes in social teaching will be contrasted in the following section with the official teaching on sexual ethics that has not experienced such changes. The three methodological areas to be considered are the shift to historical consciousness, the shift to personalism, and the acceptance of a relationality-responsibility ethical model. Each of these methodological developments will now be traced.

Shift to Historical Consciousness[7]

Historical consciousness is often contrasted with classicism. Classicism understands reality in terms of the eternal, the immutable, and the unchanging; whereas historical consciousness gives more importance to the particular, the contingent, the historical, and the individual. Historical consciousness should also be contrasted with the other extreme of sheer existentialism. Sheer existentialism sees the present moment in isolation from the before and the after of time, with no binding relationships to persons and values in the present. Historical consciousness recognizes the need for both continuity and discontinuity. This discussion about worldview tends to be primarily a philosophical endeavor, but there are relationships to the theological. The Catholic theological tradition has recognized historicity in its rejection of the axiom "the Scripture alone." The Scripture must always be understood, appropriated, communicated, and lived in the light of the historical and cultural realities of the present time. The Church just cannot repeat the words of the Scriptures. Catholicism has undergone much more development than most people think. While creative fidelity is necessary for any tradition, such creative fidelity is consistent with the philosophical worldview of historical consciousness.

These two different worldviews spawn two different methodological approaches. The classicist worldview is associated with the deductive methodology that deduces its conclusions from its premises, which are eternal verities. The syllogism well illustrates the deductive approach. Note that in such an approach one's conclusions are as certain as the premises if the logic is correct. Historical consciousness recognizes the need for a more inductive approach. However, the need to maintain both continuity as well as discontinuity argues against a one-sided inductive approach. An inductive approach by its very nature can never achieve the same degree of certitude for its conclusions as does the deductive methodology of the classicist worldview.

There can be no doubt that a significant development toward historical consciousness has occurred in the body of official social teaching. Pope Pius XI's 1931 encyclical *Quadragesimo anno* is often called in English "On Reconstructing the Social Order."[8] In this encyclical the pope proposes his plan for this reorganization, which is often called moderate corporatism or solidarism. In keeping with the traditional emphasis in the Catholic tradition, this papal plan sees all the different institutions that are part of society as working together for the common good of all. Catholic social teaching has insisted on the metaphor of society as an organism with all the parts existing for the good of the totality. According to such an outlook labor and capital should not be adversaries fighting one another, but rather they should work together for the common good. Moderate corporatism sees labor, capital, and consumers all working together and forming one group to control what happens in a particular industry. This group would set prices, wages, and the amount of goods to be produced. Then other such groups on a higher level would coordinate and direct the individual industries and professions.

Pope Pius XI proposed his plan for reconstruction as something applicable to the whole world. Of course, the world of Pius XI and his contemporaries was primarily the Euro-centric world. The deductive nature of the plan is quite evident in the encyclical. From a philosophical view of society as an organism, the pope sketched out his approach as a middle course between the extremes of individualistic capitalism and collective socialism. In reality this plan had little chance of succeeding precisely because it did not correspond to any existing historical reality, and the popes never entered into the debate of making the plan work in practice. Pope Pius XII, the successor of Pope Pius XI, spoke less and less about this plan as his pontificate continued, and Pope John XXIII basically ignored the proposal.[9]

Such a deductive methodology is in keeping with the neo-Scholastic thesis approach to theology. However, some developments gradually occurred. Pope John XXIII's 1963 encyclical *Pacem in terris* still follows a generally deductive approach, but in this and in his earlier encyclical *Mater et magistra*, Pope John XXIII did not give attention to the plan for reconstruction proposed by Pope Pius XI. However, at the end of each of the four chapters or parts of *Pacem in terris* there is a short section on the signs of the times—the special characteristics of the present day.[10] Two years later *Gaudium et spes*, the Pastoral Constitution of the Church in the Modern World of the Second Vatican Council, gives a much greater emphasis to historical consciousness. Each of the five chapters in the second part of the document deals with a specific area of concern and each begins with the signs of the times.

Pope Paul VI's Apostolic Letter *Octagesima adveniens* of 1971 shows a very heightened awareness of historical consciousness:

> In the face of such widely varying situations it is difficult for us to utter a unified message and to put forward a solution which has universal validity. Such is not our ambition, nor is it our mission. It is up to the Christian communities to analyze with objectivity the situation which is proper to their own country, to shed on it the light of the Gospel's unalterable words and to draw principles of reflection, norms of judgment, and directives for action from the social teaching of the church....It is up to these Christian communities, with the help of the Holy Spirit, in communion with the bishops who hold responsibility and in dialogue with other Christian brethren and all people of good will, to discern the options and commitments which are called for in order to bring about the social, political, and economic changes seen in many cases to be urgently needed.[11]

Only forty years earlier Pope Pius XI had put forward a plan for social reconstruction that in his mind had universal validity. The difference between the approaches of these two popes is very great.

The more inductive methodology of *Octogesima adveniens* gives great importance to contemporary developments. A large portion of the letter is devoted to two aspirations that have come to the fore in the contemporary consciousness:

> While scientific and technological progress continues to overturn human surroundings, patterns of knowledge, work, consumption, and relationships, two aspirations persistently make themselves felt in these new contexts, and they grow stronger to the extent that one becomes better informed and better educated: the aspiration to equality and the aspiration to participation, two forms of human dignity and freedom.[12]

It must be pointed out that the present pope, John Paul II, has pulled back somewhat from Pope Paul VI's insistence on historical consciousness. *Laborem exercens*, the 1981 encyclical, is a philosophical reflection on work and its meaning that is intended to address all people. In his other writings John Paul II definitely moves away from the historical consciousness of Paul VI. His Christology, for example, is a Christology from above that begins with the eternally begotten Word of God and not with the historical Jesus.

Two reasons help to explain John Paul II's reluctance to embrace historical consciousness as much as his predecessor did. By temperament and training the present pope is a philosopher who studied, taught, and wrote in the more classical philosophical mode. Such thinking and writing are clearly congenial to him. In addition, historical consciousness can be seen as somewhat of a threat to the unity and central authority in the Church. All today recognize the tensions existing between the Church universal as represented by the bishop of Rome and the national and local Churches. Local diversity and pluralism are seen as threats to the unity and authority of the Church. There can be no doubt that these existing tensions have made Pope John Paul II very wary of historical consciousness.

However, the present pope does not use a more classicist approach to avoid making some very concrete and critical statements about existing social reality. *Laborem exercens* does not shrink from criticizing many aspects of the plight of the worker today.

Recent Catholic social theology and ethics have embraced the concept of historical consciousness. Consider, for example, the whole field of liberation theology as well as the importance given to praxis and to social analysis in recent writings.

Shift to the Person with an Emphasis on Freedom, Equality, and Participation

Within the time frame of a one-hundred-year span there has been a very significant shift in Catholic social teaching away from an emphasis on human nature with a concomitant stress on order, the acceptance of some inequality, and away from obedience to the many controlling authorities, to a recognition of the vital importance of the human person with the concomitant need for human freedom, equality, and participation.

In the nineteenth century, the Catholic Church opposed freedom and the thought of the Enlightenment. Freedom in religion, philosophy, science, and politics threatened the old order in all its aspects. Individualistic freedom forgot about human beings' relationships to God, to God's law, to human society in general, and to other human beings. Continental liberalism with its emphasis on the individualistic freedom was seen as the primary enemy of the Church.[13] Even in the nineteenth century, official Catholic teaching did not condemn all slavery as always wrong.[14]

Pope Leo XIII was very much a part of this tradition. He stressed order and social cohesiveness rather than freedom. God's law and the natural law govern human existence. Leo's view of society was authoritarian or at least paternalistic. He often referred to the people as the ignorant multitude that had to be led by their rulers. (Such an approach is somewhat understandable in the light of the low state of European literacy at the time.) In social ethics freedom was seen as a threat to the social organism. Individualistic capitalism was condemned as a form of economic liberalism that claimed that one could pay whatever wage one could get away with. Leo was also no friend of democracy because no majority could do away with God's law, and freedom of religion could never be promoted but at best only tolerated as the lesser evil in certain circumstances.[15]

Development occurred in the methodology of official Catholic social teaching precisely because of changing historical circumstances. The Catholic Church's enemy, or in more recent terminology, the dialogue partner, changed. In the nineteenth century, the Church opposed the individualistic liberalism of the day. As the twentieth century advanced, the central problem became the rise and existence of totalitarian governments. In this context the Catholic Church began to defend the freedom and dignity of the human person against the encroachments of totalitarianism. Pope Pius XI in the 1930s wrote encyclical letters against fascism, nazism, and communism.[16] In theory the Roman Catholic Church opposed all forms of totalitarianism, but there can be no doubt that the Church was more willing in practice to tolerate totalitarianism from the right. After the Second World War, Catholic teaching consistently and constantly attacked communism. (Note that in the 1960s a change occurred with Pope John XXIII, and there ensued a much more nuanced dialogical approach to Marxism.)[17] In the light of this polemic Catholic teaching stressed the freedom and dignity of the individual.

Pope John XXIII's *Pacem in terris* in 1963 signals the Catholic acceptance of the role of freedom. In *Mater et magistra* in 1961 John XXIII, in keeping with the Catholic tradition, insisted in a major part of this document that the ideal social order rests on the three values of truth, justice, and love.[18] Two years later in *Pacem in terris* the pope adds a fourth element—truth, justice, charity, and freedom.[19] *Pacem in terris* develops for the first time a full-blown treatment of human rights in the Catholic tradition.[20] Before that time Catholic thought had been fearful of rights language precisely because of the danger of excessive individualism. Catholic social teaching had insisted on duties and obedience to the divine and natural law and not on rights. In its quite late embracing of the human rights tradition, *Pacem in terris* still recognizes the danger of individualism by including economic rights and by insisting on the correlation between rights and duties.

There was one major obstacle or inconsistency in Catholic social teaching in the early 1960s. While the tradition was now insisting on the importance of freedom and the dignity of the individual, official hierarchical teaching still could not accept religious freedom. One of the great accomplishments of the Second Vatican Council in 1965 was the acceptance of religious freedom as demanded by the very dignity of the human person. Religious freedom is understood as freedom from external coercion that forces one to act against one's conscience or prevents one's acting in accord with one's conscience in religious matters.[21] In accepting this teaching Vatican II had to admit that a significant development and even change had occurred in Catholic thinking because in the nineteenth and twentieth century before 1965, official Catholic teaching could not accept religious freedom.[22] In the light of present circumstances one appreciates all the more both the theoretical and the practical import of this change in Catholic teaching.

In 1971 Pope Paul VI in *Octogesima adveniens* devoted a long section of the document to two new aspirations that have become more persistent and stronger in the contemporary context—the aspiration to equality and the aspiration to participation—two forms of human dignity and freedom.[23]

Pope John Paul II has strengthened and even developed the shift to personalism. *Laborem exercens* in 1981 emphasizes that the subjective aspect of work is more important than the objective precisely because of the dignity of the human person. The personal aspect of labor is the basis for the priority of labor over capital. Thus in the twentieth century a very significant shift has occurred in the methodology of Catholic social teaching through its emphasis on the importance of the dignity and freedom of the human person. Catholic personalism is the basis for many changes in particular teachings in the area of social, political, and economic morality.

Shift to a Relationality-Responsibility Ethical Model

In general there are three generic ethical models that have been used to understand the moral life in a more systematic way. The deontological model understands morality primarily in terms of law and obedience to the law. Deontological approaches are often castigated for being legalistic in a pejorative sense, but such is not necessarily the case. (Think, for example, of the legal model developed by Kant with its categorical imperative.) The teleological model understands morality in the light of the end or the goal and the means to attain it. One first determines what is the end or the goal. Something is good if it leads toward that goal and evil if it impedes attaining the goal. In the complexity of human existence there are many various types of goals and ends—the ultimate end, less ultimate ends, subordinate ends, and so on. The relationality-responsibility model sees the human person in terms of one's multiple relationships with God, neighbor, world, and self and the call to live responsibly in the midst of these relationships. In systematic understandings of moral theory one of the models will be primary. One word of caution is necessary. Although one of these models is primary, they should not be seen as mutually exclusive. Thus, for example, in a teleological model or in a relationality-responsibility model there will always be place for some laws and norms, but the law model will not be primary.

All agree that the manuals of Catholic moral theology that existed until the time of the Second Vatican Council employed the legal model as primary. According to the manuals of moral theology, the proximate, subjective, and intrinsic norm of moral action is conscience. Conscience is the dictate of moral reason about the morality of an act. The remote, objective, and extrinsic norm of moral action is law. The function of conscience is thus to obey the law. Law is either divine law or human law. Divine law is twofold. First, the laws that necessarily follow from God as the author and creator of nature involve the eternal law, which is the order or plan existing in the mind of God, and the natural law, which is the participation of the eternal law in the rational creature. Second, divine positive law comes from the free determination of God as the author of revelation. Human law has human beings as its author and can be either church or civil law. Note that all law shares in the eternal law of God and that human law must always be seen in relationship to and subordinate to the natural law and the eternal law. Thus the manuals of moral theology view the moral life as conscience obeying the various laws.[24] More specifically, Catholic moral teaching has insisted that most of its moral teaching is based on the natural law, which in principle is knowable by all human beings since it is human reason reflecting on human nature.

The emphasis on the legal model as primary in Catholic moral theology before the Second Vatican Council is somewhat anomalous in light of the Catholic tradition. Thomas Aquinas (d. 1274) remains the most significant figure in the Roman Catholic theological tradition. However, Thomas Aquinas in his moral theory was not a deontologist but a teleologist.[25] It is true that Thomas does have a treatise on law and the different types of law just as is found in the manuals, but this treatise on law is comparatively small and appears only at the end of his discussion of ethical theory. Aquinas was an intrinsic teleologist. His first ethical consideration is the ultimate end of human beings. The ultimate end of human beings is happiness, which is achieved when the fundamental powers or drives of human nature achieve their end. The intellect and the will are the most basic human powers. To know the truth and to love the good constitute the basic fulfillment and happiness of the human being. This happiness occurs in the beatific vision. Morality in this view is intrinsic. Something is commanded because it is good for the individual and leads to the ultimate fulfillment and happiness of the individual. However, the neo-Scholasticism of the manuals of moral theology truncated Aquinas's moral thought and reduced it to a deontological model.

There can be no doubt that the Catholic social teaching in the nineteenth and early twentieth centuries basically worked out of a legal model. Even as late as 1963 *Pacem in terris* recognized the law model to be the primary structural approach of the whole encyclical. *Pacem in terris* begins by insisting that peace on earth can firmly be established only if the order laid down by God be dutifully observed. An astounding order reigns in our world, and the greatness of human beings is to understand that order. The Creator of the world has imprinted on the human heart an order that conscience reveals and enjoins one to obey.[26]

But fickleness of opinion often produces this error, that many think that the relationships between human beings and states can be governed by the same laws as the forces and irrational elements of the universe, whereas the laws governing them are of quite a different kind and are to be sought elsewhere, namely, where the Father of all things wrote them, that is, in human nature.

By these laws human beings are most admirably taught, first of all, how they should conduct their mutual dealings among themselves, then how the relationships between the citizens and the public authority of each state should be regulated, then how states should deal with one another, and finally how, on the one hand, individual human beings and states, and, on the other hand, the community of all peoples, should act toward each other, the establishment of such a community being urgently demanded today by the requirements of universal common good.[27]

This introductory section sets the stage for the four parts of the encyclical, which are the four areas mentioned above. Thus, the law model is highlighted as the approach still followed in *Pacem in terris*.

Pope Paul VI's *Octogesima adveniens* in 1971 well illustrates the shift from a legal model to a relationality-responsibility model. As noted above, Paul VI here strongly endorses a shift to historical consciousness. In such a perspective this document does not look for the order and laws inscribed in human nature. Here the historical character and the dynamism of the Church's social teaching are stressed:

> It is with all its dynamism that the social teaching of the Church accompanies human beings in their search. If it does not intervene to authenticate a given structure or to propose a ready-made model, it does not thereby limit itself to recalling general principles. It develops through reflection applied to the changing situations of this world, under the driving force of the gospel as the source of renewal when its message is accepted in its totality and with all its demands. It also develops with a sensitivity proper to the Church which is characterized by a disinterested will to serve and by attention to the poorest. Finally, it draws upon its rich experience of many centuries which enables it, while continuing its permanent preoccupations, to undertake the daring and creative innovations which the present state of the world requires.[28]

Octogesima adveniens does not see conscience in the light of obedience to law. We examined in greater detail the understanding of conscience in chapter 3. The most characteristic word to describe the function of conscience in this papal letter is discernment (§36). Pope Paul VI also introduces into Catholic social teaching the methodological importance of utopias:

> The appeal to a utopia is often a convenient excuse for those who wish to escape from concrete tasks in order to take refuge in an imaginary world. To live in a hypothetical future is a facile alibi for rejecting immediate responsibilities. But it must clearly be recognized that this kind of criticism of existing society often provokes the forward-looking imagination both to perceive in the present the discarded possibility hidden within it, and to direct itself toward a fresh future; it thus sustains social dynamism by the confidence that it gives to the inventive powers of the human mind and heart; and, if it refuses no overture, it can also meet the Christian appeal. The Spirit of the Lord, who animates human beings

renewed in Christ, continually breaks down the horizons within which one's understanding likes to find security and the limits to which one's activity would willingly restrict itself; there dwells within one a power which urges one to go beyond every system and every ideology. At the heart of the world there dwells the mystery of the human person discovering oneself to be God's child in the course of a historical and psychological process in which constraint and freedom as well as the weight of sin and the breath of the Spirit alternate and struggle for the upper hand.[29]

Octogesima adveniens ends with a recognition of shared responsibility, a call to action, and the realization of a pluralism of possible options.[30] Thus the letter definitely marks a decided shift toward the primacy of the relationality-responsibility model in Catholic social teaching. Development within official Catholic social teaching has thus occurred on three very important methodological concerns.

CATHOLIC SEXUAL TEACHING

The focus now shifts to official Catholic teaching in the area of sexual morality. Three recent documents will be examined—the "Declaration on Sexual Ethics" issued by the Congregation for the Doctrine of the Faith on December 29, 1975;[31] the "Letter to the Bishops of the Catholic Church on the Pastoral Care of Homosexual Persons" promulgated by the Congregation for the Doctrine of the Faith on October 1, 1986;[32] the "Instruction on Respect for Human Life in Its Origin and on the Dignity of Procreation" issued by the Congregation for the Doctrine of the Faith on February 22, 1987.[33] The present discussion centers on methodological issues, but something must be said briefly about the authoritative nature of these documents. There is a hierarchy of official Catholic Church documents. These three documents are not from the pope himself but from one of the Roman congregations. By their very nature such documents are not expected to break new ground. However, it is interesting that the documents have received wide public discussion. Catholics owe a religious respect to the teaching of these documents, but they are of less authoritative weight than the documents issued by the pope himself.

For our present purposes the focus is on the methodological approaches taken in these documents. This study will show that these methodological approaches differ sharply from the three methodological approaches found in the contemporary documents on Catholic social teaching. Each of these three methodological issues will be considered in turn.

Classicist Rather than Historically Conscious

The "Declaration on Sexual Ethics" of 1975 shows very little historical consciousness. In the very beginning of the document the emphasis on the eternal and the immutable is very clear:

> Therefore there can be no true promotion of human dignity unless the essential order of human nature is respected. Of course, in the history of civilization many of the concrete conditions and needs of human life have changed and will continue to change. But all evolution of morals and every type of life must be kept within the limits imposed by the immutable principles based upon every human person's constitutive elements and essential relations—elements and relations which transcend historical contingencies.

These fundamental principles, which can be grasped by reason, are contained in

> the divine law—eternal, objective, and universal—whereby God orders, directs, and governs the entire universe and all the ways of human community by a plan conceived in wisdom and love. Human beings have been made by God to participate in this law with the result that under the gentle disposition of divine providence they can come to perceive ever increasingly the unchanging truth.

This divine law is accessible to our minds (§3).

The "Letter to the Bishops of the Catholic Church on the Pastoral Care of Homosexual Persons" in 1986 bases its teaching on "the divine plan" and "the theology of creation," which tells us of "the creator's sexual design" (§§1–7). The "theocratic law" (§6) found in the Scripture also attests to the Church's teaching. Emphasis is frequently put on the will of God, which is known in the above-mentioned ways and is what the Church teaches.

This letter points out that many call for a change in the Church's teaching on homosexuality because the earlier condemnations were culture-bound (§4). The letter acknowledges that the Bible was composed in many different epochs with great cultural and historical diversity and that the Church today addresses the gospel to a world that differs in many ways from ancient days (§5). In the light of this recognition of historical consciousness one is not prepared for the opening sentence of the next paragraph: "What should be noticed is that, in the presence of such remarkable diversity, there is nevertheless a clear consistency within the Scriptures themselves on the moral issue of homosexual behaviour" (§5). Historical consciousness is mentioned *only* to deny it in practice.

The "Instruction on Respect for Human Life in Its Origin and on the Dignity of Procreation" promulgated in 1987 appeals to the unchangeable and immutable laws of human nature. The laws are described as "inscribed in the very being of man and of woman" (II, B, §4). These laws are "inscribed in their persons and in their union" (Introduction, §5).

This instruction describes its own methodology as deductive: "The moral criteria for medical intervention in procreation are deduced from the dignity of human persons, of their sexuality, and of their origins" (II, B, §7). "A first consequence can be deduced from these principles" of the natural law (Introduction, §3). In summary these documents show little or no historical consciousness in their approach to questions of sexuality.

The Emphasis Is on Nature and Faculties Rather than on the Person

In the official hierarchical teaching on sexuality, the methodology gives much more significance to nature and faculties than it does to the person. This has been a constant complaint against the older Catholic methodology in sexual ethics that has led to its teaching on masturbation, artificial contraception, sterilization, artificial insemination, homosexual acts, and so on.[34] The manuals of moral theology based their sexual ethics on the innate purpose and God-given structure and finality of the sexual faculty. The sexual faculty has a twofold purpose—procreation and love union. Every sexual actuation must respect that twofold finality, and nothing should interfere with this God-given purpose. The sexual act itself must be open to procreation and expressive of love. Such an understanding forms the basis of the Catholic teaching that masturbation, contraception, and artificial insemination even with the husband's seed are always wrong.[35]

The popular mentality often thought that Catholic opposition to artificial contraception was based on a strong pronatalist position. However, such is not the case. Catholic teaching has also condemned artificial insemination with the husband's seed, which is done precisely in order to have a child. In my judgment this condemnation points up the problematic aspect in the methodology of Catholic sexual teaching—the sexual faculty can never be interfered with and the sexual act must always be open to procreation and expressive of love. This natural act must always be present. I maintain that for the good of the person or the good of the marriage one can and should interfere with the sexual faculty and the sexual act. Chapter 5 has pointed out that the official teaching is guilty of physicalism by insisting that the human person cannot interfere with the physical, biological structure of the sexual faculty or the sexual act. There is no doubt that the official documents under discussion here continue to accept and propose this basic understanding.

The "Declaration on Sexual Ethics" points out that the sexual teaching of the Catholic Church is based "on the finality of the sexual act and on the principal criterion of its morality: it is respect for its finality that ensures the moral goodness of this act" (§5). Sexual sins are described often in this document as "abuses of the sexual faculty" (§6, also §§8, 9). The nature of the sexual faculty and of the sexual act and not the person form the ultimate moral criterion in matters of sexual morality.

The letter on homosexuality cites the earlier "Declaration on Sexual Ethics" to point out that homosexual acts are deprived of their essential and indispensable finality and are intrinsically disordered (§3). This letter points out that it is only within marriage that the use of the sexual faculty can be morally good (§7). However, there does seem to be a development in this letter in terms of a greater appeal to personalism. The teaching claims to be based on the reality of the human person in one's spiritual and physical dimensions (§2). There are more references to the human person throughout this document than in the earlier declaration, but the change is only verbal. The methodology is ultimately still based on the nature of the faculty and of the act, which are then assumed to be the same thing as the person.

The instruction on some aspects of bioethics is very similar to the letter on homosexuality in this regard. There are references to the "intimate structure" of the conjugal act and to the conjugal act as expressing the self-gift of the spouses and their openness to the gift of life. The document also appeals to the meaning and values that are expressed in the language of the body and in the union of human persons (II, B, §4). Thus the terms, the finality of the faculty and of the act and the abuse of the sexual faculty, are not used, but the basic teaching remains the same. There are many more references to the person and to the rights of persons than in the earlier documents, but the change remains verbal and does not affect the substance of the teaching.

Ethical Model

There can be no doubt that the documents in official Catholic teaching on sexuality employ the law model as primary. The "Declaration on Sexual Ethics" in its discussion of ethical methodology insists on the importance of the divine law—eternal, objective, and universal—whereby God orders, directs, and governs the entire universe (§3). This document bases its teaching on the "existence of immutable laws inscribed in the constitutive elements of human nature and which are revealed to be identical in all beings endowed with reason" (§4). Throughout the introductory comments there is no doubt whatsoever that this declaration follows a legal model:

> Since sexual ethics concern certain fundamental values
> of human and Christian life, this general teaching equally

applies to sexual ethics. In this domain there exist principles and norms which the Church has always unhesitatingly transmitted as part of her teaching, however much the opinions and morals of the world may have been opposed to them. These principles and norms in no way owe their origin to a certain type of culture, but rather to knowledge of the divine law and of human nature. They therefore cannot be considered as having become out of date or doubtful under the pretext that a new cultural situation has risen. (§5)

The "Letter to the Bishops of the Catholic Church on the Pastoral Care of Homosexual Persons" is by its very nature more concerned with pastoral care than with an explanation of the moral teaching and the ethical model employed in such teaching (§2). However, the occasional references found in this pastoral letter indicate the deontological model at work. There are frequent references to the will of God, the plan of God, and the theology of creation. Traditional Catholic natural law is the basis for this teaching. The teaching of Scripture on this matter is called "theocratic law" (§6).

The recent instruction on bioethics definitely employs a deontological ethical model:

Thus the Church once more puts forward the divine law in order to accomplish the work of truth and liberation. For it is out of goodness—in order to indicate the path of life—that God gives human beings his commandments and the grace to observe them.... (Introduction, §1)

The natural moral law expresses and lays down the purposes, rights, and duties that are based upon the bodily and spiritual nature of the human person. Therefore this law cannot be thought of as simply a set of norms on the biological level; rather it must be defined as the rational order whereby the human being is called by the Creator to direct and regulate one's life and action and in particular to make use of one's own body (Introduction, §3).

This document also cites the following quotation from *Mater et magistra*: "The transmission of human life is entrusted by nature to a personal and conscious act and as such is subject to the all-holy laws of God: immutable and inviolable laws which must be recognized and observed" (Introduction, §4). Biomedical science and technology have grown immensely in the last few years, but "science and technology require, for their own intrinsic meaning, an unconditional respect for the fundamental criteria of the moral law" (Introduction, §2).

A very significant practical difference between a law model and a relationality-responsibility model is illustrated by the teaching proposed in these documents. In a legal model the primary question is the existence of law. If something is against the law, it is wrong; if there is no law against it, it is acceptable and good. Within such a perspective there is very little gray area. Something is either forbidden or permitted. Within a relationality-responsibility model there are more gray areas. Here one recognizes that in the midst of complexity and specificity one cannot always claim a certitude for one's moral positions.

The contemporary official Catholic teaching on social issues with its relationality-responsibility model recognizes significant gray areas. *Octogesima adveniens* acknowledges the pluralism of options available and the need for discernment. The two recent pastoral letters of the United States Roman Catholic bishops on peace and the economy well illustrate such an approach. The documents make some very particular judgments, but they recognize that other Catholics might in good conscience disagree with such judgments. The bishops' letters call for unity and agreement on the level of principles, but they recognize that practical judgments on specific issues cannot claim with absolute certitude to be the only possible solution. The pastoral letter on peace, for example, proposes that the first use of nuclear weapons is always wrong but recognizes that other Catholics in good conscience might disagree with such a judgment.[36]

In the contemporary official Catholic teaching on sexual issues there is little or no mention of such gray areas. Something is either forbidden or permitted. Even in the complex question of bioethics the same approach is used. Certain technologies and interventions are always wrong; others are permitted. Thus the very way in which topics are treated—namely, either forbidden or permitted—indicates again that a legal model is at work in the hierarchical sexual teaching.

The thesis and the conclusions of this chapter are somewhat

modest, but still very significant. There can be no doubt that there are three important methodological differences between hierarchical Roman Catholic teaching on social morality and the official hierarchical teaching on sexual morality. Whereas the official social teaching has evolved so that it now employs historical consciousness, personalism, and a relationality-responsibility ethical model, the sexual teaching still emphasizes classicism, human nature and faculties, and a law model of ethics. The ramifications of these conclusions are most significant, but they go beyond the scope of this study.

Notes

1. Pope Leo XIII, *Rerum Novarum*, in *The Church Speaks to the Modern World: The Social Teachings of Leo XIII*, ed. Etienne Gilson (Garden City, NY: Doubleday Image Books, 1954), 200–244.

2. Pope Pius XI, *Quadragesimo Anno*, in *The Church and the Reconstruction of the Modern World: The Social Encyclicals of Pope Pius XI*, ed. Terence P. McLaughlin (Garden City, NY: Doubleday Image Books, 1957), 213–73.

3. Pope John XXIII, *Mater et Magistra*, in *Renewing the Earth: Catholic Documents on Peace, Justice, and Liberation*, ed. David J. O'Brien and Thomas A. Shannon (New York: Paulist Press, 1977), 44–116.

4. Pope Paul VI, *Octogesima Adveniens*, in O'Brien and Shannon, *Renewing the Earth*, 347–383.

5. Pope John Paul II, *Laborem Exercens*, in *The Priority of Labor*, ed. Gregory Baum (New York: Paulist Press, 1932), 95–152.

6. E.g., Pope Leo XIII, *Diuturnum*, in Gilson, *The Church Speaks to the Modern World*, 140–61.

7. I have developed in greater detail this shift to historical consciousness as well as the shift to personalism in my *Directions in Catholic Social Ethics* (Notre Dame, IN: University of Notre Dame Press, 1985), 6–22.

8. Gilson, *The Church Speaks to the Modern World*, 213.

9. For an interpretation that sees somewhat more continuity between Pope Pius XI and his successors, see John F. Cronin, *Social Principles and Economic Life*, rev. ed. (Milwaukee: Bruce, 1964), 130–40.

10. *Pacem in Terris* 39–45, 75–79, 126–29, 142–45, in O'Brien and Shannon, *Renewing the Earth*, 133–35, 143, 154, 158–59.

11. *Octogesima Adveniens* 4, in O'Brien and Shannon, *Renewing the Earth*, 353, 354.

12. *Octogesima Adoeniens* 22, in O'Brien and Shannon, *Renewing the Earth*, 364.

13. John Courtney Murray, "The Church and Totalitarian Democracy," *Theological Studies* 13 (1952): 525–63.

14. John Francis Maxwell, *Slavery and the Catholic Church* (London: Barry Rose Publishers, 1975), 78, 79; Joseph D. Brokhage, *Francis Patrick Kenrick's Opinion on Slavery* (Washington, DC: Catholic University of America Press, 1955).

15. John Courtney Murray, *The Problem of Religious Freedom* (Westminster, MD: Newman Press, 1965), 52–66; Fr. Refoulé, "L'Église et les libertés de Léon XIII à Jean XXIII," *Le Supplément* 125 (May 1978): 243–59.

16. McLaughlin, *The Church and the Reconstruction of the Modern World*, 299–402.

17. Arthur F. McGovern, *Marxism: An American Christian Perspective* (Maryknoll, NY: Orbis Books, 1980), 90–131.

18. *Mater et Magistra* 212–65, in O'Brien and Shannon, *Renewing the Earth*, 102–14.

19. *Pacem in Terris* 35, 36, in O'Brien and Shannon, *Renewing the Earth*, 132.

20. *Pacem in Terris* 11–34, in O'Brien and Shannon, *Renewing the Earth*, 126–32.

21. "Declaration on Religious Freedom," in O'Brien and Shannon, *Renewing the Earth*, 285–306.

22. John Courtney Murray, "Vers une intelligence du dévelopment de la doctrine de l'Église sur la liberté religieuse," in *Vatican II: La liberté religieuse, declaration 'Dignitatis humanae personae,'* ed. J. Hamer and Y. Congar (Paris: Éditions du Cerf, 1967), 111–47.

23. *Octogesima Adveniens* 22, in O'Brien and Shannon, *Renewing the Earth*, 364.

24. E.g., Marcellinus Zalba, *Theologiae Moralis Summa*, I: *Theologia Moralis Fundamentalis* (Madrid: Biblioteca de Autores Cristianos, 1952).

25. Thomas Aquinas, *Summa Theologiae, Pars Ia IIae* (Rome: Marietti, 1952).

26. *Pacem in Terris* 1–5, in O'Brien and Shannon, *Renewing the Earth*, 124, 125.

27. *Pacem in Terris* 6, 7, in O'Brien and Shannon, *Renewing the Earth*, 125, 126.

28. *Octogesima Adveniens* 42, in O'Brien and Shannon, *Renewing the Earth*, 375.

29. *Octogesima Adveniens* 37, in O'Brien and Shannon, *Renewing the Earth*, 371.

30. *Octogesima Adveniens* 47–52, in O'Brien and Shannon, *Renewing the Earth*, 378–82.

31. Congregation for the Doctrine of the Faith, "Declaration on Sexual Ethics," *Origins* 5 (1976): 485–94. References to this and the subsequent documents will be to the official paragraph numbers. These documents are also available from the Publications Office, National Conference of Catholic Bishops, 1312 Massachusetts Ave. NW, Washington, DC 20005.

32. Congregation for the Doctrine of the Faith, "Letter to the Bishops of the Catholic Church on the Pastoral Care of Homosexual Persons," *Origins* 16 (1986): 377–82.

33. Congregation for the Doctrine of the Faith, "Instruction on Respect for Human Life in Its Origin and on the Dignity of Procreation," *Origins* 16 (1987): 697–711.

34. Luigi Lorenzetti, "Tramissione della vita humana: da un'etica della natura ad un'etica della persona," *Rivista di Teologia Morale* 18, no. 71 (1986): 117–29.

35. E.g., Marcellinus Zalba, *Theologiae Moralis Summa*, II: *Tractatus De Mandatis Dei et Ecclesiae* (Madrid: Biblioteca de Autores Cristianos, 1953), 314–420.

36. United States Catholic Bishops, "The Challenge of Peace: God's Promise and Our Response," *Origins* 13 (1983): 2, 3.

Subsequent Developments

My dissent from *Humanae vitae* had significant effects on me personally. After 1968, I continued addressing methodological issues and some important specific moral issues facing the Church using mostly the essay genre. A letter from the Congregation for the Doctrine of the Faith (CDF) dated July 13, 1979, informed me that I was under investigation. I was to respond in writing to sixteen pages of Observations "concerning errors and ambiguities" in my writing. The primary issue was dissent; the specific issues included fundamental option, theory of compromise, charge of physicalism, indissolubility of marriage, abortion, and the sexual issues of contraception, masturbation, homosexuality, sterilization, and premarital sex. I responded on October 26, 1979, with twenty-three printed pages concentrating on the understanding of hierarchical magisterium, which was described as "the fundamental flaw." In February 1981, Cardinal Franjo Seper wrote that the Observations remain pertinent, and I should respond to all the other issues. The total correspondence is found in Charles E. Curran, *Faithful Dissent* (Kansas City, MO: Sheed & Ward, 1968). The correspondence continued through September 1985.

A September 7 letter from Cardinal Joseph Ratzinger, who had succeeded Seper as prefect of the CDF, asked me to retract my positions because one cannot teach in the name of the Church and at the same time deny its teaching. After that I met twice with Archbishop James Hickey of Washington, the chancellor of the university, and Cardinal Joseph Bernadin, the chair of the board of trustees, to discuss possible strategies. All of these fell through, but Cardinal Ratzinger agreed to an informal meeting with me at the Vatican to discuss the issues. The two-hour meeting at the Vatican on March 8, 1986, did not change the basic positions. I wrote to Cardinal Ratzinger on April 1, 1986, that in conscience I could not change my positions. Ratzinger ended that part of the correspondence on July 25, 1986, with the judgment approved by the pope that I was neither "suitable, nor eligible" to teach Catholic theology.

Hickey, as chancellor of CUA, informed me in August 1986 that he was initiating the process of removing me from the theology faculty at the university, but according to the statutes, I had a right to a due process faculty hearing. Later, I learned that in the meantime, I could not teach. For the next two and a half years, I went through three stages of a long, grinding, complex process involving many skirmishes. I will very briefly summarize what happened. For a further exposition, see my *Loyal Dissent: Memoir of a Catholic Theologian* (Washington, DC: Georgetown University Press, 2006). The first phase, the faculty hearing, concluded that I had a right to teach in my area of competence. In the second phase, the chancellor and the board of trustees refused to allow me to teach moral theology. (There was discussion about what was my area of competence.) After hearing from me on June 2, 1988, the board of trustees concluded that in light of the declaration of the Holy See, I was not suitable to be a professor of Catholic theology.

The third phase involved my going to court to claim that the university had broken my contract that included academic freedom. The legal process began in June of 1988 and ended with a ruling of Judge Frederick Weisberg of the Superior Court of the District of Columbia in February 1989 that there was "nothing in its contract with Professor Curran or any other faculty member promising it (CUA) will come down on the side of academic freedom" in a conflict with the Holy See. The ten-year-long process finally came to a close.

I would be remiss if I did not very briefly mention the strong support I received from my bishop Matthew Clark, colleagues, fellow theologians, and students. They nurtured and sustained me throughout this time. A special word of thanks goes to John Hunt and Paul Saunders of the law firm of Cravath, Swaine, and Moore. Paul is a litigator and had the primary role in court. I have framed in the bookcase in my study the expenses for the case of *Curran v. The Catholic University of America* totaling $1,557,280.24 with the accompanying note in bold print, "THIS IS NOT A BILL: DO NOT PAY."

During the university hearing and the court trial, I took visiting professorships at Cornell, the University of Southern California, and Auburn. I could not take a full-time tenured position, because I would then lose my tenure at CUA. It became evident that no Catholic university would hire me. These universities did not have the special relationship to the Vatican that CUA has, but apparently fear of alumni and donor reactions explain their unwillingness to hire me. But, in December 1990 I accepted a very attractive offer from Southern Methodist University (SMU) to serve as the Elizabeth Scurlock University Chair of Human Values. To give a greater prominence to ethics, SMU in the mid-1980s established two chairs that are in no school or department but report directly to the provost so they can have a larger impact on the campus as a whole. SMU has been a stimulating and very friendly home for me ever since. The Scurlock chair called for me to teach two courses a semester and work with some doctoral students. This chair also gave me more time for my research and writing. Since coming to SMU, I have edited or coedited ten more volumes in the series Readings in Moral Theology published by Paulist Press; nine monographs in the Moral Traditions Series published by Georgetown University Press, and five other books. At the present time, I am on a reduced schedule, teaching full time in the fall semester and not in the spring, but holding onto my office and some help to continue some research and writing.

A September 2018 article (Charles E. Curran, "*Humanae Vitae*: Fifty Years Later," *Theological Studies* 79 [2018]: 520–43) traced the development in the fifty years after *Humanae vitae*. A good number of Catholics left the Church because of the encyclical, but within a very short time, birth control was no longer a pressing pastoral issue. Catholics made up their own conscience on the issue, and the percentage of married Catholics using contraception was basically the same as that of all other Americans. However, the pontificates of John Paul II and Benedict XVI strongly defended *Humanae vitae* in their official teaching and in actions against me and other theologians. Pope Francis has occasionally defended the teaching and has shown no sign of changing it.

The thesis of my article was somewhat startling: the issue of contraception is more important for the Church today than it was fifty years ago. Why is this so, since Catholic people have long since solved the problem for themselves? The reality is that if the Church cannot change its teaching on contraception, it is never going to be able to change on such important moral issues as homosexuality, divorce, and other sexual and medical moral issues, and especially it will not be able to change on the most important issue of all—the role of women in the Church.

Part Three

THE ENSUING YEARS

Introduction and Context

The aftermath of Vatican II and *Humanae vitae* dominated the discussions of moral theology for about twenty years. Then, newer issues and developments also affected the ongoing revision of moral theology.

The "Setting of Moral Theology," published in my *Toward an American Catholic Moral Theology* (Notre Dame, IN: University of Notre Dame Press, 1987), is the first chapter in part 3 and the eighth chapter in this book, titled "Moral Theology in the United States 1965–1985: An Analysis." The chapter describes the setting of moral theology in the United States at that time in light of four different contexts—the ecclesial, societal, ecumenical, and academic. All of these contexts have changed greatly since 1968 and have influenced moral theology and its methodology. This changed setting brought about a new generation of moral theology in the United States. The pre–Vatican II moral theologians tended to disappear after Vatican II and *Humanae vitae*. Richard A. McCormick and I were the two primary U.S. Catholic moral theologians in the twenty-year period after Vatican II. Catholic theologians until well into the 1970s were primarily priests. European moral theologians such as Bernard Häring, Joseph Fuchs, and Louis Janssens had a great role in the United States context during this period. It was only in the 1970s that a good number of Catholic universities in this country started doctoral programs to train Catholic moral theologians. Many of the early newer moral theologians were religious women, but gradually some laymen and women began to receive doctoral degrees and started teaching and writing. This trend grew exponentially as the years went by.

Chapter 9, "Methodological Overview of Moral Theology," was published in my *Moral Theology: A Continuing Journey* (Notre Dame, IN: University of Notre Dame Press, 1982). The Catholic tradition, well illustrated in the *Summa theologiae* of Thomas Aquinas, tends to strive for a synthetic approach, putting together into a unified whole all aspects of moral theology. Most of my writing before 1985 consisted of individual essays that were then put into books. In fact, Fides Publishers and the University of Notre Dame Press published thirteen books of my essays before 1986. The need to address so many different aspects and individual problems and the fact that there were so few people writing favored the essay genre. Except for occasional sabbaticals, there was not time to stand back and try to put all these parts together in a more systematic way.

In addition, there was the growing number of people in advanced degree programs and a more academic approach to moral theology on the undergraduate level that called out for a need for textbooks. There were some good but limited attempts in the late 1970s and early 1980s to produce such texts. Chapter 8 mentions the works of Daniel Maguire and Timothy O'Connell. I was obviously thinking about the need for such an approach, but the best I could do at this time was an extended outline, which is included in this volume as chapter 9. Only in 1999 did Georgetown University Press publish my *The Catholic Moral Tradition Today: A Synthesis*.

Chapter 10, "*Veritatis Splendor*: The Moral Methodology of Pope John Paul II," was published in my *History and Contemporary Issues: Studies in Moral Theology* (New York: Continuum, 1996). John Paul II's long papacy from 1978 to 2005 had a major impact on Catholic life in general and theology in particular. John Paul II frequently referred to Vatican II and saw himself as faithfully carrying out its meaning, and at the same time he strongly supported the teaching of *Humanae vitae*. Catholic moral theologians of a revisionist perspective (which was the majority) generally supported his social teachings, but not the sexual teachings. Thus, his writings well illustrate the different methodological approaches to sexual and social issues as discussed in chapter 7. *Veritatis splendor* differs from his thirteen other encyclicals, which had a wider focus and were addressed to a broad audience, including all members of the Church and all people of good will. *Veritatis splendor* deals very specifically with the methodology of moral theology and hence is addressed simply to the bishops of the Church and not to a broader audience.

Chapter 11, "Pope Francis: Reform in the Catholic Moral Tradition," was published in my *Tradition and Church Reform* (Maryknoll, NY: Orbis Books, 2016). Pope Francis began his service as Bishop of Rome in March 2013. His background was primarily as a pastor, and thus he differed from his predecessor, John Paul II, who had been a professor whose writings often dealt with issues of love, marriage, and sexuality. In fact, John Paul II exerted a significant influence on Pope Paul VI's decision to reiterate the condemnation of birth control. The different backgrounds and visions definitely affected their somewhat different emphases in dealing with moral theology. This chapter shows that Francis supports *Humanae vitae* but does not refer to it as much as John Paul II did. Francis emphasizes the love and mercy of God and our response to God's gift. This centrality of mercy also comes through in his insistence that pastors should smell like the sheep and deal with people in the situations in which they find themselves.

Chapter 12, "Methodological Approach in Dealing with Particular Social Issues," was the only plenary address given to almost five hundred Catholic moral theologians at the July 28, 2018, conference sponsored by Catholic Theological Ethics in the World Church (CTEWC) in Sarajevo. The organizers asked me to propose the best methodological approach in the Catholic moral tradition to deal with the concrete social issues troubling society today, such as economic inequality, justice, peace, the environment, and climate. The chapter proposes that what is distinctive about Catholic ethics (which also include most other religious perspectives) is the need not just to point out what is right or wrong, but also to propose how what is right and just can be brought into existence in contemporary society. Christians are called to bring about a greater justice in our world.

Chapter 13, "Pluralism in Contemporary U.S. Catholic Moral Theology," was published as the conclusion of my book *Diverse Voices in Modern U.S. Moral Theology* (Washington, DC: Georgetown University Press, 2018). The present volume has frequently recognized historical consciousness as the most significant methodological approach coming from Vatican II. This short chapter builds on the concept of historical consciousness to recognize the important role of *sitz-im-leben*. *Diverse Voices* uses the reality of *sitz-im-leben* to explain the diversity and pluralism in contemporary Catholic moral theology. The pluralistic nature of moral theology today contrasts sharply with the manuals of moral theology that existed sixty years ago, which assumed that moral theology was the same all over the world. However, this very brief chapter also points out there are still some common elements in the contemporary diverse approaches to moral methodology.

8. Moral Theology in the United States 1966–1985

An Analysis

This chapter was published in my *Toward an American Catholic Moral Theology* (Notre Dame, IN: University of Notre Dame Press, 1987), 20–42.

To analyze the development of moral theology in the United States in the twenty years since the end of the Second Vatican Council is no simple task. To facilitate such a study this chapter will consider the contexts of Catholic moral theology in the United States, will give a brief overview of its content, and will conclude with an analysis of the tensions in the Church created by these developments. The context within which moral theology is done obviously has a great influence on the approach and the very content of moral theology.

The Contexts of Moral Theology

There are four important contexts of moral theology in the United States that help to explain what has happened in the last twenty years—the ecclesial, the societal, the ecumenical, and the academic.

Ecclesial Context

Since moral theology like all theology is in the service of the Church, it is only natural that what happens in the life of the Church will have a significant impact on moral theology. In general, moral theology in the United States was unaware of the renewal of moral theology that was brought to a head by the Second Vatican Council. There were no leading figures in moral theology in the United States at the time who were really calling for a change in the basic orientation and method of the discipline. The primary purpose in teaching moral theology was to train confessors for the sacrament of penance, especially in terms of the role of judge, and the method of the manuals of moral theology was generally followed.

The renewal of moral theology that began in Europe and was encouraged by Vatican II called for both a new orientation and a some-what different methodology. Moral theology, as chapter 1 pointed out, could no longer view its function primarily as training priests to be confessors in the sacrament of penance. Within the context of this narrow orientation, moral theology was basically interested in determining what was sinful and the degree of sinfulness involved in particular acts. The renewal of moral theology called for a life-oriented moral theology that reflects on the totality of the Christian life, including the gospel call to perfection and holiness. The newer methodological approach above all stressed the important role of the Scriptures, the need to overcome the gulf between faith and daily life, as well as between the supernatural and the natural, the importance of historicity, and the necessity for moral theology to be in dialogue with other theological disciplines.

One of the first and most significant consequences of the renewal in moral theology was the fact that the leading moral theologians in the United States before the council were not prepared to deal well with the newer developments in orientation and methodology. As a result the leadership in post–Vatican II moral theology in the United States passed to a very few younger theologians who were just beginning to teach moral theology in the 1960s. Throughout the period after the council there were no real leaders in Catholic moral theology who had been in the field for a great number of years.

Moral theology in the United States could not avoid the practical issues that confronted the Church in this period. The North American penchant for dealing with practical problems also influenced moral theology in this country. The most significant issue in the early post–Vatican II period was that of artificial contraception for married couples. Chapter

5 has discussed the related issues of contraception, natural law, and absolute moral norms. Chapter 6 dealt with teaching authority in the Church and the legitimacy of dissent from noninfallible authoritative teaching.

The lively debates sparked by *Humanae vitae* in 1968 heavily influenced the course of moral theology in the United States and in the world. The two questions of the existence of absolute norms and the proper response to the noninfallible hierarchical Church teaching have dominated the concerns of moral theology since that time.

There can be no doubt that a strong division exists among United States' theologians in general and moral theologians in particular on these two issues that are very closely intertwined. Most Catholic theologians in the United States belonged to the Catholic Theological Society of America, which came into existence in 1946. Until the late 1970s this was primarily a clerical organization of seminary professors. However, the complexion of the membership began to change. In 1955 the first national meeting of the Society of Catholic College Teachers of Sacred Doctrine was held with the purpose of strengthening the teaching of theology in Catholic colleges. Later this society changed its name to the College Theology Society and became ecumenical, but it still remains a predominantly Catholic group.[1]

The vast majority of the membership of these two academic societies became generally associated in the 1970s with the revisionist and progressive trends in Catholic theology, although obviously all the members did not accept these positions. Perhaps the most publicized illustration of this development was the publication in 1977 of *Human Sexuality: New Directions in United States Catholic Thought*.[2] This volume was actually the report of a committee established by the Board of Directors of the Catholic Theological Society of America in 1972. The committee report, like all other previous reports, was received by the Board of Directors and never actually approved by the board or by the membership at large. The book disagreed with a number of magisterial teachings on sexuality. *Human Sexuality* evoked a significant debate, thus fulfilling one of its intended purposes. The methodological approach and the solution of particular problems proposed in the book were also criticized by some revisionists.

To counteract this growing tendency among Roman Catholic theologians and to defend the need for adherence to the hierarchical magisterium, a number of more conservative Catholic scholars founded the Fellowship of Catholic Scholars in 1977. Unfortunately the relationships between the two different approaches and the two different groups have not always been cordial and dialogical. These tensions and divisions continue to mark Catholic theology and especially Catholic moral theology in the United States today. In the judgment of some, these tensions are often exacerbated by ultraconservative groups and newspapers.[3] However, all concerned should strive for a greater openness to dialogue and mutual respect.

The two questions posed in the wake of the discussion over artificial contraception have continued to be two of the most important concerns addressed by Catholic moral theology in the United States as developed in chapter 5. In addition, both sides have continued to debate the question of the proper response due by theologians and by the faithful at large to the noninfallible teaching of the hierarchical magisterium as treated in chapter 6. Here revisionist theologians have had support from a good number of ecclesiologists who have generally recognized the right to dissent in certain circumstances.

The fact that there exist two generic positions called, for lack of better terms, the conservative and the revisionist, should not hide the fact that there are also many differences within these approaches. In the future it will be beneficial for all concerned to recognize these rather significant differences within each group. Such a recognition will avoid overly simplistic characterizations and should facilitate dialogue and criticism not only between the two groups but also within the two general positions.

Not only the life of the universal Church but also the life of the local Church has affected moral theology in the United States. Perhaps the most distinctive aspect of this local Church influence has been the recent involvement of the American Catholic bishops in social issues especially through their two pastoral letters on peace and the economy. American theologians had been giving some attention to these areas, but the leadership taken by the bishops has focused attention on both issues. As a result, Catholic moral theologians have devoted more attention to these two very significant questions and to the whole area of social ethics.

Societal Context

A second important context for moral theology is the societal influence. A number of factors in the United States in the last twenty years have emphasized the importance of ethics. In the 1960s the struggle against poverty, racial discrimination, and war raised the consciousness of the society at large to the importance of ethics. The shock of Watergate in the 1970s only increased the importance of ethical considerations. Questions of law, conscience, and public policy have been discussed at great length. Concern about population growth, energy resources, especially nuclear energy, ecology, and the role of women in society have all contributed to the heightened awareness of the need for ethics.

Within this atmosphere so conducive to the role of ethics a number of significant developments have occurred. Perhaps the most important from the academic perspective has been the interest of philosophy in substantive ethical questions. Until recently this country's philosophical ethics was dominated by the linguistic analysis approach and primarily interested in metaethical questions. But now philosophical journals and books are dealing with all the many ethical questions facing society. Contemporary philosophical work has stimulated moral theology and become an important dialogue partner with moral theology.

Another result of the widespread interest in ethics has been the establishment of different commissions by the government to study problems especially in the area of recent developments in bioethics. The best known and most productive commission is "The President's Commission for the Study of Ethical Problems in Medicine and Biomedical and Behavioral Research," which was active from January 1980 to March 31, 1983. The commission, whose power was only advisory, produced ten reports, five appendix volumes, and a guidebook for institutional review boards. The reports dealt with such topics as defining death, deciding to forego life-sustaining treatment, making health-care decisions, protecting human subjects, screening and counseling for genetic choices, securing access to health care, splicing life, and whistleblowing in biomedical research.[4]

Support for ethical studies has come not only from the government but also from private-sector funding. Think tanks and research institutions have sprung up to study and assess the ethical aspects of the many different questions facing society. Sometimes theologians, philosophers, and ethicists are part of larger interdisciplinary groups, whereas at other times the institutes tend to be primarily composed of ethicists. This widespread interest in ethics with the resulting growth in institutional support for ethical concerns is a great help to ethics in general, but in my judgment the contribution to moral theology is somewhat ambivalent.

Moral theology and Christian ethics reflect on the moral life in the light of the Christian and Catholic self-understandings. The United States, however, is a pluralistic country in which many people do not share these Christian beliefs. Questions that arise from these differences have both theoretical and practical dimensions. From the theoretical perspective the question concerns whether there exists one moral order that is the same for Christians and for all others or whether there is a unique morality for Christians and another morality for non-Christians. The question has often been addressed in this country in terms of the distinctiveness of Christian ethics and Christian morality. On the basis of both contemporary and traditional Catholic theological insights, I maintain there is only one moral order and that the specific content of Christian morality does not differ from what human morality calls for. However, the fact that the explicit material content of Christian morality is per se available to all human beings does not mean that moral theology, or Christian ethics, and philosophical ethics are the same. Moral theology explicitly reflects on the Christian life and the one human moral order in the light of explicitly Christian realities.[5]

The recognition that the specific moral content is the same, but that moral theology and philosophical ethics are not the same because of their different sources, should guide reaction to what is often happening in the United States today. The American Catholic bishops have recognized in their pastoral letters that they are addressing two different audiences—their fellow believers in the Church and the broader public that does not necessarily share their beliefs. In addressing the public at large, the pastoral letters prescind from the appeal to specifically Christian sources.[6] Such an approach is certainly legitimate and appropriate.

There exists, however, a danger in some institutes and commissions dealing with public policy. Here the tendency is often to prescind from any Christian sources and to discuss issues in a purely philosophical manner. There is a very apparent problem here for the discipline of moral theology as such. Within such institutes and commissions often there is no room for Christian ethics or Jewish ethics or Muslim ethics. As a result the discipline of moral theology is not helped by such commissions and institutes. At times I can understand why public commissions especially should prescind from religious differences; but, on the other hand, pluralism does not always require that everything should be reduced to the least common denominator. Perhaps even here efforts could be made to show how different religious perceptions can agree but also even disagree on particular issues facing society. The problem is very difficult, but it should be noted that the broad support for ethical institutes and commissions has not necessarily had a positive effect on the development of the discipline of moral theology as such.

The societal context has also brought to the fore the differences between the moral order and the legal order. Catholic moral theology as illustrated in the approach of Thomas Aquinas has always distinguished between the two orders. The emergence of constitutional government, especially as it appeared in the United States with the emphasis given to the freedom of the citizen, has stressed even more the differences between the moral order and the legal order. In my judgment the best approach to this question in theory is found in the principles enshrined in Vatican II's Declaration on Religious Freedom. This document recognizes that the freedom of individuals should be respected as far as possible and curtailed only when and insofar as necessary. Public order with its threefold aspect of justice, peace, and public morality is the criterion that justifies the proper intervention of the state. In addition, laws must be just and enforceable, and also the feasibility of passing such legislation is most significant in supporting possible laws. Unfortunately, it seems that many Catholics in the United States do not consciously realize the practical scope of the difference between the two orders.

In practice, discussions about law and morality have quite frequently occurred in the United States. In the last three presidential elections the question of abortion law has come to the fore in the light of the liberal law now existing in this country. In my judgment the criteria proposed above can justify a more strict law or even the existing law depending on whether one gives more importance to the criterion stressing justice and the need to protect the rights of the innocent or the criteria giving the benefit of the doubt to the freedom of individuals and invoking feasibility. Despite some significant statements to the contrary there is no basis for saying that there is only one Catholic position on the legal aspects of abortion in this country.

The role of the United States in the contemporary world has become, especially since the Vietnam era, an important object of discussion and criticism within the society at large. Without a doubt the two most significant questions today involve peace and the economy. Both these issues have important domestic and international aspects, especially in terms of relationships with the Third World and with the nations of the Southern Hemisphere. Catholic ethicists in dialogue with many others of differing backgrounds have been discussing the issues of war and peace. Some Catholic moralists have used the just war principles in an effort to limit the possible use of nuclear weapons and the arms race. Some have become nuclear pacifists, while a comparatively small but growing and determined group have embraced a total pacifism.[7] As mentioned earlier, the recent pastoral letter of the United States bishops has given a very significant impulse for further study in this area. Catholic moral theologians have given less sustained attention to the issue of economics and the relationship of the United States to the world economic order. Here the American bishops have provided important leadership. The process leading to a pastoral letter on the economy has stimulated much study in this area. Human rights has been an important area of concern both domestically and internationally, and Catholic scholars have been addressing this issue out of the context of the developing Catholic tradition.[8]

The role of women in society and feminism have become very significant issues in the United States. Some feminists have declared that Christianity is opposed to feminism and have moved beyond Christianity. Christian feminists strive to show that feminism and Christianity are compatible. Christian feminist ethics is already emerging as a special approach in Christian ethics.[9] There is a growing number of women writing today in the area of moral theology. Feminism is much more than merely a women's issue, but the ever-increasing number of well-trained women theologians will ensure that the feminist approach receives its proper place in ethics. Catholic feminists often feel that the institutional Church is not open and sympathetic. In practice I think that the most crucial, and unfortunately divisive, issue facing the Catholic Church in the United States is the role of women in Church and society. The rightful role and function of women in society and the Church is not simply a women's issue but truly a human issue involving human rights and the good of humanity in general, and a Christian issue concerning the community of equal disciples of Jesus.

Ecumenical Context

A third important context for moral theology in the United States is the ecumenical context. This is an entirely new phenomenon that has only emerged in the last twenty years as a result of Vatican II but is very characteristic of the contemporary discipline of moral theology. This ecumenical aspect is now present in such a way that it cannot be dismissed as merely a passing fad.

There are various ways in which the ecumenical emphasis has been institutionalized. There is no society of Catholic moral theologians in the United States. Moral theologians before 1965 belonged almost exclusively to the Catholic Theological Society of America and to the College Theology Society, as it is now called. The Society of Christian Ethics, as it is now called, was founded in 1959 primarily by Protestant seminary professors of Christian social ethics. This society itself has grown considerably from 117 members in 1960–61 to 664 in 1983. In its earliest years the society, which meets once a year and now publishes an annual, was predominantly male, white, and Protestant. Since then there has been a marked increase in the number of female, black, and Roman Catholic members. According to the recently published history of the society, beginning with the year 1965 Roman Catholics began joining the society at the rate of about five or six per year through the '60s. The first Roman Catholic became president of the society in 1971. By 1983, 145 Catholics belonged. The programs and the new history of the society bear out the ecumenical aspect of the group.[10]

There are other significant ways in which the ecumenical aspect of moral theology has been institutionalized. Some Catholic moral theologians now teach in denominational, private, and state institutions. A good number of somewhat younger Catholic moral theologians have been trained in and received their degrees from Protestant or independent institutions. The literature in moral theology in the last few years in the United States well illustrates the ecumenical dimension of the discipline. With encouragement from the Society of Christian Ethics and others, the *Journal of Religious Ethics* began publishing in 1973 as an independent, ecumenical, academic enterprise dealing with all aspects of religious ethics. The ecumenical character of moral theology is nowhere better illustrated than in the literature reviewed in the "Notes on Moral Theology" that have regularly appeared at least once a year in *Theological Studies*. "Notes on Moral Theology" critically reviews the most important articles that have appeared in the preceding year. Before 1965 the literature reviewed was almost totally Roman Catholic, but now the "Notes" are truly ecumenical without losing their Catholic bases. The contemporary authority, success, and importance of these "Notes" is due to the incisive and penetrating work of Richard A. McCormick, who composed them for nineteen years before passing on the role to others in 1984.

There can be no doubt that the ecumenical aspect has had an impact on Catholic moral theology in the United States, but this has also been a two-way influence, with Catholic ethics also affecting Protestant ethics. One must also remember that the ecumenical dialogue occurs as part of a larger context within which Catholic moral theology is being renewed.

There has been a growing rapprochement between Protestant and Roman Catholic ethics. James M. Gustafson, a University Professor at the University of Chicago and a most respected analyst of Christian ethics, has aided this growing rapprochement in his study of these developments. In the area of practical moral reasoning Protestantism has been consciously moving away from a "wasteland of relativism," whereas Roman Catholics coming from the opposite pole have been searching for responsible openness. To strengthen the discipline Protestantism has been seeking some philosophical base to overcoming the seeming vagaries of historicism and existentialism, whereas Roman Catholics have been revising natural law to overcome its excessive rigidity. From a theological viewpoint christological concerns and a striving to overcome an extrinsic understanding of nature and grace within the Catholic tradition have brought the two approaches closer together.[11]

Gustafson's analysis is quite accurate, but there is one important aspect missing in his book that the Chicago professor himself has recognized in his study. Gustafson considers only the revisionist moral theologians. The more conservative moral theologians are not mentioned or discussed. As a general rule it is true that the ecumenical aspect is more pronounced among revisionist Catholics than among the more conservative Catholic moral theologians.

However, this general statement must be properly nuanced. A number of more conservative Catholic moral theologians frequently appeal to more conservative Protestants such as Paul Ramsey. Ramsey's positions in medical ethics have often echoed the conclusions of conservative Catholic positions. The *Linacre Quarterly* is the official journal of the National Federation of Catholic Physicians' Guilds, which every year presents its Linacre Quarterly Award for the best article that appeared in the journal in the previous year. The 1978 award was presented to Paul Ramsey for his article "Euthanasia and Dying Well Enough" that appeared in the February 1977 issue.[12] It is interesting to note that Ramsey and two other somewhat conservative religious ethicists are members of the editorial advisory board of this journal, but there are no longer any Catholic revisionist moral theologians on the board.

There can be no doubt that especially in areas of sexual and medical ethics Ramsey's conclusions are generally congenial to more conservative Roman Catholics. However, all should recognize that from a methodological viewpoint a great difference exists between Ramsey's approach and traditional Catholic emphases. Ramsey adopts a deontological methodology based on faithful, covenant love. The Thomistic tradition has an entirely different methodological approach with its emphasis on the ultimate end of human beings and the good. The retired Princeton University professor is strongly opposed to any teleology. It is true that Ramsey has often dealt favorably with the Catholic tradition in areas such as just war and medical ethics, especially the care for the dying. In addition Ramsey has at times spoken favorably about Catholic natural law methodology. However, Ramsey has never really accepted the Catholic concept of natural law. From a theological perspective Ramsey's heavy emphasis on *agape* and his unwillingness to accept the Catholic concept of mediation have always made it somewhat difficult for him to ground theologically any understanding of natural law. From a philosophical viewpoint, even when Ramsey was speaking favorably of Jacques Maritain's approach to natural law, the American Methodist never really accepted the ontological aspect of natural law proposed by the French Thomist. While it is true that Ramsey has dealt extensively with traditional Catholic issues such as just war and ordinary-extraordinary means to preserve life, his treatment of these issues is from his own *agape*-based deontological methodology. Although Ramsey's conclusions are often in agreement with the teachings of the hierarchical magisterium, his methodology considerably differs from traditional Catholic approaches.[13]

In my view the ecumenical dialogue shows the primary differences between Roman Catholic and Protestant ethicists to center on the characteristic Catholic acceptance of mediation. Mediation is distinctive of Catholic theology and is manifested in all aspects of that theology. The revelation of God is mediated through Scripture and tradition. The word and work of God are mediated in and through Jesus, and in and through the human instrumentality of the Church. The moral call to follow Jesus is mediated in and through the human and human experience. From a theological perspective traditional Catholic natural law theory illustrates the reality of mediation. Catholic ethics appeals, not immediately to the will or word of God, but rather to the human that mediates the divine will and word. It is necessary to remember that one danger in mediation is to absolutize what is only a mediation, and this has often occurred, as exemplified in Catholic ecclesiology.

It is precisely the Catholic insistence on mediation that I see as the critical difference between the Catholic tradition and the theocentric ethics recently proposed by James M. Gustafson. Recall that Gustafson has been quite appreciative of many of the recent developments among Catholic moral theologians. However, his new two-volume study shows again that mediation is often the continuing point of difference between Protestant ethicists of all types and Catholics be they liberal or conservative. Gustafson claims to be following the Reformed tradition in emphasizing the glory of God. The Chicago professor rejects most of contemporary Christian ethics as being too anthropocentric and too much based on the human. God, and not human beings, is the center of meaning. Human fulfillment or human happiness cannot be the primary concern of Christian ethics. Human experience itself underscores the tragic aspects of human existence, and at times human beings must be angry with the God who brings this about. However, in the Catholic tradition there has never been the need to choose between the glory of God and human fulfillment. The glory of God is the human person come alive. The glory of God is seen in and through human fulfillment and happiness. Thus the contemporary dialogue indicates that Protestant and Catholic ethicists often differ over the methodological significance of mediation, whereas Catholics of all different stripes are usually in agreement on this important theological issue.

The analysis given of the ecumenical aspect of moral theology in the United States indicates that the ecumenism involved is a true ecumenism and not just a watering down of one's own Catholic tradition. The integrity of the moral theologians themselves would ensure that this is the case. One further illustration of the more substantive differences between Protestant and Catholic ethicists came to the fore in a dispute over abortion occasioned by "A Call to Concern" signed by 209 scholars mostly from the field of Christian ethics and including many well-known Protestant ethicists but noticeably lacking in Catholic support. The document rejected the absolutist position on abortion, supported the 1973 Supreme Court rulings, called for the government to fund abortions for poor people, and expressed sorrow at the heavy institutional involvement of the bishops of the Roman Catholic Church in favor of the absolutist position.[14] It is true that there is a great diversity among Catholic theologians on the question of the legal aspect of abortion and even some diversity on the moral question itself. However, "A Call to Concern" was rejected by the vast majority of Roman Catholic moral theologians. In his recent history of the Society of Christian Ethics Edward LeRoy Long maintains that one of the most valuable meetings in the life of the society involved an honest and frank discussion over "A Call to Concern" at the 1978 meeting.[15]

Academic Context

A fourth significant context of moral theology in the United States is the academic context. For all practical purposes, moral theology and all Catholic theology in the United States were not looked on as academic disciplines before the 1960s. Theology was primarily identified with seminary education, which in the pre–Vatican II period meant separation from all other worlds. It is true that theology was taught at all

Catholic colleges, but for the most part it was treated as a catechetical rather than an academic enterprise. The professors were usually clerics, many of whom did not have advanced degrees. The very fact of priestly ordination was often judged to be sufficient preparation for teaching theology.

The beginning of the College Theology Society in 1954 indicated an incipient move toward a greater professionalization in the teaching of what was then called sacred doctrine. At the time only priests and brothers were admitted into the Catholic Theological Society of America. Women religious and laity with advanced degrees in theology were looking for a professional organization. This declericalization and continued professionalization of theology began to grow especially after the 1960s. Corresponding to this was the increase in the number of Catholic universities offering a doctorate degree in theology. Theology both in its undergraduate and graduate setting was striving for academic respectability alongside all the other academic disciplines. Vatican II only heightened the interest in and concern for theology as a respected academic discipline in the Catholic college and university.

At the same time the self-understanding of Catholic colleges and universities began to change. Academic freedom had been a hallmark of American higher education throughout its existence. Colleges and universities must be free and autonomous centers of study with no external constraints limiting their autonomy or their freedom.[16] In the post–World War II period, Catholic colleges and universities realized that they were more and more a part of American higher education in general. Before 1960 most Catholic educators still thought there was a basic incompatibility between Catholic institutions of higher learning and the American understanding of a college or university with its autonomy and freedom. However, with a growing understanding on the part of American Catholic educators, they realized they should be and could be an integral part of American higher education, and the theological developments highlighted at Vatican Council II also influenced a new approach.[17] The most significant illustration of the new approach was the so-called Land O'Lakes Statement issued by twenty-six leaders in Catholic higher education in the United States and Canada in 1967. The statement makes its point succinctly and forcefully:

The Catholic university today must be a university in the full modern sense of the word with a strong commitment to and concern for academic excellence. To perform its teaching and research functions effectively, the Catholic university must have a true autonomy and academic freedom in the face of authority of whatever kind, lay or clerical, external to the academic community itself. To say this is simply to assert that institutional autonomy and academic freedom are essential conditions of life and growth and indeed of survival for Catholic universities as for all universities.[18]

The Catholic literature on academic freedom before the 1960s was invariably negative and defensive. However, the middle 1960s saw a growing acceptance of the place for and need of academic freedom in American Catholic higher education. A dissertation accepted at the Catholic University of America in 1969 made the case for the full acceptance of academic freedom for Catholic institutions of higher learning and for Catholic theology,[19] even though a dissertation published in 1958 held the exact opposite position.[20] Perhaps the contemporary scene is best illustrated by the fact that in 1984 a Roman Catholic layman defended a doctoral dissertation, "Academic Freedom in the American Roman Catholic University," at Drew University, a graduate school with ties to the Methodist Church![21]

In this context Roman Catholic theology in general and moral theology in particular are looked upon as academic disciplines like other academic disciplines existing within Catholic institutions of higher learning that claim for themselves academic freedom and autonomy. Such a context does not deny anything that is essential to Catholic theology and moral theology as such. Catholic theology can and must recognize the role of the hierarchical teaching office in the Church. However, judgments about the competency of Catholic scholars that affect their right to teach in Catholic institutions can only be made by academic peers and not by any authority, clerical or lay, which is external to the academic community itself. Such judgments about competency to teach Catholic theology must give due weight to the teaching of the hierarchical magisterium. The academic freedom of the Catholic institution and of Catholic theology is in the eyes of most United States theologians compatible with a

Catholic understanding of the proper role of the hierarchical magisterium and of theologians within the Church. Archbishop Rembert Weakland of Milwaukee maintains that the acceptance of academic freedom is not merely a compromise with secular reality but makes Catholic institutions of higher learning more effective in their service to the Church.[22] A minority of Catholic scholars, in particular those associated with the Fellowship of Catholic Scholars, would not accept such an understanding of academic freedom as applied to Catholic institutions and theology.

The academic context of Catholic theology in the United States means that the theologian cannot see one's role and function in terms of a commissioning to teach given by the hierarchical magisterium in the Church. Theology very definitely is in the service of the Church, but it is also an academic discipline as such. Recent canonical legislation has been viewed by many as threatening the understanding of theology as an academic discipline and as questioning whether Catholic institutions of higher learning can belong to the mainstream of American higher education.

The academic context of Catholic moral theology comes primarily from the place, the academy, in which theology is done. However, there are different places where theology is being done today. Commissions and think tanks or institutes have already been mentioned. Very often these institutes are ecumenical and multidisciplinary in their approach. Theologians of various denominations work together with other humanists and scholars in debating the problems facing society and the world. One of the best known of such institutes is the Institute of Society, Ethics, and the Life Sciences, commonly called the Hastings Center, which publishes a very significant journal, *The Hastings Center Report*. Georgetown University, which is a Catholic institution, houses and sponsors the Kennedy Institute of Ethics, which is ecumenical in its membership and approach. However, other institutes have been set up primarily as Catholic centers as such. The best example of such institutes is the "Pope John XXIII Medical-Moral Research and Education Center" originally founded in 1973. This center publishes a newsletter and occasional books, sponsors workshops, including an annual workshop for bishops, and arranges meetings for various groups. The center tends to adopt a more conservative position on the issues of medical ethics.

In general in the last twenty years the academic aspect of Catholic theology has been stressed with a resulting strengthening of the position that the Catholic theologian cannot be seen merely as an extension of the hierarchical teaching office in the Church.

CONTENT OF MORAL THEOLOGY

This second section will briefly discuss Catholic moral theology in the United States from the perspective of the content of moral theology itself. In the light of the very nature of the discipline as well as the context discussed above, moral theology will be involved in discussing the major problems faced by both the Church and the society.

The areas of sexual and medical ethics have already been briefly mentioned. Here the majority of moralists contributing have adopted a revisionist methodology that argues against some, but by no means all, of the positions maintained in older Catholic approaches. According to revisionists the primary problem of the older methodology is a physicalism that identifies the human moral aspects with merely the physical or the biological aspect of the act. The revisionist approach appeals to historical mindedness and personalism to argue against absolute moral norms, in which what is always forbidden is described in physical or biological terms, for example, contraception or direct killing. Many maintain that such physical or premoral evil can be done for a proportionate reason. Especially in the areas of sexual and medical morality much tension has arisen because here the revisionists propose that one can dissent from the authoritative noninfallible teaching of the hierarchical magisterium. Proponents of the older position often modify the older natural law arguments but accuse the revisionists of gnosticism in failing to give enough importance to the physical aspects of embodied humanity.

Within the area of social ethics there again exists what is usually called a "conservative-liberal" dispute, but this difference is not exactly the same and does not necessarily involve the same people as the discussion in sexual and medical ethics. In the area of social ethics the American bishops with their earlier statements and especially with their recent pastoral letters on peace and the economy are generally judged to belong to the liberal approach. The more conservative position, as exemplified in *A Lay Letter* on the economy as an alternative to the bishops' approach, is much more supportive of the American economic system and more ready to defend the need for a strong nuclear defense policy than are the American bishops.[23] Michael Novak, who is the most prominent and prolific author in this area, proposes a realism that accepts human limitations and sinfulness, rejects utopian solutions, and faults the Catholic tradition for its insistence on distribution rather than on the call to creatively produce more wealth.[24] In this area too there is an ecclesiological discussion, with many of the more conservative authors maintaining that the hierarchical Church should not be so specific in its teaching on social issues and should not adopt its generally liberal approach.[25]

How is one to evaluate the consistency of the hierarchical teaching in these two different areas? The United States bishops themselves, under the leadership of Cardinal Bernardin, have been arguing for a consistent life ethic affecting all life issues such as abortion, war, and capital punishment.[26] In general I think there is great merit to such an approach, but there is a tendency to become too unnuanced and to forget the distinction between law and morality.

In my judgment a lack of consistency exists between the positions taken by the American Catholic bishops and the universal hierarchical teaching office in the sexual and medical areas and the approaches taken in social ethics, for two different methodologies appear to be at work in official hierarchical teaching. In the social area official Church documents strongly recognize the importance of historical consciousness, and they turn to the subject with an emphasis on the person. These emphases with all their logical conclusions are missing in contemporary hierarchical approaches in the areas of sexual and medical ethics. Chapter 7 has examined this difference in great detail.

In the general area of methodology and fundamental moral theology much work remains to be done. Most attention up to now has been given to the question of norms in moral theology, with Richard A. McCormick doing the most work to develop a theory of proportionalism, while Germain Grisez has strongly defended universal norms with his theory based on an understanding of the modes of responsibility and basic human goods. Speaking as a revisionist, I recognize the need to develop exactly what is meant by proportionate reason and to study all the ramifications of the theory in all aspects and areas of moral theology. Other methodological issues such as the use of Scripture in moral theology, the distinctiveness of Christian ethics, and, to a lesser extent, the role of the sciences in moral theology have been discussed.

One fascinating aspect of the ecumenical dialogue has been the recent Protestant emphasis on virtue, character, and the importance of narrative and story, shown especially in the writings of Stanley Hauerwas.[27] As a result Roman Catholics are now much more conscious of what has been such a fundamental aspect of Catholic moral theology but has been generally overlooked in the last few years. However, sustained and systematic studies of the Christian person as agent and subject are needed. Moral development has received quite a bit of attention, especially in dialogue with Kohlberg, Gilligan, and other psychologists. Many articles and even some books have been written on conscience, but much remains to be done. In all these areas of fundamental moral theology one is conscious of the need for interdisciplinary approaches in order to do justice to the anthropological realities involved.

With all the significant changes in the discipline and the manifold specific questions that have emerged, it is natural that there have been few attempts to construct a systematic moral theology. Timothy O'Connell's *Principles for a Catholic Morality*, with its heavy dependence on the work of Joseph Fuchs, deals from a contemporary viewpoint with the issues raised by the older manuals in fundamental moral theology.[28] Daniel Maguire's *The Moral Choice* presents a lively and innovative approach to the specific issue of moral choice.[29] As helpful as these books are, especially for use with students, they are not intended to be systematic studies of all moral theology.

Bernard Häring's three-volume *Free and Faithful in Christ* is really the first attempt at a systematic discussion of contemporary moral theology in a manual-type approach.[30] It is fitting that Häring's book, which was written in English, should be the first attempt at a systematic contemporary moral theology on the American scene. Häring has lectured widely and taught in many different Catholic, Protestant, and state institutions in this country in the past twenty years. It is safe to say that Häring has had a greater influence on the totality of the American Catholic Church than any other moral theologian. Recently Germain Grisez has published *The Way of the Lord Jesus*, volume 1, *Christian Moral Principles*, a thousand-page treatise that is the first of a projected four-volume systematic moral theology.[31] Grisez here develops again his basic theory of moral responsibility and norms, but he tries to incorporate this within a larger and systematic moral theology.

Notes

1. Rosemary Rodgers, *A History of the College Theology Society* (Villanova, PA: College Theology Society, 1983). *Horizons* is the journal of the College Theology Society.

2. Anthony Kosnik et al., *Human Sexuality: New Directions in American Catholic Thought* (New York: Paulist Press, 1977). For what can accurately be called a conservative response to the above, see Ronald Lawler, Joseph Boyle Jr., and William E. May, *Catholic Sexual Ethics: A Summary, Explanation, and Defense* (Huntington, IN: Our Sunday Visitor, 1985).

3. Raymond E. Brown, "Bishops and Theologians: 'Dispute' Surrounded by Fiction," *Origins* 7 (1978): 673–82.

4. President's Commission for the Study of Ethical and Legal Problems in Medicine and Biomedical and Behavioral Research, *Summing Up: Final Report on Studies of the Ethical and Legal Problems in Medicine and Biomedical and Behavioral Research* (Washington, DC: U.S. Government Printing Office, 1983).

5. For many different viewpoints on this question, see Charles E. Curran and Richard A. McCormick, eds., *Readings in Moral Theology No. 2: The Distinctiveness of Christian Ethics* (New York: Paulist Press, 1980). Other volumes edited by Curran and McCormick in this series are: *Readings in Moral Theology No. 1: Moral Norms and Catholic Tradition*; *Readings in Moral Theology No. 3: The Magisterium and Morality*; *Readings in Moral Theology No. 4: The Use of Scripture in Moral Theology* (New York: Paulist Press, 1979, 1982, 1984).

6. "The Pastoral Letter on War and Peace: The Challenge of Peace: God's Promise and Our Response," *Origins* 13 (1983): 3, 4.

7. Thomas A. Shannon, ed., *War or Peace? The Search for New Answers* (Maryknoll, NY: Orbis Books, 1980). This volume is in a sense a festschrift for Gordon C. Zahn, who has written most extensively on Christian pacifism from the Catholic perspective.

8. David Hollenbach, *Claims in Conflict: Retrieving and Renewing the Catholic Human Rights Tradition* (New York: Paulist Press, 1979); Alfred Hennelly and John Langan, eds., *Human Rights in the Americas: The Struggle for Consensus* (Washington, DC: Georgetown University Press, 1982); Margaret E. Crahan, ed., *Human Rights and Basic Needs in the Americas* (Washington, DC:

Georgetown University Press, 1982). All three volumes were written in connection with the Woodstock Theological Center in Washington.

9. Margaret A. Farley, "Feminist Ethics in the Christian Ethics Curriculum," *Horizons* 11 (1984): 361–72; June O'Connor, "How to Mainstream Feminist Studies by Raising Questions: The Case or the Introductory Course," *Horizons* 11 (1984): 373–92.

10. Edward LeRoy Long Jr., *Academic Bonding and Social Concern: The Society of Christian Ethics 1959–1983* (Notre Dame, IN: Religious Ethics, 1984).

11. James M. Gustafson, *Protestant and Roman Catholic Ethics: Prospects for Rapprochement* (Chicago: University of Chicago Press, 1978).

12. "Presentation of the *Linacre Quarterly* Award to Dr. Paul Ramsey by John P. Mullooly, M.D.," *Linacre Quarterly* 46 (1979): 7, 8.

13. Gustafson, *Protestant and Roman Catholic Ethics*, 151. For a fuller development of my analysis, see Curran, *Politics, Medicine, and Christian Ethics: A Dialogue with Paul Ramsey* (Philadelphia: Fortress Press, 1973).

14. "A Call to Concern," *Christianity and Crisis* 37 (1977): 222–24.

15. Long, *Academic Bonding and Social Concern*, 136.

16. Richard Hofstadter and Walter P. Metzger, *Academic Freedom in the United States* (New York: Columbia University Press, 1955).

17. Neil G. McCluskey, ed., *The Catholic University: A Modern Appraisal* (Notre Dame, IN: University of Notre Dame Press, 1970).

18. "Land O'Lakes Statement," in McCluskey, *The Catholic University*, 336ff.

19. Frederick Walter Gunti, "Academic Freedom as an Operative Principle for the Catholic Theologian" (STD diss., The Catholic University of America, 1969).

20. Aldo J. Tos, "A Critical Study of American Views on Academic Freedom" (PhD diss., The Catholic University of America, 1958).

21. James John Annarelli, "Academic Freedom and the American Roman Catholic University" (PhD diss., Drew University, 1984).

22. Archbishop Rembert G. Weakland, "A Catholic University: Some Clarifications," *Catholic Herald* (March 21, 1985): 3.

23. Lay Commission on Catholic Social Teaching and the U.S. Economy, *Toward the Future: Catholic Social Thought and the U.S. Economy: A Lay Letter* (North Tarrytown, NY: Lay Commission, 1984).

24. For Novak's latest work on the subject, see Michael Novak, *Freedom with Justice: Catholic Social Thought and Liberal Institutions* (San Francisco: Harper and Row, 1984).

25. J. Brian Benestad, *The Pursuit of a Just Social Order: Policy Statements of the U.S. Catholic Bishops, 1966–1980* (Washington, DC: Ethics and Public Policy Center, 1982).

26. Joseph Cardinal Bernardin, "Fordham University Address on the Need for a Consistent Ethic of Life," *Origins* 13 (1984): 491–94; "Enlarging the Dialogue on a Consistent Ethic of Life," *Origins* 13 (1984): 705–9.

27. For the most systematic treatment of his position, see Stanley Hauerwas, *The Peaceable Kingdom* (Notre Dame, IN: University of Notre Dame Press, 1983).

28. Timothy E. O'Connell, *Principles for a Catholic Morality* (New York: Seabury Press, 1978).

29. Daniel C. Maguire, *The Moral Choice* (Garden City, NY: Doubleday, 1978).

30. Bernard Häring, *Free and Faithful in Christ: Moral Theology for Clergy and Laity*, 3 vols. (New York: Seabury Press, 1978, 1979, 1981).

31. Germain Grisez, *The Way of the Lord Jesus*, vol. 1, *Christian Moral Principles* (Chicago: Franciscan Herald Press, 1983).

9. Methodological Overview of Fundamental Moral Theology

This chapter was published in my *Moral Theology: A Continuing Journey* (Notre Dame, IN: University of Notre Dame Press, 1982), 35–61.

Moral theology, like all theology, bases its reflections on the word of God in the Scriptures, on tradition, on the teaching of the Church, on the signs of the times, and on the eschatological pull of the future. In the last few years great attention has been paid to the signs of the times. The signs of the times, which are important for moral theology in the United States, include both the cultural milieu with its understanding of moral problems and the thematic and systematic reflection, which is the discipline of ethics, both in its religious and philosophical contexts.

To read the signs of the times always involves a prudential discernment and the risk of being wrong. Traditionally American life and ethos have given great importance to freedom in all aspects of life, but there has also been a recognition of the limits of freedom that has especially come to the fore in recent years. The contemporary American scene has witnessed the end of an era in which easy optimism and even naiveté characterized much of the country's self-understanding. Self-criticism and doubt have been more apparent ever since the Vietnam War, Watergate, continuing world crises, and the energy shortage. At times there is a feeling of pessimism and even helplessness, but this self-critical attitude has raised in the public consciousness a greater interest in ethics and the morality of the decisions that must be made to guide our future life. No one is unaware of the multitude of problems calling out for a solution: nuclear energy and weapons; poverty throughout the world and at home; hunger in the world; human rights and wars of liberation; the contemporary trouble spots in the globe—the Near East, Indochina,

Africa, Central and South America; world trade and economic policies; multinational corporations; technology; energy; the environment. There appears to be a widespread feeling that Americans must be willing to face these problems and also to change their own lifestyles away from the consumerism and materialism that have so often characterized our society. At the same time there exists a great interest in contemplation, in the personal struggle for growth, and in the meaning of life and death.

The influence of specifically Catholic thought and theology on the American cultural and intellectual life has not been great. Over twenty years ago John Tracy Ellis criticized American Catholicism for its failures in making any noticeable contribution to the wider scene of American intellectual and cultural life.[1] Since that time individual Catholics and groups have made some contributions, but generally speaking there has been little that is specifically theological in these individual contributions.

On the reflective level of ethics as such, Catholic moral theology in the United States is related to and influenced by religious ethics, especially Protestant Christian ethics, and philosophical ethics. Protestant ethics has had a significant influence in the United States. Perhaps there is no intellectual figure who had a greater impact on American foreign policy in the middle years of the twentieth century than theologian Reinhold Niebuhr.[2] Before the Second Vatican Council there was little or no dialogue between Protestant and Catholic ethicists, but that situation has changed dramatically since the 1960s. Not only dialogue but also rapprochement characterizes the relationship between Catholic moral theology and Protestant ethics. As one very knowledgeable and competent Protestant scholar has pointed out, Catholic moral theology now gives more stress to aspects of ethics that were previously identified as typically Protestant emphases—becoming, process, dynamism, change, freedom, history, grace, and gospel. On the other hand, Protestants have striven to give more importance to Catholic concerns such as being, structure, order, continuity, nature, and law.[3] Close contact and dialogue with Protestant Christian ethics characterizes moral theology in the United States, but moral theology still attempts to remain firmly rooted in its own tradition. At the same time there is increasing communication with philosophical ethics both on methodological and on substantive questions. Philosophical ethics is no longer dominated by an analytic approach that shuns substantive and content questions. Now there is a growing interest of philosophers in the ethical questions facing society and in theoretical issues such as justice and the justification of moral norms.[4] Catholic moral theology exists in an intellectual milieu in the United States in which it is in contact and dialogue with Protestant and philosophical ethics. In the light of these signs of the times this chapter will discuss method in moral theology.

I approach the question of method in moral theology with the presupposition that errors and mistakes in method generally arise not so much from positive error as from the failure to consider all the aspects that deserve discussion. In moral theology itself in the last few years there has been an unfortunate tendency, readily understandable in the light of the contemporary controversies, to reduce moral theology merely to the question of norms and the morality of specific actions. The questions of specific actions and of norms are significant questions in moral theology, but there are other questions that are of greater or equal importance. In my judgment the following areas must be investigated in any systematic reflection on Christian moral life: the perspective or stance; the ethical model; Christian anthropology; concrete Christian decision-making and norms. These different aspects will now be discussed in greater detail.

STANCE

The question of stance or perspective is the most fundamental and logically first consideration in moral theology. Catholic moral theology has not explicitly posed the question of stance, but in the American Protestant tradition James Sellers has insisted on stance as the first consideration in moral theology, logically prior to any other consideration and the source of other criteria.[5] James Gustafson employs a similar concept of perspective or posture to indicate the fundamental angle of vision that directs the entire enterprise of Christian ethics.[6]

Two cautions should be kept in mind in any discussion of stance. First, it is impossible to say that one stance is right and another wrong. The adequacy of the stance depends on how well it accomplishes its purpose as being the logically prior step that structures our understanding of moral reality, serves as a critique of other approaches, and is a source of other ethical criteria. Second, although stance as a logically prior step seems to have something of the a priori about it, in reality my own stance developed in an a posteriori way based on a critique of other positions. To properly fulfill its critical function and be proved adequate, the stance cannot rest merely on an a priori deduction or assumption.

My stance consists of a perspective based on the fivefold Christian mysteries of creation, sin, incarnation, redemption, and resurrection destiny. The reason for accepting these as aspects of the stance are obvious for the Christian, but the adequacy of this fivefold stance must be shown. The stance functions both methodologically and substantively. From a methodological viewpoint the stance both serves as a negative critique of other methodologies and provides a positive approach of its own.

Roman Catholic natural law theory rightly recognizes that the Christian finds ethical wisdom and knowledge not only in the Scriptures and in Jesus Christ but also in human nature and human reason. On the basis of creation by a good and gracious God, human reason reflecting on human nature can arrive at ethical wisdom and knowledge. Insistence on the goodness of the natural and the human with its corollary that grace builds on nature and is not opposed to nature, stands as a hallmark of the Catholic theological tradition. Some Protestant theologians deny the goodness of creation and the possibility of ethical wisdom and knowledge based on human nature and human reason for a number of different reasons—Scripture alone is the source of ethical wisdom for the Christian; a narrow Christomonism sees Christ as the only way into the ethical problem; sin so affects human nature and human reason that they cannot serve as the basis of true knowledge; an unwillingness to accept an analogy between creation and the Creator.

However, from the viewpoint of the proposed stance, the natural law approach is deficient because it does not integrate the natural or creation into the total Christian perspective. The natural law theory rightly recognizes creation and incarnation, but sin, redemption, and resurrection destiny do not receive their due. Catholic moral theology may have overstressed sin in terms of particular actions, but it never paid sufficient attention to the reality of sin as present in the world and affecting, without however destroying, human nature and human reason. Likewise, natural law theory gives no place to grace, or redemption and resurrection destiny as the stance describes this reality, so that often Catholic moral theology became based exclusively on the natural to the neglect of what was then called the supernatural.

On the contrary, a Lutheran two-realm theory recognizes the reality of sin but overemphasizes sin and fails to give enough importance to the reality of creation and to moral wisdom based on it, to the integrating effect of the incarnation, to the recognition that redemption also affects the world in which we live, and to a more positive appreciation of the relationship between resurrection destiny and the present world.

Protestant liberalism arose in the nineteenth century, and its most significant ethical manifestation in the United States was the Social Gospel school.[7] This approach, especially in its more extreme forms, stressed the goodness of creation, the integrating effect of the incarnation on all reality, and the presence of redemption in the world, but sin and resurrection destiny as a future gift at the end of time were neglected.

Liberalism was succeeded in Protestant theology by neoorthodoxy with its Barthian and Niebuhrian approaches. Barthian ethics flourished in Europe, but its most significant American exponent is Paul Lehmann.[8] Barthian ethics emphasized the centrality of redemption and of Christ and made Christ the sole way into the ethical problem. There was no place for philosophical ethics or natural law for the Christian. Within such a perspective, sin, incarnation, redemption, and resurrection destiny could all be given due importance, but creation and its ethical ramifications in terms of human reason were denied. Niebuhrian Christian realism, which ultimately exerted such a great influence on American thought and foreign policy, recognized some ethical import in creation even though it was infected by sin, but in the final analysis gave too much to the presence of sin and failed to appreciate the effects of incarnation, redemption, and a more positive relationship between the world of the present and the fullness of resurrection destiny in the eschaton. However, in many ways Niebuhr tried to account for all the elements in the stance but overemphasized the role of sin and downplayed the others.

In the 1960s in Protestant theology some approaches similar to the older liberalism came to the fore in the form of the theologies of the death of God and of secularization. Once again there was a tendency to overstress creation, incarnation, and redemption and to neglect the reality of sin and the fact that resurrection destiny is future and its fullness comes only as God's gracious gift at the end of time. In the light of the proposed stance subsequent developments were healthy. A theology of secularization gave way to a theology of hope with the primacy on resurrection destiny as future. However, at times there was still not enough emphasis on sin and on some discontinuity between this world and the next. Jürgen Moltmann as a Protestant and Johann Baptist Metz as a Catholic both went through a development similar to that outlined above and then put greater emphasis on discontinuity by highlighting the role of suffering as Moltmann wrote about *The Crucified God* and Metz talked about the future "*ex memoria passionis eius.*"[9]

In the 1960s in conjunction with the Second Vatican Council, Roman Catholic theology rightly attempted to overcome the dichotomy between nature and grace, between gospel and daily life, between Church and world. But in overcoming the dichotomy there emerged the danger of making everything grace and the supernatural. In other words, there was a tendency to forget sin and the fact that resurrection destiny is future and exists always in discontinuity, as well as in continuity, with present reality. Catholic thinking in this period often suffered from a collapsed eschaton because of which people thought that the fullness of the kingdom would come quickly, readily, and without struggle or suffering.

In contemporary Catholic theology, liberation theology, with its attempt to integrate redemption and the gospel into our understanding of political and economic life in society, marks an improvement over the exclusive natural law approach that formerly characterized Catholic social ethics as exemplified in the papal social encyclicals. However, in liberation theology there exists among some a tendency to forget the reality of sin as affecting to some extent all reality (too often the impression is given that sin is all on one side) and a tendency to think that the fullness of the eschaton will come too readily and quickly. On the contrary, liberation will involve a long, hard, difficult struggle and will never be fully present in this world. At times liberation theology fails to recognize complexity in this world, for among some there is a great confidence in being able to know quite easily what God is doing in this world. The opposite danger maintains that reality is complex, and sin so affects all reality that one cannot know what God is doing in the world. I want to avoid both these extremes.

Not only does the stance embracing the fivefold mysteries of creation, sin, incarnation, redemption, and resurrection destiny serve as a critique of many other theories in moral theology as pointed out above, but at the same time it provides a positive methodology and perspective for approaching moral theology. Creation indicates the goodness of the human and human reason; but sin touches all reality, without, however, destroying the basic goodness of creation. Incarnation integrates all reality into the plan of God's kingdom. Redemption as already present affects all reality, while resurrection destiny as future exists in continuity with the redeemed present but also in discontinuity because the fullness of the kingdom remains God's gracious gift at the end of time.

The stance also addresses some substantive issues; but since the stance is the logically prior step in moral theology and by definition remains somewhat general, one cannot expect the stance to provide specific and detailed substantive content. A primary contribution of the stance is in giving a direction and general perspective to our understanding of some of the most basic issues in Christian ethics. The first question concerns the meaning of human existence in this world and the relationship between this world and the kingdom. In the past, Protestant theology often addressed the same basic question in terms of the relationship between Christ and culture as illustrated in the work of H. Richard Niebuhr, who points out five different typologies for understanding this relationship.[10] The position derived from the stance corresponds to Niebuhr's type of Christ-transforming culture. The fullness of the kingdom will only come at the end, but in this world the kingdom strives to make itself more present. The individual Christian and the community of believers must recognize that the mission of the Church and of the gospel calls for them to struggle for peace and justice in the world.

The stance also sheds light on the meaning of death for the Christian. Death seems to point to total discontinuity between this world and the next for the individual person, but in the light of the stance, death can be seen in a transformationist perspective. All created reality will die, but sin has added an important negative dimension to the Christian understanding of death. Even more importantly death is understood in the light of the mystery of the incarnation, death, and resurrection of Jesus, so that death is neither the end nor the beginning of something totally discontinuous but rather the transformation of earthly life and reality into the fullness of life and love.

The stance serves as an interpretive tool in understanding the basic mysteries of the Christian life. Especially in a sacramental and mystical perspective the Christian life is often described in terms of living out the paschal mystery of Jesus into which we are baptized. The paschal mystery can be interpreted in different ways depending on the stance. Some have interpreted it in paradoxical terms to show that life is present in the midst of death, joy in the midst of sorrow, and light in darkness. A transformationist understanding recognizes that there are some paradoxical aspects to the Christian life, but also at times God's life is known in human life, God's love in human love, God's light in human light, and God's joy in human joy. The paschal mystery understood in this perspective gives us a better understanding of Christian life and death and the relationship between the two. Life involves a constant dying to selfishness and sin to enter more fully into the resurrection, and so death itself can be seen as the moment of growth par excellence—dying to the present to enter most fully into life itself.

Perhaps this is the best place to mention briefly the debate about a distinctively Christian ethic. I deny that on the level of material content (actions, virtues, attitudes, and dispositions) there is anything distinctively Christian because non-Christians can and do share the same material content of morality even to the point of such attitudes as self-sacrificing love. Unlike some others, I base this, not on a common human nature abstractly considered, but rather on the fact that in the present existential order all are called to share in the fullness of God's love. However, Christians thematize their understanding in a specifically Christian way. Since ethics, as distinguished from morality, is a thematic and systematic reflection, moral theology and Christian ethics must be based on Christian realities even though some of these (e.g., creation) are not distinctively Christian.

ETHICAL MODEL

The second logical step in the systematic reflection, which is moral theology, concerns the model in view of which one understands the Christian life. In this section I develop somewhat differently the explanation of the model found in chapter 3. Three different models have been proposed in both philosophical and theological literature. The teleological model views the ethical life in terms of the goal or end to be achieved, but in the complexity of existence one distinguishes ultimate goals from intermediate and subordinate goals. Something is morally good if it is conducive to achieve the goal and is evil if it prevents the attainment of the goal. It should be pointed out that these models are very broad umbrellas. Thomas Aquinas, who begins his ethical consideration with a discussion of the last end, serves as a good example of the teleological model, but utilitarians also fit under the same model. A deontological model views the moral life primarily in terms of duty, law, or obligation. The categorical imperative of Immanuel Kant well illustrates a deontological approach to ethics. Popular Christian piety frequently adopts such an approach by making the Ten Commandments the basis of the moral life. The manuals of moral theology, although thinking they were in the tradition of Thomas Aquinas, by their heavy emphasis on law as the objective norm of morality and conscience as the subjective norm, belong to the deontological model. A relationality-responsibility model views the moral life primarily in terms of the person's multiple relationships with God, neighbor, world, and self and the subject's actions in this context.

I opt for a relationality-responsibility model as the primary ethical model. Such an option does not exclude some place for teleological and deontological concerns, but the relationality-responsibility model is primary and forms the perimeters within which the ethical life is discussed. Within a relationality-responsibility model one must avoid the danger of a narrow personalism that views the moral life only in terms of the perspective of an "I-thou" relationship. The Christian is related to God, neighbor, the world, and self. The failure to give due weight to all these relationships will distort the meaning of the Christian life. The basic reality of the Christian life has been described in different ways— love, conversion, life in Christ, the law of the Spirit. All of these descriptions can be used, but they must be understood in terms of a relationality model that includes all the aspects mentioned above.

Just as the fundamental, positive understanding of the Christian life is viewed in relational terms, so too the negative aspect of sin should be seen in the same perspective. A deontological model defines sin as an act against the law of God. A teleological model views sin as going against God, the ultimate end. But from the earliest pages of Genesis sin is described in terms of our relationship with God, neighbor, the world, and self. A contemporary theology of sin in terms of the fundamental option should also be interpreted in relational terms. Mortal sin is primarily not an act against the law of God or going against the ultimate end, but rather the breaking of our relationship of love with God, neighbor, world, and self. Venial sin is the diminishing of these fundamental relationships. In this perspective all the aspects of sin become apparent, especially social sin and its influence on our political, social, and economic structures.

Changes in the understanding of the sacrament of penance well illustrate the shift to a more relational model of the Christian life. In the context of a deontological ethical model the sacrament of penance was called confession from the name of the primary act—the confession of sins according to number and species. Today the sacrament is called reconciliation—a relational term that includes our multiple relationships with God, neighbor, world, and self.

A relationality-responsibility model also influences our approach to particular questions. Take the example of lying. An older approach, based on the teleology inscribed by nature in the faculty of speech, defined the malice of lying as frustrating the God-given purpose of the faculty of speech, which according to God's plan is to express on one's lips what is in one's mind. Within such a context it was necessary to resort to a casuistry of mental reservations to deal with some of the problems that arise. Lately a different approach employing a relationality model has seen the malice of lying in the violation of my neighbor's right to truth. There are cases in which the neighbor does not have the right to truth, and my false speech does not involve the moral malice of lying. Similarly, in questions of sexuality, contraception and sterilization were condemned on the basis of the innate teleology inscribed in the sexual faculty. To go directly against the procreative purpose of the sexual faculty is always wrong. A more relational approach sees the sexual faculty related to the human person and the person related to others, especially to the marriage partner. For the good of the marriage relationship contraception or sterilization can be justified. A relationality-responsibility model not only determines our understanding of basic moral considerations but also results in different solutions to concrete ethical questions.

CHRISTIAN ANTHROPOLOGY

A third step in the development of a method for moral theology concerns Christian anthropology, or the subject existing in the midst of these multiple relationships. In ethics the basic importance of the person is twofold. First, individual actions come from the person and are expressive of the person. Actions are ethically grounded in the person placing the actions. As the Scriptures remind us, the good tree brings forth good fruit, or those who live in the Spirit should produce the fruits of the Spirit. Second, the person, through one's actions, develops and constitutes oneself as a moral subject. In the transcendental terms to be developed later, through one's actions one fulfills the drive to authentic self-transcendence. Individual acts are not the most fundamental ethical category because they are both expressive of the moral subject and constitutive of the moral being of the subject.

The importance of the moral subject underscores the place of growth and development in the Christian life. The Christian is called to be perfect even as the heavenly Father is perfect. Although the fullness of response to God's gracious gift will never be achieved, the Christian strives to grow in wisdom, age, and grace before God and human beings. The call to continual conversion also highlights the importance of growth in the Christian life. Philosophically this growth is grounded in the drive of the subject toward authentic self-transcendence. Through actions the subject continually transcends self and thereby contributes to true growth. Psychologists, too, have been paying much attention to the importance of moral growth in human life. Lawrence Kohlberg has proposed his theory of moral development involving six stages, with the last stage exemplifying postconventional morality and described as the full development of an interior, self-directed moral sense with an orientation of conscience toward ethical principles that appeal to logical comprehensiveness, universality, and consistency.[11] Catholic thinkers are appreciative of Kohlberg's work but are beginning to deal with Kohlberg in a critical way.[12] In my judgment Kohlberg's basic limits come from the formal aspect of his approach that is conditioned both by his Kantian philosophy and by his attempt to come up with a model of moral development acceptable and usable in a pluralistic context. As a result his approach is based on the formalities of justice but does not give enough importance to content, to questions of dispositions and virtues, and to aspects other than a rationalistic understanding of justice.

Intimately connected with the person are the attitudes, virtues, and dispositions, which are expressed in action and which also constitute the subject as morally good and form an essential part of the growth and development of the moral subject.[13] These dispositions or virtues affect the various relationships within which the subject finds oneself. It is impossible to describe in detail all the dispositions that should characterize the different relationships within which the Christian person exists as subject, but some of the more significant ones can be mentioned.

Traditionally the relationship of the individual to God is characterized by the three theological virtues of faith, hope, and charity. In the light of a better integrated view of the moral life of the Christian based on the stance, some other important dispositions and attitudes should be developed. The attitude of worship and thanksgiving must characterize the Christian, who recognizes God as the author of love, life, and all good gifts. The Christian is primarily a worshiper. Here one can see the intimate connection between liturgy and the moral life of the Christian. The liturgy with its celebration of the encounter of God's giving and of human response mirrors the basic structure of life. A second very fundamental attitude for the Christian is openness and receptivity to the word and work of God. The Scriptures frequently allude to the importance of this basic virtue—be it done unto me according to your will. This disposition is the true humility of spirit that the Scriptures portray as the great characteristic of the poor of Yahweh. The privileged people in the kingdom—the poor, children, and sinners—underscore the importance of this disposition of openness to God's saving gift. A self-sufficiency, which so often characterizes the rich, the proud, and the important, is the antithesis of the disposition of openness or true humility of spirit.

Within the traditional triad of faith, hope, and charity more importance must be given to hope than was true in the manuals of moral theology. This emphasis comes from the contemporary theological highlighting of eschatology and of the pilgrim nature of our existence. Struggle and suffering are an integral part of our existence.

Relationships to neighbor are characterized by the generic dispositions of love and justice. These general attitudes are then specified by the different relationships one has to specific neighbors—parent, friend, teacher, coworker, client, supervisor, employer, person in authority. In this context one cannot underscore enough the Christian insistence on love for the poor, the needy, and the outcast. This habitual attitude constantly calls one out of one's own narrowness and selfishness and strives to make ever broader and more universal the horizons of our love.

The relationship to the world and to earthly realities involves a number of specific relationships. The basic Christian attitude is that the goods of creation exist to serve the needs of all. The purpose of the goods of creation is to serve all God's people, and no one has a right to arrogate superfluous goods to oneself at the expense of the neighbor in need. Unfortunately an overemphasis on private property has too often blinded us to the basic attitude toward the goods of creation.[14] Selfishness and sinfulness have too often turned the goods of creation into the means of personal gratification and aggrandizement at the expense of others. The question of the best economic system is complex, but the guiding principle must be how well the system fulfills the basic principle that the goods of creation exist to serve the needs of all. An attitude of respectful gratitude for the gifts of creation serves as the basis for an environmental ethics. Our relationships with the different types of material goods will make more specific and spell out this general understanding of their universal destiny.

Our relationship to self is governed by the basic attitude of stewardship, using our gifts, talents, and selves in the living out of the Christian life. Here, too, the individual must always struggle against the opposite attitude of selfishness. As in our other relationships there is place for a proper Christian asceticism, which uses our lives, our gifts, and our bodies for the service of the kingdom and our own proper development.

DECISION-MAKING AND NORMS

The fourth and final level of ethical reflection in describing a method for moral theology concerns concrete decision-making and the morality of particular actions. In the contemporary context the two most important questions are the grounding of moral norms and the role and function of conscience.

There has been much discussion in Catholic moral theology, in Protestant Christian ethics, and in contemporary philosophical ethics about norms and the grounding of moral norms. Among a good number of Roman Catholic theologians throughout the world there has been a dissatisfaction with the existence of certain negative moral absolutes and the grounding of these norms in a particular understanding of natural law. As mentioned in earlier chapters, the problem arises from a concept of natural law as coinciding with the physical structure of the act, so that the physical structure of the act becomes morally normative—an act described in physical terms is said to be always and everywhere wrong. I am not saying that the physical structure of the act and the moral reality of the act cannot coincide, but the moral must include much more than merely the physical structure of the act and the grounding of the moral meaning involves more than merely a consideration of the physical structure of the act.

Many revisionist Catholic moral theologians at the present time solve the problem by distinguishing between moral evil and premoral, physical, or ontic evil, which, in the understanding of the manuals on questions such as double effect or sterilization, was called moral evil. Physical, ontic, or premoral evil can be justified if there is a commensurate or proportionate reason.[15]

In my view such an approach is in the right vein but does not go far enough. The physical is but one aspect of the moral, which is the ultimate human judgment and includes all the other aspects—the psychological, the sociological, the pedagogical, the hygenic, and so on. It is necessary to reveal what is meant by premoral or ontic evil and commensurate reason. This raises the question of the different values involved. In general, norms exist to protect and promote values. But the question arises of how norms are arrived at and grounded.

Before discussing the precise way in which norms as the safeguard of values are to be grounded, a word should be said about the source of conflict situations, which bring about the tensions existing between and among different values. Again, in keeping with a general presumption in favor of complexity, there appear to be numerous sources for the conflict situations that arise and might call for modifications or exceptions in moral norms. From a strictly ethical perspective Catholic moral theology has recognized one source of conflict in its distinction between the objective moral order and the subjective. Objectively a particular act is morally wrong (e.g., drunkenness), but for this individual subject in these particular circumstances (e.g., an alcoholic) there is no subjective guilt or the guilt is greatly diminished. Philosophical ethics recognizes the same reality in its distinction between circumstances that justify an act (which makes it right) and circumstances that excuse an act (take away guilt without making it right).

There exist other sources of conflict situations in moral theology that can be reduced to three—eschatological tension, the presence of sin, and human finitude. Eschatological tension results from the fact that the fullness of the eschaton is not here, and in this pilgrim existence the eschatological exigencies cannot always be fully met. In this light I have argued against an absolute prohibition of divorce and remarriage.

The presence of sin in the world also causes some conflict situations. There can be no doubt that the presence of sin in the world has justified certain moral actions that would not be acceptable if there were no sin. Think of the justifications given for war, capital punishment, revolution, occult compensation. An older Catholic theology explicitly recognized that the justification of private property was grounded in the fact of original sin and not in human nature as such. In the light of my stance and contention that at times Catholic moral theology has not explicitly given enough importance to the reality of sin, it seems there might be other cases in which the presence of sin might justify an action that could not be justified if sin and its effects were not present. In the past I have referred to this as the theory of compromise. Such a theory is more a theological explanation of the source of the conflict and tension rather than a tightly reasoned ethical analysis of how it is to be applied in practice. Compromise was chosen to describe this reality in order to recognize the tension between justifying such actions because of the presence of sin and the Christian obligation to try to overcome sin and its effects. However, at times in this world sin and its presence cannot be overcome—a fact that the Catholic tradition has recognized in its discussion of war and private property; but perhaps a greater emphasis on the compromise aspect of these two ethical realities might have made us more cautious in dealing with them.

A third source of tension and conflict in establishing moral norms as preservers of values stems from human finitude. Values will at times conflict and clash because it is impossible to obtain or safeguard *one* value without losing or diminishing another value. At the very least moral theology should recognize the sources of the conflict situations that often arise in questions involving norms. However, the recognition of the different sources of conflict does not help to resolve the question of how norms are grounded and the question of modifications or exceptions in some norms that have been accepted as absolute in the manuals of moral theology.

In approaching the question of grounding norms much can be learned from a dialogue with contemporary philosophical ethics. The question is often phrased in terms of a deontological or teleological grounding of norms. According to the deontological grounding of norms, certain actions are right or wrong no matter what the consequences. No matter how much good might result, suicide, for example, is always morally wrong. Such an approach has been called a Catholic position and certainly coincides with what has often been presented in Catholic philosophy and theology. However, some revisionist Catholic moralists maintain that norms are derived teleologically and this was true even for the Catholic understanding in the past. Norms were based on whether or not the particular action was judged good or evil for the human person and for society.

Many of the revisionist Catholic theologians, who have proposed a teleological grounding for norms, have employed an approach according to which commensurate reason can justify premoral or ontic evil and, thereby, have challenged some of the absolute norms defended in the manuals of moral theology. As a result some other Catholic theoreticians claim that such approaches are consequentialist, basing morality solely on the consequences of the action.[16]

An overview of the contemporary philosophical discussion about the grounding of norms indicates there are three different positions and not just two, but the terminology is confusing and not uniform. The one position is clearly deontological—some actions are always wrong no matter what the consequences. A second position is truly consequentialist, utilitarian, or strictly teleological and derives norms and the morality of actions solely on the basis of consequences. In this context there has been much debate about the difference between act and rule utilitarianism.

However, it is evident that there also exists a third position mediating between the two and called by different names including teleology and prima facie obligationalism.[17] This position rejects deontology but

also disagrees with a strict teleology or consequentialism. In disagreement with strict consequentialists or utilitarians, this middle position
maintains the following three points: (1) moral obligations arise from
elements other than consequences, such as promises, previous acts of
gratitude or evil; (2) the good is not separate from the right; and (3) the
way in which the good or the evil is obtained by the agent and not just
the end result is a moral consideration.

The existence of three different positions on the grounding of the
moral norm indicates there are more than just two different approaches
to this question. In my judgment, the middle position is best described as
a distinct approach based on a relationality-responsibility grounding of
norms. Such a position grounds the norm on the basis of what is experienced as good for the person and for the total human society, and this on
the basis of a relational criterion that gives importance to consequences
but also gives moral value to aspects other than consequences.

In general, a relational grounding of the norm sees the norm as
protecting and promoting values. Such an approach avoids the absolut-
ism of a deontological approach and also the simplistic approach of a
consequentialism that gives moral significance only to consequences. By
highlighting the continued importance of the social dimension of human
existence, such an approach recognizes that often norms are required for
the good of all living together in human society.

The difference between my approach and that of Germain Grisez,
as developed in chapter 5, helps to give a clearer understanding of how
my approach works. According to Grisez there are eight basic human
goods that the individual person can never directly go against.[18] My relational approach does not see the individual face-to-face with eight separate, basic goods but rather views the individual in multiple relationships
with others and sees these goods as also related among themselves. At
times there might be a conflict among these eight basic goods, and one
might have to be sacrificed for other important values. In my methodology a relationality-responsibility model not only serves as the basic
model of the Christian moral life but also grounds and establishes moral
norms.

Conscience is the guide and director of the moral life of the individual. This section both overlaps with and develops somewhat differently what is found in chapter 3. The understanding of conscience found

in the manuals of moral theology can be criticized for being legalistic, minimalistic, overly rational, and too deductive. A better notion of conscience must be integrated within the understanding of the stance, model, and anthropology described above. For example, a relational model will not accept as primary the deontological understanding of conscience as the subjective norm of morality trying to conform to the objective norm of morality that is law in all its different aspects—divine, natural, and positive. Conscience is grounded in the subject, who is called to respond to the gospel message in the midst of the multiple relationships of human existence and thereby live out the thrust for authentic self-transcendence. Conscience thus partakes of the dynamism of the self-transcending subject.[19] The authentic life of the person as subject calls for self-transcendence that on the moral level reaches its fulfillment when the subject exists in a loving relationship with God, neighbor, the world, and self. An older faculty metaphysics situated conscience in the practical intellect. In my perspective conscience should be seen as an operation of the subject. In this way one can better integrate the creative and affective aspects of conscience and avoid a one-sided rationalism.

Conscience is the operation of the subject guiding and directing the moral life. Conscience is stimulated in many different ways—through parables, stories,[20] symbols, the liturgy, through the example of others as models, and through a myriad of life experiences. In its pursuit of values and self-transcendence the subject in many different ways comes to know, appreciate, love, and create the attitudes that should mark the life of the Christian. Conscience is seriously impoverished when it is reduced merely to a knowledge of the law, for it should be seen as an operation of the self-transcending subject trying to live out the fullness of the relationship with God, neighbor, the world, and self.

What about the decision of conscience about a particular action to be done here and now? In accord with a transcendental approach in the context of a relational model of ethics, the judgment of conscience is grounded ultimately in the self-transcending subject. The ultimate criterion of the truth of conscience is not conformity to the truth existing out there but is the self-transcendence of the human subject striving for authentic development. Authentic subjectivity is genuine objectivity.

The judgment of conscience is virtually unconditioned. The self-transcending subject with its thrust toward the true and the good constantly asks questions. The criterion of a true judgment exists when the subject rests at peace because there are no more pertinent questions to ask. The subject is always dealing with the data and reality before it and asking questions precisely to comprehend the moral meaning. Of course, there are dangers that the drive for authentic self-transcendence and the questioning based on it will be blunted and short-circuited, but the mature moral subject will be aware of these possible pitfalls and struggle against them.

The Christian tradition has talked about the peace and joy of conscience as being the sign of a good conscience. A transcendental theory grounds this peace and joy in the judgment of conscience as virtually unconditioned in which the subject, constituted by its dynamic thrust toward self-transcendence, arrives at the true and the good and is at peace. The subject rests in the achievement of the true and the good. In this whole process the self is constantly asking questions about the entire moral act, end and circumstances, and takes all the steps that are appropriate in a discerning process including prayer, reflection, and counsel.

The dilemma of conscience has always arisen from the recognition that the individual must act in accord with one's own conscience, but conscience might be wrong. The generic limitations of conscience, especially in the light of the stance, are finitude and sinfulness. The person striving for true self-transcendence must be aware of these limitations and strive to overcome them. In this context, from a purely ethical viewpoint, which is obviously strengthened in the light of Catholic ecclesiology, one can see the importance of the Church as a moral teacher because by definition the community of believers guided by the Spirit through various offices and charisms exists in diverse times and places and is aided in the struggle against sin. The Church helps to overcome the twofold generic limitation of human conscience.

This study has attempted to sketch the method that should be employed in moral theology, especially in the light of the cultural and academic situation in the United States. On the basis of a presupposition recognizing great complexity in the moral life in general and in the systematic reflection on that experience, four general areas of reflection have been considered—the stance, the ethical model, anthropology, and norms and concrete decision-making.

Notes

1. John Tracy Ellis, "American Catholics and the Intellectual Life," *Thought* 30 (1955): 351–88.

2. See Ronald Stone, *Reinhold Niebuhr: Prophet to Politicians* (Nashville: Abingdon Press, 1971); also *Reinhold Niebuhr: His Religious, Social and Political Thought*, ed. Charles W. Kegley and Robert W. Bretall (New York: Macmillan, 1956).

3. James M. Gustafson, *Protestant and Roman Catholic Ethics: Prospects for Rapprochement* (Chicago: University of Chicago Press, 1978).

4. See, e.g., *Ethics and Problems of the 21st Century*, ed. K. E. Goodpaster and K. M. Sayre (Notre Dame, IN: University of Notre Dame Press, 1979). On questions of justice much discussion has been sparked by John Rawls, *A Theory of Justice* (Cambridge, MA: Harvard University Press, 1971).

5. James Sellers, *Theological Ethics* (New York: Macmillan, 1966), 29–68.

6. James M. Gustafson, *Christ and the Moral Life* (New York: Harper and Row, 1968), 240–48.

7. The standard account of this movement remains Charles Howard Hopkins, *The Rise of the Social Gospel in American Protestantism, 1865–1915* (New Haven, CT: Yale University Press, 1940).

8. Paul Lehmann, *Ethics in a Christian Context* (New York: Harper and Row, 1963); Lehmann, *The Transfiguration of Politics* (New York: Harper and Row, 1975).

9. Jürgen Moltmann, *The Theology of Hope* (New York: Harper and Row, 1967); Moltmann, *The Crucified God* (New York: Harper and Row, 1974); Johannes B. Metz, *Theology of the World* (New York: The Seabury Press, 1969); Metz, "The Future in the Memory of Suffering," *New Concilium* 76 (1972): 9–25.

10. H. Richard Niebuhr, *Christ and Culture* (New York: Harper Torchbook, 1956).

11. Kohlberg has published his stages of moral development in many different places. For a recent elucidation, see Lawrence Kohlberg, "The Implications of Moral Stages for Adult Education," *Religious Education* 72, no. 2 (March–April 1977): 183–201.

12. Illustrative of this critical approach are the following: Paul J. Philibert, "Conscience: Developmental Perspectives from Rogers and Kohlberg," *Horizons* 6 (1979): 1–25; Walter E. Conn, "Post-conventional Morality: An Exposition and Critique of Lawrence Kohlberg's Analysis of Moral Development in the Adolescent and Adult," *Lumen Vitae* 30 (1975): 213–30.

13. A significant factor on the American scene is the interest by Protestant ethicians in the subject and in character. See James M. Gustafson, *Christian Ethics*

and the Community (Philadelphia: Pilgrim Press, 1971), 151–216; also in his
Christ and the Moral Life; Stanley Hauerwas, *Character and the Christian Life:
A Study in Theological Ethics* (San Antonio, TX: Trinity University Press, 1975).

14. The universal destiny of the goods of creation to serve the needs of all
has been highlighted in more recent statements of the hierarchical magisterium;
but John A. Ryan, the leading figure in American Catholic social ethics in the first
half of the twentieth century, insisted on such a first principle in his discussions
of the goods of creation and the system of private property. See John A. Ryan,
Distributive Justice (New York: Macmillan, 1916), 56–60. See also Reginald G.
Bender, "The Doctrine of Private Property in the Writings of Monsignor John A.
Ryan" (STD diss., The Catholic University of America, 1973).

15. For a book of readings in English of significant articles originally
written on this topic in various languages, see *Readings in Moral Theology No.
1: Moral Norms and the Catholic Tradition*, ed. Charles E. Curran and Richard
A. McCormick (New York: Paulist Press, 1979). On the American scene Rich-
ard A. McCormick has done the most to carry on a dialogue on this question
of norms both with Catholic moral theologians throughout the world and with
Protestant and philosophical ethicians in the United States. See especially his
"Notes on Moral Theology" that appear regularly in *Theological Studies* and also
Doing Evil to Achieve Good: Moral Choice in Conflict Situations, ed. Richard A.
McCormick and Paul Ramsey (Chicago: Loyola University Press, 1978).

16. John R. Connery, "Morality of Consequences: A Theological
Appraisal," *Theological Studies* 34 (1973): 396–414; reprinted in *Readings in
Moral Theology No. 1*, 244–66.

17. This third or mediating position is held by a large number of philosophers. See, e.g., Rawls, *A Theory of Justice*, 25ff.; William K. Frankena, *Ethics*
(Englewood Cliffs, NJ: Prentice-Hall, 1963), 13ff.

18. Germain Grisez, *Abortion: The Myths, the Realities and the Argu-
ments* (New York: Corpus Books, 1970), 311–21; Germain Grisez and Russell
Shaw, *Beyond the New Morality: The Responsibilities of Freedom* (Notre Dame,
IN: University of Notre Dame Press, 1974). For his critique of what he calls con-
sequentialism, see Germain Grisez, "Against Consequentialism," *The American
Journal of Jurisprudence* 23 (1978): 21–72.

19. For a detailed development of this notion of conscience, see Walter
E. Conn, *Conscience: Development and Self-Transcendence* (Birmingham, AL:
Religious Education Press, 1981).

20. For a strong insistence on the importance of story, see Stanley Hauerwas, with Richard Bondi and David B. Burrell, *Truthfulness and Tragedy: Further Investigations into Christian Ethics* (Notre Dame, IN: University of Notre
Dame Press, 1977), esp. 15–98.

10. *Veritatis Splendor*

THE MORAL METHODOLOGY OF POPE JOHN PAUL II

This chapter appeared in my *History of Contemporary Issues: Studies in Moral Theology* (New York: Continuum, 1996), 216–38.

Pope John Paul II's encyclical *Veritatis splendor*, officially signed on August 6, 1993, has the "central theme" of the "reaffirmation of the universality and immutability of the moral commandments, particularly those which prohibit always and without exception intrinsically evil acts" (§115).[1]

The pope directs his remarks primarily to the state of Catholic moral theology today, but since the Catholic approach always saw its moral teaching affecting society as a whole, the encyclical makes important remarks about life in the world today. The pope had publicly mentioned his intention of writing such an encyclical on August 1, 1987, the second centenary of the death of Alphonsus Liguori, the patron saint of moral theologians and confessors (§5). Rumors about the preparation, the primary authors, the central themes, and even the possible scrapping of the whole idea surfaced in the intervening years. The pope himself refers to the encyclical as "long awaited" and proposes as one reason for the delay that the *Catechism of the Catholic Church* be published first (§5).

OVERVIEW OF THE ENCYCLICAL

The encyclical is addressed to "the venerable brothers in the epis-copate who share with me the responsibility of safeguarding 'sound teaching'" (§5). The occasion for the new encyclical is the "new situation" within the Catholic Church itself. "It is no longer a matter of limited and occasional dissent, but of an overall and systematic calling into question of traditional moral doctrines on the basis of certain anthropological and ethical presuppositions" (§4). These dissenting positions are heard even in seminaries and theological faculties with regard to questions of the greatest importance for the life of the Church and souls (§4). This reality constitutes "a genuine crisis" for the Church (§5).

At the root of these unacceptable presuppositions causing the present crisis are currents of thought that end by detaching human freedom from its essential and constitutive relationship to truth (§4). This explains the whole thrust of the encyclical with its title of the "Splendor of Truth" and with the very first paragraph of the introduction citing 1 Peter 1:22 about the need for "obedience to the truth." The whole structure of the document with its three chapters follows logically and coherently from the understanding of the occasion for it and the root causes of the problem.

The first chapter involves an extended reflection on the story in Matthew 19:16ff. of the rich young man who came to Jesus with the question, "What good must I do to have eternal life?" Jesus's response is that he should obey the commandments and give up all his possessions and come follow him. This comparatively long biblical reflection involves a somewhat new approach in papal teachings on moral matters. Catholic moral theology is traditionally based on human reason and natural law. However, similar but shorter reflections on biblical passages can be found in other encyclicals of the pope.[2] The pope uses this scriptural passage to point out that God's revelation includes moral commandments and that the moral life is intimately connected with faith. However, in no way does the pope abandon the Catholic emphasis on natural law, as the second chapter makes abundantly clear.

The real import of the first chapter comes from its relationship to the purpose of the entire document. "Jesus' conversation with the rich young man continues in a sense in every period of history including our own" (§25). The Church ("the pillar and bulwark of the truth"—2 Tim 3:15) continues the teaching role of Jesus with the "task of authentically interpreting the word of God...entrusted only [sic] to those charged with the Church's living magisterium, whose authority is exercised in the name of Jesus Christ" (§27).[3] These quotations come from the end of the first chapter and make the point that the pope today continues the work of Jesus in teaching the commandments to guide the moral life of all the followers of Jesus.

The way in which Scripture is used depends on the purpose of the one using it. Here the pope's purpose has shaped and limited the use of the Scripture. The moral life is understood primarily in terms of commandments (to the exclusion and underplaying of other elements such as the change of heart, virtues, vision, attitudes, moral imagination, goals, and so forth), and the role of Jesus and consequently of the Church is reduced to teaching commandments. Jesus as exemplar or paradigm is left out. The risen Jesus through the Spirit as the enabler and empowerer of the Christian life is not mentioned. The moral life itself is understood in light of a legal model, with the pope following the role of Jesus proposing the commandments "with the reaffirmation of the universality and immutability of the moral commandments, particularly those prohibiting always and without exception intrinsically evil acts" (§115).

The second chapter has an entirely different feel and approach. The pope, carrying on the moral teaching function of Jesus, points out and condemns certain interpretations of Christian morality that are not consistent with sound teaching. The pope explicitly denies any intention "to impose upon the faithful any particular theological system, still less a philosophical one" (§29). However, in reality John Paul II strongly reasserts the nineteenth- and twentieth-century neo-Scholasticism of the manuals of moral theology within his more personalistic framework.

The general error pointed out in this section fails to recognize the importance of truth in moral theology and absolutizes freedom of conscience, cutting off their basic relationship to truth. The pope specifically mentions and condemns the most important aspects of the so-called revisionist school of Catholic moral theology (he does not use that term) that has been evolving since Vatican II—an autonomous ethic, the charge of physicalism made against the accepted Catholic teaching in sexual and medical ethics, the theory of fundamental option, and the ethical theory of proportionalism. All these in their own way have called into question the existence of some intrinsically evil acts. *Veritatis splendor* in this chapter also strongly criticizes in the broader context the absolutization of freedom, false autonomy, subjectivism, individualism, and relativism.

Chapter 3 develops a number of related points. The first stresses the bond between freedom and truth. Commitment to the truth above all shows forth in the willingness of people to give their lives for the truth of the gospel of Jesus. Although martyrdom represents the high point of witness to moral truth, and one to which few people are called, all Christians must daily be ready to make a consistent witness at the cost of suffering and sacrifice (§93). Second, universal and unchangeable norms are at the service of persons and of the society, thus showing the necessary connection between freedom and truth. Only a morality that acknowledges certain norms and rights as valid always, everywhere, and without exception can guarantee an ethical foundation of social coexistence on both the national and international levels (§§95–101). Third, the chapter recalls that God's grace transforms and strengthens weak and sinful human beings to be able to obey God's law (§§102–5). A final section on morality and evangelization contains an important section dealing with the roles of the magisterium and of moral theologians who are called to be an example of loyal assent, both internal and external to the magisterium's teaching (§§106–17).

Early reaction to the encyclical has followed a somewhat predictable course.[4] Proponents of what has been called revisionism in Catholic moral theology have tended to be quite negative,[5] whereas more conservative moral theologians have been quite positive although some want the pope to go even further to a definitive and infallible magisterial judgment on the received teaching on intrinsically evil acts and to the same kind of judgment on certain understandings of faith and revelation that are even more fundamental.[6] Some more evangelically rooted scholars have lauded the pope's great emphasis on Scripture and the gospel, but perhaps they do not give enough importance to how strongly the second chapter of the document holds on to neo-Scholastic philosophy.[7] Feminists readily find fault with the methodology involved.[8] A good number have been appreciative of the pope's dealing with the broader societal issues.[9] All of us interpret and react to the document in the light of our own understandings and interests, but we all must be careful to try to understand precisely what the pope is saying before entering into dialogue with him. In this spirit I recognize that I am coming from a revisionist position and have disagreed over the years with the papal teaching on intrinsically evil acts and dissent in the Church. One commentator has pointed out that the encyclical is directed at my work.[10] However, I also find myself in agreement with many points made in the encyclical.

POSITIVE EVALUATION

I find myself in agreement with many of the pope's problems with some contemporary ethical thinking, with the positive points he makes against them, and with the applications especially in the area of social ethics. Moral truth is most important. Freedom and conscience can never be absolutized. There are many things one should not do (§§35–53). The Catholic tradition in the past often failed to give enough importance to freedom as exemplified in its long-standing opposition to religious freedom and the continuing problems with academic freedom. However, as the twentieth century developed, the Catholic Church, in reaction to the danger of totalitarianism, began to give a greater role to human freedom. A very significant development occurred in Pope John XXIII's writings within two years. In *Mater et magistra* in 1961 he claimed that the ideal social order was founded on the values of truth, justice, and love.[11] In *Pacem in terris* in 1963 he added freedom to this triad.[12] Freedom is very significant, but it must be seen in its relationship to other values. The pope in *Veritatis splendor* is concentrating on freedom's relationship to truth, but it is fair to say he is not denying the other important relationships of freedom with justice and charity. One is not free to deny fundamental human rights.

Just as freedom cannot be absolutized so too conscience cannot be absolutized. Conscience cannot make something right or wrong (§§54–64). Adolph Eichmann claimed that he only followed his conscience, but he was rightly convicted of crimes against humanity. Conscience is called to recognize and respond to moral truth. Intimately connected with the absolutization of freedom of conscience is the false autonomy of the individual. The individual is not autonomous in the sense that the individual makes something right or wrong on her own. Here too, however, the Catholic tradition has not given enough importance to the role of creativity and the initiative of the individual. But one cannot go to the other extreme and proclaim the absolute autonomy of the individual.

Any theistic morality sees the individual in relationship to and dependent on God.

The challenge is to avoid both a one-sided autonomy or a one-sided heteronomy. *Veritatis splendor* deals well with this aspect of autonomy in the first part of the second chapter (§§38–42). To its credit the Catholic tradition with its emphasis on participation has been able to provide a very satisfactory approach to this question. Too often the issue is proposed in terms of a competition between the divine and the human. If you have one hundred points to assign to both, then you might assign eighty to God and twenty to the human. But maybe human beings should have more and God less. The traditional Catholic emphasis on participation and mediation as mentioned in the encyclical avoids such an either-or approach. The glory of God is the human person come alive. God wants us to attain our happiness and our perfection. The basic insight of Thomas Aquinas well illustrates this approach. In the Second Part of the *Summa*, Aquinas speaks of the human being as an image of God because like God she is endowed with intellect, free will, and the power of self-determination.[13] The human person imitates God by using her intellect, free will, and the power of self-determination. Traditional Catholic moral theology following the teaching of Thomas Aquinas sees the natural law as the participation of the eternal law in the rational creature. Human reason reflecting on God's created human nature can arrive at the plan of God for us, which involves our own fulfillment.[14] All theists and even some nontheists would join the Catholic tradition in denying the absolute autonomy of the human being. But the Catholic tradition does not want to embrace a heteronomy that downplays the place of self-direction and human fulfillment.

Likewise the pope properly points out the related danger of individualism in our society (§33). The absolutization of freedom, conscience, and autonomy logically leads to individualism. The individual becomes the center of all reality and not enough importance is given to the community in general, the various communities to which we all belong, and the relationships that tie us to other human beings. In the past, the Catholic tradition has not given enough importance to the individual and sometimes in the name of community restricted the role and rights of the individual. Think of the acceptance of torture in some cases and the failure to recognize the right of the defendant not to incriminate herself. Until this century it was universally held that the state could and should use capital punishment to protect itself, but now many Catholics, recognizing more the dignity of the person, strongly oppose capital punishment. A greater emphasis is being given to the rights of the individual vis-à-vis the state, but contemporary Catholic thought in keeping with the best of its own tradition rightly rejects individualism. In the United States society today many are criticizing American individualism in the name of a more communitarian understanding of human anthropology.[15] The Catholic tradition strongly supports such a communitarian critique of individualism.

Subjectivism logically follows from all the above-mentioned approaches. The pope correctly condemns the subjectivism that makes the subject the center of right and wrong and does not give enough significance to objective reality (§32). Here again the Catholic tradition in the past has not given enough importance to the subject, and many recent developments in Catholic theology and philosophy have embraced the turn to the subject but this does not entail a radical moral subjectivism.

This radical subjectivism often appears in our society but without much philosophical grounding. The morality accepted by many people today proclaims that you do your thing and I'll do my thing. Just don't interfere with each other. Such subjective individualism destroys any possibility of a community of shared truths and values. To have a community one needs such shared moral values. The pope rightly points out there are rights that are always and everywhere to be acknowledged and protected. There are actions such as torture, arbitrary imprisonment, and treating workers as mere instruments of profit that should never be done (§§95–97). The dangers of individualism and subjectivism are present in our contemporary American society.

Finally, John Paul II points out the danger of relativism for human social living (§§96–101). The Catholic tradition by definition stands opposed to relativism. Catholic means universal and the pope insists on the existence of universal principles and norms. The danger in the Catholic tradition has been not to give enough importance to diversity in all its different forms. Think, for example, of the insistence on the universal language for liturgical prayer before Vatican II so that almost no Catholic understood the language of the Eucharist. The Catholic emphasis on universality too easily claimed universality for what was a historically or culturally conditioned reality. Feminism reminds us how easy it was for those in power to impose patriarchy in the name of universality.

One of the most significant debates in contemporary ethics focuses on the possibility of universality in ethics, with many either theoretically or practically denying the possibility of such universality.[16] However, the Catholic tradition with its emphasis on the one God who is Creator, Redeemer, and Sanctifier of all can never accept a relativism. We are brothers and sisters of all other human beings and called to live together with them in peace and harmony. In the midst of the pluralism and diversity of our world, universalism is more chastened than in the past and more difficult to ground and explain. I think that the pope tends to gloss over too easily some of the objections to universalism, too readily grounds it in Thomistic natural law, and at times claims too much for it. However, the Catholic tradition has correctly insisted on universality.

The signs of the times also demand some universality. We experience the lack of unity in many countries in the world including our own. Religious, ethnic, and tribal differences are the cause of war and disintegration in many nations. In the society of our own United States the divisions based on color and economic class are evident in every one of our cities. In our world, with its growing interrelatedness, we badly need to be able to communicate with one another despite religious, linguistic, ethnic, and cultural differences. In many ways the challenge to our society today is how to achieve unity in the midst of the great diversity that exists on all levels.

NEGATIVE EVALUATION

My strong disagreements with the papal letter center on his understanding of and approach to contemporary Catholic moral theology and what might be described as the churchly aspect of moral theology as distinguished from Catholic social ethics. As I have already identified myself as a revisionist Catholic moral theologian, one would expect such differences to be there. Naturally, I disagree with the position that condemns the revisionist developments in moral theology, but I am even more disturbed by other aspects of the papal document.

The Role and Understanding of Law

The first objection comes from the moral model that the pope proposes in *Veritatis splendor*. Here John Paul II understands morality primarily on the basis of a legal model. Such an approach, which characterized the manuals of moral theology, sees morality primarily in terms of obedience to the law or the commandments of God. No one can doubt that *Veritatis splendor* employs such a model. The very first paragraph emphasizes the need for obedience to the truth but recognizes that such obedience is not always easy. The pericope of the rich young man stresses Jesus as the teacher proposing the commandments that are to be obeyed. The first and longest of the four parts of chapter 2 deals with freedom and the law (§§35–53). Chapter 2 especially emphasizes the role of the natural law. Positive precepts of the natural law are "universally binding" and "unchanging." The negative precepts of the natural law oblige always and in every circumstance—*semper et pro semper* (§52). The third chapter continues this approach with its emphasis on laws and commands and the Church's firmness in defending the universal and unchanging moral norms (§96).

In the judgment of many, the legal model is not the best and most adequate model for moral theology or any ethics. At the very minimum the legal model cannot adequately cover all the moral decisions that a person makes. In fact, the vast majority of moral decisions are not made on the basis of existing laws. Law directly enters into comparatively few of the moral decisions by which we live our lives. In addition, the legal model tends to restrict moral considerations only to acts and forgets about the more important realities of change of heart, vision, attitudes, and dispositions. Thomas Aquinas did not follow a legal model, but rather a teleological model based on what is the ultimate end of human beings. For Aquinas the ultimate end of human beings is happiness, and actions are good if they bring one to that end and evil if they prevent one's arriving at that end. Reality of course is quite complex, so there exists not only the ultimate end but also other ends that are not ultimate and interrelated with one another. In addition, Thomas Aquinas developed the moral life primarily in terms of human powers and habits and only brings in law at the end of his discussion of what we call fundamental moral theology.[17] The manuals of moral theology, the textbooks in the field before Vatican II, did adopt a legal model. Much has been said about the legal model, but for our present purposes it suffices to point out the inadequacy of the model and the fact that Thomas Aquinas himself adopted a different approach.

One might defend the legal model in *Veritatis splendor* precisely because the pope is dealing primarily with the existence of universal and immutable moral commandments, especially those that prohibit always and without exception intrinsically evil acts. However, at the very minimum the encyclical should have pointed out that the legal model is not the most adequate model for moral theology, and this document is dealing only with one aspect of moral theology. Neither explicitly nor implicitly does the pope make such an admission. *Veritatis splendor* thus gives the impression that it is describing the model for moral theology in general.

Ironically, someone in the Catholic tradition using the legal model tends to weaken the basic assertion of the entire encyclical that there is no opposition between freedom and law. Historically the manuals of moral theology with their legal model, ever since the seventeenth century and later debates over probabilism, tended to posit an opposition between law and freedom. This assertion needs further explanation.

The Catholic tradition as illustrated in Thomas Aquinas has always insisted on an intrinsic morality. Something is commanded because it is good. For Aquinas the ultimate end of human beings is happiness. Morality involves what is good for me as a person and ultimately makes me flourish. There is no opposition between freedom and moral obligation because the moral obligation is based on what is good for the individual. This is the central point to which the pope so frequently returns in his document. However, in the manuals of moral theology ever since the probabilism controversy, a greater opposition rather than harmonious agreement exists between freedom and law. Probabilism maintains that one may follow a truly probable opinion, going against the existence of a law, even if the opinion favoring the existence of the law is more probable. The so-called reflex principle used to defend this position holds that a doubtful law does not oblige—an adage more attuned to human law than anything else. The individual starts out with one's freedom, and this freedom can only be taken away by a certain law.[18] Ironically the law model as it was employed in the manuals of Catholic moral theology in the light of the probabilism controversy emphasizes the tension and apparent opposition between freedom and law rather than the harmony that the pope wants to emphasize.

Laws That Always and Everywhere Oblige

The major thrust of the encyclical insists on universal, immutable moral commandments that prohibit always and without exception intrinsically evil acts. In this context, note that the pope never cites the fifth commandment, "Thou shalt not kill." Everyone recognizes that killing is not always and everywhere wrong. We have justified killing in cases of self-defense and war. In fact, after much discussion and nuancing, the manuals of moral theology came to the conclusion that the intrinsically evil act that is always forbidden is the following: direct killing of the innocent on one's own authority. Thus we allowed indirect killing, killing in self-defense or in war, and capital punishment.[19]

Notice the difference between the two. Killing is a physical act that in some circumstances can be permitted. The second rule tries to account for all the possible justifying circumstances and thus states the norm that admits of no exceptions. But one has to circumscribe quite severely the generic "no killing." The pope himself in this document does not cite this very specific absolute norm that was developed in Catholic moral theology.

What, then, is the papal example of the universal, immutable condemnation of an act that is always and everywhere wrong? The answer: murder. Thus in the passage about the rich young man in Matthew, Jesus begins the commandments with, "You shall not murder" (§13). All would agree that murder is always wrong, because by definition murder is unjustified killing. Thus we have here three different types of norms dealing with killing. The pope cites only the very formal norm of no murder.

But there is a problem in *Veritatis splendor* from the pope's own perspective, because of a fourth formulation that is proposed. The pope wants to illustrate the point that there are intrinsically evil acts that are always and per se such on account of their very object and quite apart from the intention of the agent and circumstances. He quotes the Pastoral Constitution on the Church in the Modern World, paragraph 27, to illustrate this thesis (§80). The quote begins, "Whatever is hostile to life itself such as any kind of homicide...." However, homicide is not an intrinsically evil act. Homicide is the physical act of killing a human being. Our language recognizes that homicide can be justifiable in certain circumstances.

But the problem might not come primarily from the pope. The official Latin version of the encyclical in its citation from the Pastoral Constitution on the Church in the Modern World uses the word *homicidium*.[20] *Homicidium* in the Latin can refer either to murder or homicide. As mentioned above, in this case the pope is citing a text from the Pastoral Constitution on the Church in the Modern World of Vatican II. Two unofficial English translations of the documents translate *homicidium* as murder.[21] However, the official translation of the papal encyclical that came from the Vatican uses the word "homicide." The error might rest with the translator and the approval of that translation by the Vatican. However, at the very minimum this goes to show how intricate and difficult it is to speak about norms that are always and everywhere obliging without any exception.

In fact, the list of actions found originally in the Pastoral Constitution on the Church in the Modern World and quoted in *Veritatis splendor* contains some actions that are not always and everywhere wrong. Both documents include abortion under the category of "what is hostile to life itself." However, the Catholic tradition has always recognized the existence of some conflict situations and concluded that direct abortion is always wrong. Indirect abortion can be justified for a proportionate reason so that abortion is not always and everywhere wrong. One would have to be stretching the point beyond belief to claim that the original clause of "whatever is hostile to life itself" means that homicide is murder and abortion is direct abortion. The reality is that any homicide or abortion is hostile to life itself, but in some circumstances might be justified.

The second category of those actions in both documents that are now claimed by the pope to be always and everywhere wrong concerns "whatever violates the integrity of the human person such as mutilation...." However, Catholic moral theology has consistently recognized justified mutilation. In fact, the principle of totality in medical ethics justifies a mutilation of a part of the body for the sake of the whole.[22] Here again one cannot appeal to the opening clause "whatever violates the integrity of the human person" to show that the mutilation in such a context excluded medical mutilation for the good of the whole person. If the heading were the dignity or total good of the human person then one could make such a claim. By definition all mutilation goes against the physical integrity of the person, but the Catholic tradition does not say that all mutilation is wrong. The pope's efforts to uphold laws that are intrinsically or always and without exception wrong by reason of the object is fraught with difficulties. There are such actions when the act is described in merely formal terms such as murder. One could also make the case that there are such acts when the significant circumstances are included. In reality, *Veritatis splendor* itself does not succeed in making a consistent case to prove its own position about acts that are always and intrinsically evil by reason of the object alone.

Evaluation of Contemporary Moral Theology

Veritatis splendor strongly disagrees with and condemns many of the developments in Catholic moral theology since Vatican II and stands opposed to the revisionist moral theology in general.

However, *Veritatis splendor* distorts and does not accurately describe the various positions attributed to so-called revisionist moral theologians. The first part of the second chapter disagrees with a school of autonomous ethics that first arose in Germany (§§36–37). I have disagreed with the name "autonomous" but accept the reality proposed in the sense that the moral content for life in this world is the same for Christians as for non-Christians. In my judgment, this position is in keeping with the traditional assertion that the Christian brings the human to its perfection and fulfillment. Like *Veritatis splendor* I have also disagreed with the contention that the Scripture provides only *parenesis*, or exhortation, as some hold.[23] However, the supporters of autonomous ethics in the Catholic tradition would strongly disagree with the following description of their position: "Such norms…would be the expression of a law which man [*sic*] in an autonomous manner lays down for himself and which has its source exclusively in human reason. In no way could God be considered the author of this law except in the sense that human reason exercises its autonomy in setting down laws by virtue of a primordial and total mandate given to man by God" (§36).

Veritatis splendor in the same first part of chapter 2 points out that some Catholic moral theologians have disagreed with the teachings of the hierarchical magisterium in the area of sexual morality because of their "physicalism" and "naturalistic" argumentation (§47). Such a statement is correct. In my opinion physicalism is the a priori identification of the human or the moral aspect with the physical, natural, or biological process. So far, so good. But the pope goes on to explain this theory in this way:

> A freedom which claims to be absolute ends up treating the human body as a raw datum devoid of any meaning and moral values until freedom has shaped it in accordance with its design. Consequently, human nature and the body appear as presuppositions or preambles, materially necessary for freedom to make its choice, yet extrinsic to the person, the subject, and the human act....The finalities of these inclinations would be merely "physical" goods, called by some *premoral*. To refer to them, in order to find in them rational indications with regard to the order of morality, would be to expose oneself to the accusation of physicalism or biologism. In this way of thinking, the tension between freedom and a nature conceived of in a reductive way is resolved by a division within man [*sic*] himself. (§48)

Those who charge the hierarchical magisterium's teaching on sexuality with physicalism do not "treat the human body as a raw datum devoid of any meaning." The physical is one aspect of the moral or the fully human. The moral or the fully human must embrace all the aspects of the human—the physical and the spiritual, the sociological and the psychological, the eugenic and the hygienic. In keeping with the Catholic tradition, one should never be guilty of a reductionism that reduces the fully human to just one aspect of the human no matter what that aspect is. Yes, there are times when the physical is the same as the moral and the truly human, but this needs further justification to make the point.[24] In this very citation, the pope contradicts his own assertion. *Veritatis splendor* refers to this physical aspect as physical or premoral goods. Note the word "goods." They are not just a "raw datum" or "extrinsic to the person." Those making the charge of physicalism take seriously the position of Pius XII that the physical and the bodily exist to serve the higher spiritual good of the person.[25] That one in theory can interfere with the physical or biological process, because of the good of the total person as a whole, seems to be very much in accord with any kind of personalism. But at the very least *Veritatis splendor* distorts the position of those who characterize hierarchical Catholic sexual teaching as guilty of physicalism. We do not absolutize freedom and we do not deny any value or meaning to the physical. In our judgment the hierarchical magisterium in this matter has absolutized the physical and the biological at the expense of the truly and the fully human.

The second part of chapter 2 deals with the relationship between conscience and truth. However, John Paul II also dealt with that question earlier in the encyclical. The pope claims that those who invoke the criterion of conscience as "being at peace with oneself" (he puts the words in quotation marks) are guilty of absolutizing freedom, forgetting the claim of truth, and subjectivism (§32).

Chapter 3 proposed a theory of conscience that "attempts to explain in a more systematic and reflective way the traditionally accepted notion that joy and peace mark the good conscience which is the adequate criterion of good moral judgment and decision."[26] I explicitly point out that my approach disagrees with the position of the manuals that the judgment of conscience is based on conformity with the truth "out there." I developed this theory in dialogue with the transcendental approaches of Karl Rahner and Bernard Lonergan. However, I insist that one's judgment has to attain the true and the real value. I do put great emphasis on the subject but insist that "thus we have established the radical identity between genuine objectivity and authentic subjectivity."[27] Such an approach is proposed as a theory and others might readily disagree with it, but it does not "exalt freedom to such an extent that it becomes an absolute" nor "adopt a radically subjectivistic conception of moral judgment" (§32).

In the second part of chapter 2 on conscience, it seems that the pope's insistence on the relationship between conscience and truth has influenced him to take a position that at the very least is in opposition to the generally accepted position in Catholic moral theology. *Veritatis splendor* states, "It is possible that the evil done as the result of invincible ignorance or a nonculpable error of judgment may not be imputable to the agent; but even in this case it does not cease to be an evil...." (§63). Thomas Aquinas maintained that invincible ignorance renders the act involuntary and excuses from sin. In other words, the evil act done in invincible ignorance is never imputable to the agent. The encyclical does not go as far as Aquinas and simply says that it "may not be imputable to the agent." However, St. Alphonsus Ligouri, the patron saint of moral theologians and confessors, goes even further than Aquinas. Alphonsus maintains that an act done out of invincible ignorance is not only not imputable but it is actually meritorious. This opinion of Alphonsus became the more common position among Catholic theologians.[28] Louis Vereecke, now an emeritus professor of the history of moral theology at the Accademia Alfonsiana in Rome and a consultor to the Holy Office, concludes his article on conscience in Alphonsus Liguori by claiming that Alphonsus's moral doctrine on conscience embraces three values— the importance of truth, the importance of reason and conscience, and the importance of freedom.[29] By so emphasizing and perhaps even absolutizing the relationship of conscience to truth, *Veritatis splendor* not only does not accept the position of Alphonsus but does not even accept the position of Thomas Aquinas, which does not go as far as Alphonsus.

The third part of chapter 3 addresses the theory of the fundamental option. Here also the theory is distorted. For example, the encyclical speaks of the theory as separating "the fundamental option from concrete kinds of behavior" (§67, see also §70). The theory of fundamental option distinguishes the different levels of human freedom and of transcendental and categorical acts, but it does not separate them. As Joseph Fuchs, who has written much on the fundamental option points out, the encyclical distorts the meaning of the theory by failing to recognize that the fundamental option and categorical acts happen on different levels and thus the fundamental option does not occur in the area of reflex consciousness.[30]

The fourth part of chapter 3 deals with the moral act, insists on acts that are intrinsically evil by reason of their object, and condemns teleological and proportionalist theories that hold "that it is impossible to qualify as morally evil according to its species—its 'object'—the deliberate choice of certain kinds of behavior or specific acts apart from a consideration of the intention for which the choice is made or the totality of the foreseeable consequences of that act for all persons concerned" (§79). On a number of occasions the pope points out that a good intention is not sufficient to determine the morality of an act (§§67, 78). But no Catholic moral theologian I know has ever claimed that the intention alone suffices to determine the morality of an act.[31] Above I pointed out that as a revisionist I accept some acts as always and everywhere wrong if the significant circumstances (not the totality of the foreseeable consequences) are included.

I have no doubt that the pope disagrees with all these recently developed theories in Catholic moral theology, but the encyclical tends to distort them and thus does not reflect their true meaning. In a certain sense they are made into straw people that then are much easier to reject. However, this is not the worst distortion in the encyclical about the present state of Catholic moral theology.

The pope claims that the "root of these presuppositions [of the dissenting Catholic moral theologians] is the more or less obvious influence of currents of thought which end by detaching human freedom from its essential and constitutive relationship to truth" (§4). This sentence is found in the opening introduction to the entire document. The introduction to chapter 2 points out "these tendencies are at one in lessening or even denying the dependence of freedom on truth" (§34). Note some qualification in these statements, but the fundamental problem the pope has with revisionist Catholic moral theologians is their tendency to detach or lessen human freedom's relationship to truth. Such an assertion itself is not accurate. I know no Catholic moral theologian who absolutizes freedom or detaches conscience from truth. The real question remains the proverbial one—what is truth?

As a result of this misreading of the present state of Catholic moral theology, the pope apparently sees no difference between Catholic revisionist moral theologians and the proponents of absolute freedom, conscience separated from truth, individualism, subjectivism, and relativism. Non-Catholic colleagues or any fair-minded interpreter of the present state of Catholic moral theology would readily recognize that revisionist Catholic moral theologians are not absolutizing freedom or conscience and are not supporting individualism, subjectivism, and relativism. Catholic revisionist moral theologians strongly agree with the pope in opposing these positions. That is why I made it a point earlier in this chapter to stress my strong agreement with the pope on these points.

Everyone recognizes that the pope strongly disagrees with and condemns revisionist Catholic moral positions, but the problem here is the understanding of revisionist moral theologians. Their theories are caricatured, but even worse the pope falsely accuses them of absolutizing freedom and separating it from truth and wrongly identifies them with subjectivists, individualists, and relativists.

What is going on here? I do not know. Some have blamed the pope's advisers.[32] Such an approach is a familiar Catholic tactic. When Catholics disagree with the pope it is always easier to blame it on the advisers than on the pope. On the other hand, I have never heard anyone who agreed with a papal statement say that they agreed with the pope's advisers! Popes obviously have advisers, but the final document is the pope's and not theirs. More worrisome is the fact that the pope's area of expertise is ethics. Does he really think that Catholic moral theologians who dissent on some Church teachings, especially in the area of sexuality, are subjectivists, individualists, and relativists?

A realistic assessment of the contemporary state of Catholic moral theology differs considerably from the picture painted in *Veritatis splendor*. The differences between the pope and revisionist moral theologians are by no means as great as *Veritatis splendor* states. Yes, different methodologies are often at work, but revisionist moral theologians have generally agreed with the papal teaching in the area of social ethics. Likewise, revisionist moral theologians are willing to accept some intrinsically evil acts when the object of the act is described in formal terms (murder is always wrong, stealing is always wrong) or when the act is described in terms of its significant circumstances (not telling the truth when the neighbor has a right to the truth).

The primary area of disagreement concerns the understanding of the moral object: the encyclical claims that morality is determined by the three sources of morality—the object, the end, and the circumstances—and that some actions are intrinsically evil by reason of their object (§§71–83). The question is, how does one describe the object? As mentioned above, revisionist theologians would be willing to admit intrinsically evil acts by reason of the object if the object were described in a broad or formal way or with some significant circumstances. The earlier discussion about always obliging laws pointed out a very significant problem in the encyclical itself in describing the moral object.

Revisionists in general object to those cases in which the moral act is assumed to be identical with the physical structure of the act. These areas occur especially in the area of sexuality. As pointed out, not every killing, mutilation, taking something that belongs to another, and false speech are always wrong. Contraception, however, describes a physical act. The physical act described as depositing male semen in the vagina of the female can never be interfered with. Some people have mistakenly thought that the hierarchical teaching against contraception was based on a pronatalist position. Such is not the case. The hierarchical teaching also condemns artificial insemination with the husband's seed even for the good end of having a child. The reason why both contraception and AIH are judged wrong is because the physical act must always be there and one can never interfere with it no matter what the purpose.[33]

The charge of physicalism is intimately connected with the theory of proportionalism. Rather than describe the physical act or object as morally wrong, this theory speaks of premoral, ontic, or physical evil that can be justified for a proportionate reason. This challenges the hierarchical teaching on contraception but also explains the existing hierarchical teaching on killing, mutilation, and taking property. There is no doubt that Catholic moral theologians are calling for a change in hierarchical teaching especially in the area of sexuality, but they are precisely challenging these areas in which the moral aspect has been a priori identified with the physical aspect of the act. Thus the differences between these revisionist moral theologians and the pope are much less than the encyclical recognizes. The problem is not that dissenting moral theologians absolutize freedom and/or conscience or separate them from truth. The question remains, what is moral truth?

Hierarchical Magisterium and Theologians

The confrontation and differences within Catholic moral theology in the last few decades have centered not only on the moral issues themselves but on the ecclesiological questions of the role and functioning both of the hierarchical magisterium and of theologians. *Veritatis splendor* explicitly addresses these issues in the third chapter (§§106–17), although the role of the hierarchical magisterium is mentioned throughout the document.

The encyclical itself deals primarily with moral truth. The ultimate question for both the hierarchical magisterium and for moral theology is what is moral truth and how do we arrive at moral truth? *Veritatis splendor* condemns many approaches in moral theology and in the broader ethical world but it never really explicitly addresses the question about how the hierarchical magisterium itself arrives at moral truth. In fact, the encyclical gives the impression that the hierarchical magisterium simply has the truth. However, the hierarchical magisterium like everyone else has to learn the moral truth. How is this done? The most frequently used phrase in this regard in the encyclical is the "assistance of the Holy Spirit." Mention is also made of the revelational aspect of morality and the hierarchical magisterium's role as the protector, guarantor, and interpreter of revelation.

The entire second chapter with its discussion of very complex theories and positions shows that the hierarchical magisterium also uses human reason in its attempt to know and explain moral truth. The Catholic insistence on mediation means that God works in and through the human and does not provide short circuits around the human. The assistance of the Holy Spirit does not exempt the hierarchical magisterium from using all the human reason necessary to arrive at moral truth. The tradition of Catholic natural law once again affirmed and developed in this encyclical maintains that its moral theology is based on human reason and accessible to all human beings. Yes, the encyclical reminds us (correctly) that human sin affects all our reasoning processes, but sin does not take away human reason's ability to arrive at moral truth (§§86–87). In learning moral truth the hierarchical magisterium must use human reason like everyone else.

In the last few decades, many theologians have also pointed out the experience of Christian people as a source of moral knowledge. Once again, sin affects human experience and a proper discernment is required. One cannot just work on the basis of a majority vote. However, the hierarchical magisterium itself in its Declaration on Religious Freedom of Vatican II recognized the experience of Christian people as a source of moral wisdom. The fathers of the council took careful note of these desires for religious freedom in the minds of human beings and proposed to declare them to be greatly in accord with truth and justice.[34] However, *Veritatis splendor* never mentions even implicitly that the hierarchical magisterium can and should learn from the experience of Christian people. The pope explicitly says the fact that some believers do not follow the hierarchical magisterium or consider as morally correct behavior that their pastors have condemned cannot be a valid argument for rejecting the moral norms taught by the hierarchical magisterium (§112).

The Thomistic moral tradition that the hierarchical magisterium claims to follow has insisted on an intrinsic morality—something is commanded because it is good and not the other way around. The hierarchical magisterium does not make something right or wrong, but the hierarchical magisterium must conform itself to the moral truth. Thus the hierarchical magisterium must use all the means available to arrive at that truth.

In addition, the Thomistic tradition recognizes that one cannot have the same degree of certitude about practical truths as about speculative truths.[35] The hierarchical magisterium has a role in guaranteeing and protecting revelation under the inspiration of the Holy Spirit but must also use all the human means available to arrive at moral truth and live with the reality that practical truths do not have the same degree of certitude as speculative truths. One cannot expect an encyclical to say everything on the subject, but a document dealing with the splendor of truth might have been expected to say something about the nature of moral truth and how the hierarchical magisterium itself learns and knows this moral truth.

As pointed out in chapter 6, the teaching of the hierarchical magisterium in moral matters has been wrong in the past and has developed or changed. John Noonan has recently documented this change in the areas of usury, marriage, slavery, and religious freedom.[36] The fact that past teachings of the hierarchical magisterium in morality have been wrong must have some influence on how one understands the pronouncements of the hierarchical magisterium today.

The Catholic tradition itself has rightly recognized a hierarchy of truths,[37] and even the pre–Vatican II theology developed a system of theological notes to determine how core and central teachings are in Catholic faith.[38] All interpreters would admit that most of the papal teaching (I would say all, as would many others) on specific moral issues involves the noninfallible teaching office of the pope. The fact that something is *noninfallible* does not mean that it is necessarily wrong or that Catholics can disagree with it, but by definition it means that it is *fallible*. Catholic moral theologians as well as the hierarchical magisterium today must do more work to develop and talk about these different categories in the light of the general insistence on the hierarchy of truths and the older theological notes. At the very minimum the hierarchical magisterium itself must also be willing to recognize the more tentative and peripheral nature of some of its pronouncements. In addition, the hierarchical magisterium has never come to grips with the fact that some of its teachings in the past have been wrong and subsequently changed.

Veritatis splendor understands the role of the moral theologian in the light of its understanding of the hierarchical magisterium. The assumption is that the hierarchical magisterium with the assistance of the Holy Spirit has the moral truth and proclaims it. Therefore moral theologians are to give an example of loyal assent, both internal and external, to the hierarchical magisterium's teaching (§110).

Veritatis splendor in an adversative clause acknowledges "the possible limitations of the human arguments employed by the magisterium," but calls moral theologians to develop a deeper understanding of the reasons underlying the hierarchical magisterium's teaching and to expound the validity and obligatory nature of the precepts it proposes (§110). Thus there might be limitations in the arguments proposed by the hierarchical magisterium, but these in no way affect the validity of the precepts it proposes.

In condemning dissent, the present document follows the approach of *Donum veritatis*, the 1990 document of the Congregation for the Doctrine of the Faith on the role of theologians.[39] Dissent, in the form of carefully orchestrated protests and polemics carried on in the media, is opposed to ecclesial communion and to a proper understanding of the hierarchical constitution of the people of God. Opposition to the teaching of the Church's pastors cannot be seen as a legitimate expression either of Christian freedom or of the diversity of the Spirit's gifts (§113). I know no Catholic moral theologian who dissents from Church teaching who would propose what she or he has done in those terms. One might argue that such a definition of dissent leaves the door open for a different type of dissent. However, the encyclical itself calls for moral theologians to give an example of loyal assent, both internal and external, to the magisterium's teaching (§110).

The consideration here of the hierarchical magisterium does not intend to be a thorough discussion of the role of the hierarchical magisterium or of the moral theologian. This discussion is sufficient to point out the differences that exist. Revisionist Catholic moral theologians recognize the role of the hierarchical magisterium, but insist that its teachings cannot claim an absolute certitude on specific moral issues, have been wrong in the past, and might in some circumstances be wrong today. In this light dissent is at times a legitimate and loyal function of the Catholic moral theologian. However, *Veritatis splendor* at the very minimum does not admit any kind of tentativeness or lack of absolute certitude about the teachings of the hierarchical magisterium, and in no way explicitly recognizes a positive role for dissent.

Ever since the pope announced his intention in August 1987 of writing an encyclical dealing more fully with the issues regarding the foundations of moral theology in the light of certain present-day tendencies, any student of moral theology had a pretty good idea of what the encyclical would do. The pope was certainly not going to change any of the teachings that have recently been reinforced nor was he going to abandon the reasoning process behind those teachings. As a result then no one should be surprised by those aspects found in *Veritatis splendor*.

What is surprising is the fact that the pope caricatures the positions of Catholic revisionist moral theologians and refuses to recognize the great areas of agreement between them and himself. One can only wonder why *Veritatis splendor* proposes such an "either-or" or "all-or-nothing" understanding of the positions taken by Catholic revisionist moral theologians. The fundamental question remains: What is moral truth?

Notes

1. Pope John Paul II, *Veritatis splendor*, *Origins* 23 (1993): 297–334. References will be given in the text to the paragraph numbers in the encyclical.

2. E.g., the parable of the prodigal son in *Dives in misericordia* 6–7. See Pope John Paul II, *Dives in misericordia*, in *Proclaiming Justice and Peace: Papal Documents from* Rerum Novarum *through* Centesimus Annus, ed.

Michael Walsh and Brian Davies (Mystic, CT: Twenty-Third Publications, 1991), 344–47.

3. This passage is a citation from *Dei verbum*, the Constitution on Divine Revelation of the Second Vatican Council, §10.

4. Symposia on *Veritatis splendor* have appeared in *Commonweal* 120 (October 22, 1993): 11–18; *First Things* 39 (January 1994): 14–29. *The Tablet* (London) devoted a series of eleven articles to the encyclical beginning with the October 16, 1993 issue, 1329ff.

5. Bernard Häring, "A Distress That Wounds," *The Tablet* 247 (October 23, 1993): 1378–79; Richard A. McCormick, "Killing a Patient," *The Tablet* 247 (October 30, 1993): 1410–11; Daniel C. Maguire, "The Splendor of Control," *Conscience* 14, no. 4 (Winter 1993/1994): 26–29.

6. John Finnis, "Beyond the Encyclical," *The Tablet* 248 (January 8, 1994): 9–10; Robert P. George, "The Splendor of Truth: A Symposium," *First Things* 39 (January 1994): 24–25; Germain Grisez, "Revelation vs. Dissent," *The Tablet* 247 (October 16, 1993): 1329–31.

7. Stanley Hauerwas, "*Veritatis Splendor*," *Commonweal* 120 (October 22, 1993): 16–17; L. Gregory Jones, "The Splendor of Truth: A Symposium," *First Things* 39 (January 1994): 19–20; Oliver O'Donovan, "A Summons to Reality," *The Tablet* 247 (November 27, 1993): 1550–52.

8. Lisa Sowle Cahill, "Accent on the Masculine," *The Tablet* 247 (December 11, 1993): 1618–19.

9. E.g., Mary Tuck, "A Message in Season," *The Tablet* 247 (December 4, 1993): 1583–85.

10. Maguire, *Conscience* 14, no. 4 (Winter 1993/94): 28.

11. Pope John XXIII, *Mater et Magistra* 212, in *Catholic Social Thought: The Documentary Heritage*, ed. David J. O'Brien and Thomas A. Shannon (Maryknoll, NY: Orbis, 1992), 118.

12. Pope John XXIII, *Pacem in Terris* 35, in O'Brien and Shannon, *Catholic Social Thought*, 136.

13. Thomas Aquinas, *Summa Theologiae* (Rome: Marietti, 1952), I II, Prologue.

14. Ibid., q. 91, a. 2. John Paul II cites this passage in *Veritatis splendor* 43.

15. E.g., Robert Bellah et al., *The Good Society* (New York: Alfred A. Knopf, 1991); Amitai Etzioni, *The Spirit of Community* (New York: Crown, 1993).

16. For my response to this debate, see *The Church and Morality: An Ecumenical and Catholic Approach* (Minneapolis: Fortress, 1993), 96–109.

17. Aquinas, *Summa*, I II.

18. See, e.g., John Mahoney, *The Making of Moral Theology* (Oxford: Clarendon, 1987), 224–45.

19. Marcellinus Zalba, *Theologiae moralis summa II: Tractatus de mandatis Dei et ecclesiae* (Madrid: Biblioteca de autores cristianos, 1953), nos. 243–66, pp. 255–86.

20. *Acta apostolicae sedis* 85, no. 12 (December 9, 1993): 1197.

21. *The Documents of Vatican II*, ed. Walter M. Abbott (New York: Guild, 1966), 226; *Vatican Council II: The Conciliar and Post-conciliar Documents*, ed. Austin Flannery (Northport, NY: Costello, 1975), 928.

22. Zalba, *Theologiae moralis summa II*, nos. 251–52; pp. 263–68.

23. Charles E. Curran, *Toward an American Catholic Moral Theology* (Notre Dame, IN: University of Notre Dame Press, 1987), 57–59.

24. Charles E. Curran, *Directions in Fundamental Moral Theology* (Notre Dame, IN: University of Notre Dame Press, 1985), 127–37, 156–61.

25. Pope Pius XII, "The Prolongation of Life" (November 24, 1957), in *Medical Ethics: Sources of Catholic Teachings*, ed. Kevin D. O'Rourke and Philip Boyle (St. Louis: Catholic Health Association, 1989), 207.

26. Curran, *Directions in Fundamental Moral Theology*, 244.

27. Curran, *Directions in Fundamental Moral Theology*, 242.

28. Louis Vereecke, *De Guillaume d'Ockham à Saint Alphonse de Liguori* (Rome: Collegium S. Alfonsi de Urbe, 1986), 555–60; James Keenan, "Can a Wrong Action Be Good? The Development of Theological Opinion on Erroneous Conscience," *Église et théologie* 24 (1993): 205–19. However, Aquinas, Alphonsus, and Pope John Paul II all recognize that the external act remains an objective disorder and is wrong.

29. Vereecke, *De Guillaume d'Ockham*, 566.

30. Joseph Fuchs, "Good Acts and Good Persons," *The Tablet* 247 (November 6, 1993): 1445.

31. Richard A. McCormick, "Killing A Patient," *The Tablet* 247 (October 30, 1993): 1410–11.

32. Fuchs, *The Tablet* 247 (November 6, 1993): 1445; McCormick, *The Tablet* 247 (October 30, 1993): 1411.

33. See "Artificial Insemination," and "Contraception," in O'Rourke and Boyle, *Medical Ethics*, 62, 92–95.

34. Declaration on Religious Freedom 1, in *Documents of Vatican II*, 676.

35. Aquinas, *Summa*, I II, q. 94, a. 4.

36. John T. Noonan, "Development in Moral Doctrine," *Theological Studies* 54 (1993): 662–77.

37. Decree on Ecumenism 11, *Documents of Vatican II*, 354.

38. Sixtus Cartechini, *De Valore notarum theologicarum* (Rome: Gregorian University Press, 1951).

39. Vatican Congregation for the Doctrine of the Faith, "Instruction on the Ecclesial Vocation of the Theologian," *Origins* 20 (1990): 117–26.

11. Pope Francis

Reform and the Catholic Moral Tradition

This chapter was published in my *Tradition and Church Reform* (Maryknoll, NY: Orbis Books, 2016), 261–80.

There is no doubt that Pope Francis is a reformer. This forcibly struck me as I watched his first public appearance on the balcony of St. Peter's after he was elected. Three aspects stood out in those few minutes.

First, the name Francis. No pope had ever taken the name Francis. There was already something new and different—perhaps even startling—about this name. Church historians recognize that Francis was not an establishment figure; in fact, he was often suspect by some in the institutional Church. Later the pope explained that he chose the name of St. Francis of Assisi because of his great love for the poor. He wanted a Church that is poor and for the poor. Francis also appreciated his great concern for peace and all of God's creation.

Second, the first words from Francis after he appeared on the balcony in St. Peter's square were *buona sera*—good evening. What was so unusual about that? For one thing, previous popes never began with such a greeting. Why not? Meetings with the pope, even to this day, are called papal audiences. The Oxford English Dictionary describes an audience in this sense as a formal interview or hearing, especially granted by a monarch. Monarchs do not greet their subjects with a friendly and informal *buona sera*. Francis, however, made it clear he was not a monarch speaking to his subjects, but a father greeting his children or a believer greeting fellow believers as one of them.

Third, the first official act of the pope in the appearance just after his election in the balcony of St. Peter's was to give his first blessing to

209

the crowd as the new pope. Francis broke the long-standing tradition by first asking the crowd to pray for him. Then he bowed as they prayed for him before he gave them his papal blessing.

This chapter will consider the reform of Pope Francis under four headings—style, priorities, the Church, and moral teaching and life. The first three aspects, however, also have ramifications for his approach to moral teaching and life.

REFORM IN STYLE

A more simple style characterizes this pope. Perhaps the best sign of this is when he chose to break the hundred-year-old tradition that popes live in the papal apartment in the apostolic palace. Francis, however, chose to live with many others in the Domus Sanctae Marthae, a five-story guesthouse on the edge of Vatican City. The building has 105 two-room suites and 21 singles. It was built originally to house the cardinals coming for the conclave to elect the pope, but most of the time the building houses priests working in the Vatican and also has a number of guest rooms for visitors. Pope Francis chose room 201. He eats his meals in the common dining room downstairs and usually presides at the seven a.m. Eucharist for Vatican employees in the chapel of the building. The pope himself pointed out that the papal apartments in the apostolic palace are not luxurious but large and tastefully decorated, but he wanted to live a life in community with others. This was a very important personal reality for him. Recall that even as the cardinal archbishop in Argentina he had lived in a small apartment and often traveled in the city by public transport.

Stories and anecdotes abound about the simple lifestyle of the pope. He discarded much of the formal papal garb for a simple white cassock. He has dropped in unannounced to eat in the cafeteria with Vatican workers. Pope Francis was photographed receiving the sacrament of reconciliation (going to confession) in St. Peter's Basilica. Francis has often been quoted as saying that a simple lifestyle is good for us, helping us to better share with those in need. Many people were startled the day after his election when he went back personally to pay what he owed at the guesthouse where he stayed before the conclave.

In his daily activities he comes across as concerned, caring, and merciful, especially to those in need. His participation in the rite of washing feet on Holy Thursday well illustrates his approach. His recent predecessors had presided at the liturgy in St. Peter's and there washed the feet of twelve priests. In 2013 at a juvenile detention center in Rome, he washed and kissed the feet of twelve people who included two women and two Muslims. In 2014, he washed and kissed the feet of twelve disabled people. On Holy Thursday 2015, the pope visited a prison in Rome and washed the feet of twelve prisoners—six men and six women, plus a very small child of one of the women. These symbolic actions reinforce his understanding of the papal ministry to be one of service to God's people, especially those on the margins.

One endearing story reported in Spanish newspapers tells of his telephone call to a young Spanish man who had been sexually abused by a priest. The man had written the pope a five-page letter about his suffering. The pope called him on the telephone to ask forgiveness for what the Church had done to him. The Spanish press even reported the supposed conversation. The pope asked to speak with Daniel (not the real name of the person). Daniel asked who was calling. The pope identified himself as Father Jorge. Daniel responded that the caller must have the wrong number, because he did not know any Father Jorge. Then the voice on the other side said, "I am Pope Francis." Daniel could not speak for a time, because he was so overcome with emotion. The pope then told him how moved he had been in reading Daniel's letter and wanted to call and ask for his forgiveness.

The press continues to report stories about the pope's style. Yesterday's paper, for example, ran the story of 150 homeless people who were invited to see the famous Sistine Chapel. Who was there to greet them? Pope Francis!

The style of Pope Francis is perhaps best described as pastoral. Francis himself follows the advice he has given to bishops, priests, and theologians to be "shepherds living with the smell of sheep." As cardinal archbishop of Buenos Aires, he spelled out some details of that metaphor. A priest who limits himself just to carrying out his administrative duties for a tiny flock is not a true shepherd. He is a hairdresser putting curlers on sheep rather than going out to look for the lost ones. The reality today is the mirror image of the gospel story of the shepherd who left the ninety-nine to go out looking for the one who was lost. Today, there is one in the pen, and we are called to go out looking for the other ninety-nine.

REFORM OF PRIORITIES

Francis insists on giving priority to what is most important. The most important Christian reality is the good news of the kerygma—the joy of the gospel. He has opposed a pastoral ministry obsessed with the transmission of a disjointed multitude of errors to be opposed or moral obligations that must be obeyed. Pope Francis worries that priorities will be undermined and the beauty of the kerygma will be replaced by a grim sexual morality. When this happens, the moral edifice of the Church is likely to fall like a house of cards. We have to put first things first.[1]

Pope Francis's first important official document, the apostolic exhortation of November 2013, bears the title *Evangelii gaudium*—the joy of the good news. The very first paragraph clearly summarizes the point. The joy of the gospel fills the hearts and lives of all who encounter Jesus. Those who accept the offer of salvation are set free from sin, sorrow, inner emptiness, and loneliness. With Christ, joy is constantly born anew. The good news of God's love for us is the basis for the whole of Christian faith and Christian life.[2]

Pope Francis sees the good news of God's love for us primarily in terms of God's mercy. He explicitly recognizes in his own experience the primacy of God's mercy. The motto of his papal coat of arms reads *miserando atque eligendo* (literally: by having mercy and choosing). This shows the importance he gives to God's mercy. The first question raised by Antonio Spadaro in the famous interview with the pope that appeared simultaneously in many Jesuit publications throughout the world was: "Who is Jorge Mario Bergoglio?" The answer was: "I am a sinner whom the Lord has looked upon with mercy." He reacted in a similar way when asked by the cardinals if he accepted his election as bishop of Rome: "I am a sinner, but I trust in the infinite mercy and patience of our Lord Jesus Christ" (18–20).

From a theological perspective, the primacy of mercy emphasizes that the recipient is a sinner as Francis said. But the believer is also the beneficiary of God's good creation and a recipient of God's redeeming love. To see the essence of God's love totally in terms of mercy is some-what restrictive and leaves out some dimensions of God's loving gifts to us believers. Yes, we are sinners, but we are also part of God's good creation, and above all we are redeemed by God's grace and become friends of God. There is no doubt, however, that Francis definitely sees mercy as the primary manifestation of God's love and logically recognizes himself, then, as a sinner.

Pope Francis, in addition, sees mercy as most important for the Church as a whole. On March 13, 2015, he announced that he was convoking a jubilee year to be called the Holy Year of Mercy to make ever more evident the mercy of the Church as a witness of God's mercy. The bull spelling out the jubilee of mercy begins by recognizing: "Jesus Christ is the face of the Father's mercy. These words might well sum up the mystery of the Christian faith." According to the pope, the motto of this holy year is "merciful like the Father."[3]

His reflection describing the holy year heavily depends upon Scripture. In this context, he cites Luke 6:37–38 about not judging and not condemning. If anyone wants to avoid God's judgment, the individual should not judge the sister or the brother. Human judgments touch no deeper than the surface, whereas the merciful God looks into the very depths of the soul (§14). One recalls in this context the famous remark made by the pope in a press conference on the plane returning to Rome from Brazil when asked about gays—who am I to judge. These statements, however, must be seen in a larger context. The pope in this document directs the invitation to conversion ever more fervently to those whose behavior distances themselves from the grace of God. He refers there to people who belong to criminal organizations and those who perpetuate or participate in corruption (§19). These statements exist, thus, in some tension with the judge-not statements. It is also notable that in this context he does not mention sexual sins.

In this document, the pope also discusses the relationship between justice and mercy. For God, mere justice is not enough. God goes beyond justice with mercy and forgiveness. But justice still has a place. Anyone who makes a mistake must pay the price, but this is just the beginning of conversion (§21).

In a true sense, every pope or Christian leader should always have as the first priority the good news of God's gift of love and life to us.

What then is so distinctive about the approach of Pope Francis? First, Francis chooses to describe this priority in terms of mercy. No one content virtue or attitude can ever exhaust the total reality of God's gift to us. Any content virtue or description of God's gift to us is necessarily limited, precisely because there are so many other virtues that have a different content. Francis chooses to see God's gracious gift in terms of mercy. What explains this choice? As already mentioned, his own personal spiritual experience is an important factor. He experiences himself as a sinner who has received God's gracious mercy. But I think there is another factor. In the present Church, Francis does not think the proclamation of the mercy of God comes across to most people. Other aspects in the Church's life and circumstances have received more emphasis, so that many today do not experience the primacy of God's mercy in the life, teaching, and proclamation of the Church. These two factors help to explain why Francis has made mercy, and not love for example, the distinctive aspect of the good news of the gospel.

A second characteristic aspect of Francis's approach is to emphasize that the primacy of mercy must become visible and present in every aspect of the life of the Church. Mercy is not just the primary aspect that is first considered and then one moves on to other realities. All that the Church is and does must bear witness to God's mercy. The ministers of the Church have the special call to emphasize the priority of God's mercy in their proclamations, their ministry, and their life. The insistence on the need for the Church in its life and ministry to bear primary witness to God's mercy again comes from the recognition that the Church today is often perceived as a lawgiver or a judge.

Third, in terms of the priorities for the Church, it is important to recognize a hierarchical ordering of what the Church should do. In the interview with Spadaro, the pope points out that the particular teachings of the Church on moral matters, such as abortion, homosexuality, divorce, and contraception are not of the highest priority. These teachings are very well known by all. He is in no way challenging or disagreeing with these teachings, for he is truly a son of the Church. The pope acknowledges that others in the Church have criticized him for not speaking more about these issues. For Francis, however, it is a matter of priorities. The Church and its ministers must above all proclaim, show, and live the mercy of God. The most essential things come first. We have to find a new and better balance. The proclamation of God's mercy comes before moral and religious imperatives. The message of the gospel cannot be reduced to certain aspects that are relevant but do not go to the heart of the message of Jesus. When we do speak of these particular moral issues, we have to talk about them in the context of God's love and mercy (54–59).

The most important social issue that takes priority over all other social issues concerns poverty and the liberation of the poor. *Evangelii gaudium* discusses the issue in two different places. It is the first challenge of today's world mentioned in chapter 2: "Amid the Crisis of Communal Commitment." We must say no to an economy of exclusion, a new idolatry of money, and a financial system that rules rather than serves. Here he opposes the absolute autonomy of the market and a trickle-down economic theory, which has never really worked in practice and places a crude and naive trust in the goodness of those wielding economic power (§§53–58).

The inclusion of the poor in society is the first specific issue mentioned in chapter 4: "The Social Dimension of Evangelization." Here Francis calls for both a change of heart and attitudes as well as a change of structures. The word *solidarity* has become a little worn and at times poorly understood. Solidarity calls for the recognition of the social function of property and the universal destiny of created goods to serve the needs of all. These aspects are more important than private property. Property must serve the common good, which is the basis for the pope's strong assertion that solidarity calls for us to restore to the poor what belongs to them (§189). Unfortunately at times, human rights are used as a justification for an inordinate defense of individual rights or the rights of the rich. We must put into practice the option for the poor (§§186–208). Pope Francis here is following in the footsteps of his predecessors, but he gives priority to this option for the poor.

Reform of the Understanding and Structure of the Church

A third important area of reform concerns the Church. This section will consider first the general understanding of the Church and then the institutional structure of the Church. Pope Francis firmly accepts and follows the teaching often mentioned at Vatican II—the Church is always in need of reform. To support his thesis that the Church is always in need of reform, Francis cites in *Evangelii gaudium* his predecessor Paul VI. According to Paul VI, the Church must look within itself with penetrating eyes, pondering the mystery of her own being. A vivid and lively self-awareness inevitably leads to a comparison between the ideal image of the Church as Christ envisioned her and the actual image that the Church presents to the world today. Francis also cites Vatican II that Christ summons the Church to a continual reformation in her pilgrim journey to be ever more faithful to her own calling (§§25–26).

When asked to describe the Church by Father Spadaro, Francis answers with the words of the Constitution on the Church of Vatican II. Francis sees the Church as the holy faithful people of God. The people of God is on a journey through history with joys and sorrows. He recognizes that all are called to holiness and sees this sanctity in their daily activities in the world. Here he emphasizes holiness and the patience of the people of God. This patience means not only responsibility for the events and circumstances of life but also as a constancy in going forward day by day (49–51).

Pope Francis emphasizes the role of the laity in two areas that previously have not received much attention. The first is the laity's role in evangelization. In the past, the work of proclamation belonged to the clergy and religious in the Church, but this is not the approach of Francis. His first section in chapter 3 of *Evangelii gaudium*, "The Proclamation of the Gospel," insists that the entire people of God proclaims the gospel. In all the baptized, the sanctifying power of the Spirit is at work compelling all to evangelization. The new evangelization calls for personal involvement on the part of all the baptized. Evangelization is not something done by professionals in the Church with the rest of the faithful as the passive recipients. The second area concerns the important role of popular piety in the Church. All the baptized have an effective conaturality born of love. In the years after Vatican II, the Church has become more conscious of the important role of popular piety. Popular piety, the living of faith and the gospel in a particular time and place, has much to teach the whole Church. Expressions of popular piety constitute a *locus theologicus*—the traditional name for a place in which the Church learns about theology and faith. Popular piety, the piety of the people, is a form of evangelizing (§§111–34).

A Missionary and Poor Church

In *Evangelii gaudium*, the pope proposes the dream he has for the Church to be a missionary Church that has an impulse capable of transforming everything the Church is and does for the evangelization of today's world rather than for her own self-protection and promotion. A missionary and evangelizing community knows that the Lord has taken the initiative and therefore we can move forward, boldly take our initiatives, go out to others especially those who have fallen away, stand at the crossroads, and welcome the outcast. A missionary and evangelizing community gets involved by word and deed in people's daily lives; it bridges differences; it is willing to abase itself if necessary; and it embraces human life, touching the suffering flesh of Christ in others. The Church takes on the smell of the sheep, and the sheep are willing to hear her voice (§§24–27).

Francis wants a Church that is bruised, hurting, and dirty because it has been out on the street rather than a Church that is unhealthy because it is centered on and clings to its own security. He does not want a Church claiming to be the center of all things, which ends up caught in a web of obsessions and procedures. The Church should be moved not by the fear of going astray but by the fear of being shut up within structures that give a false sense of security, within rules that make us harsh judges, within habits that make us feel safe, while at our door people are starving and looking for something to eat (§49). This document is truly Francis's "I Have a Dream" document.

In this vision of the Church, the two priorities of mercy and the poor come to the fore. In the interview with Father Spadaro, the pope speaks of his vision and his dream of a Church that is truly mother and shepherdess. The Church's ministers must be merciful, accompanying people like the good Samaritan who comforts, cleanses, and raises up the neighbor in need. The pope clearly sees that what the Church needs today is the ability to heal wounds and warm hearts. The Church is a field hospital after battle. The first task is to heal the wounds of those who are suffering (54–55). The poor have a very special place in his vision of the Church. The Church must go out to everyone, but the pope asks to whom should she go first. The gospel gives us a clear indication—not to your friends and wealthy neighbors but above all to the poor and the sick—those who are usually despised and overlooked. The gospel message is clear: the poor are the privileged recipients of the good news. There is an inseparable bond between our faith and the poor. We can never abandon them (48).

In *Evangelii gaudium*, Francis again insists on a Church that is poor and for the poor. It is not just a question of the Church helping and ministering to the poor. The poor have much to teach us. Not only do they share with us the *sensus fidei*, but in their difficulties they know the suffering Christ. We need to let ourselves be evangelized by them. The new evangelization is an invitation to acknowledge the saving power at work in the lives of the poor and to put them at the center of the Church's pilgrim way. We are called to find Christ in them, to lend our voice to their causes, but also to be their friends, to listen to them, and to embrace the mysterious wisdom that God wishes to share with us through the poor (§198).

In addition to his understanding of the Church and its role, Francis in *Evangelii gaudium* has also recognized the need for a change of structures and institutions in the Church. In his apostolic exhortation *Evangelii gaudium*, the renewal of structures comes from the need to make the Church more mission-oriented, to make pastoral activity on every level more inclusive and more open. The pope points out he himself must think about conversion and finding new ways to exercise his office in the Church. The papacy and the central structure of the universal Church need to hear the call for change and conversion. Here the pope puts his finger on what advocates of Church reform have indicated is the primary problem in Church structures and institutions. Excessive centralization according to the pope rather than proving helpful complicates the Church's life and her missionary activity. In this document, the pope briefly insists on the need for collegiality and synodality in the Church and fruitful ways to realize these realities. Collegiality, however, has not been fully realized in the Church. The juridical status and doctrinal authority of bishops' conferences has not yet been elaborated (§32).

In his major interview that appeared in Jesuit publications, Francis mentioned the great number of cases involving a suspicion of orthodoxy that are sent to Rome. He points out these cases should be investigated by the local bishops' conferences that can also rely on the Vatican and should not be sent to the Vatican (61). The pope with some regularity talks about the need for collegiality and synodality in the Church.[4] Although Pope Francis has spoken in general about the problem of over-centralization and the need for collegiality and synodality, there has been no real detailed development of the ramifications of these principles.

Particular Structural Changes

This section will now discuss some of the particular structural and institutional aspects that have changed since Francis became the bishop of Rome in 2013. Vatican II called for the role of local, national, and regional bishops' conferences, but later popes have greatly curtailed their role and authority. Francis, as noted above, calls explicitly for more genuine doctrinal authority for these conferences, but this basic principle has not been developed in practice. Francis, however, in practice has taken a very significant step forward. In his first apostolic exhortation, he cites documents from international conferences of bishops about twenty times. This is something entirely new in papal documents. Not only does it recognize some genuine doctrinal authority in these documents, but it also shows that the universal Church can and should learn from the local conferences of bishops. Up until this time, papal documents employed a top-down approach. The word went out from the pope to all the Churches throughout the world, but now there is a true two-way street working.

In October 2014, an Extraordinary Synod of Bishops met to discuss topics related to the family. In October 2015, a larger synod called the Ordinary Synod met to discuss the same topic. Vatican II called for this new structure of the international synod of bishops. Later Paul VI accepted the idea and established them but limited their role to give advice to the pope. They did not have doctrinal authority as such. Many at Vatican II and afterward thought these international synods of bishops should have some doctrinal authority of their own and not just be advisory to the pope. Obviously, the pope himself would be a part of these synods. In reality, the synods were not free to discuss the disputed issues in the Church but were carefully controlled by curial authorities. The approach of Francis was completely different. Francis urged all the participants in the synod to speak boldly. Francis did not want anyone to say they feared to speak out for fear of what others might think or say. As a result of this, the first synod involved very open discussion and differences among the participants. For the first time since Vatican II, Catholics in the whole world have heard their bishops publicly discussing and disagreeing about what is good for the Church. It remains to be seen exactly what doctrinal authority these international synods of bishops might have.[5]

The curia is the bureaucracy that assists the pope in his role as universal pastor. Here Francis has not only talked about reform but has set up a process to bring it about. One month after his election, the pope appointed a group of cardinals (eventually numbering nine) to advise him in the government of the universal Church and to prepare a plan for restructuring the curia. The conclave before the election of Francis had talked about the need for such a reform. The curial reform is twofold. First, the role of the curia is to be of service based on the principle of subsidiarity—that is to be of service to local churches throughout the world rather than to exercise centralized power in the Church. The curia has been a primary instrument in bringing about the centralization in the Church and control over all churches throughout the world. This is both a theological issue of trying to overcome the overcentralization in the Church, but also a turf battle, because local bishops and cardinals have themselves experienced the tendency of the curia to exercise control over them in their dioceses. Too often the curia forgets that the local bishop has the primary responsibility for the local Church. The local bishop is not simply a franchisee of the papal government. The second part of the envisioned reform is to reorganize the many offices in the curia. This group, formally called the Council of Cardinals, has met quite frequently but has not yet submitted any detailed plan of reform.

One very startling related event was the speech the pope gave to the curia in the annual address to give Christmas greetings to his collaborators in the curia. This address was far from a stylized Christmas greeting; in Francis's own words it was an examination of conscience in preparation for the Feast of Christmas. He identifies fifteen curial diseases that can weaken our service to the Lord. Among these diseases are thinking ourselves as immortal or indispensable, spiritual petrification, rivalry and vainglory, gossiping and backbiting, idolizing superiors, worldly profit, or self-exhibition.[6] I am sure that none of his hearers expected such a talk. It shows that the pope was very serious about reform of the curia and its members.

Pope Francis has also initiated other instances of institutional and curial reform. The pope has made new appointments and proposed new reforms for the Vatican bank. He also established a Pontifical Commission for the Protection of Minors to advise on child protection policies for the Church. The commission comprises seventeen members, one of whom is a survivor of clerical sexual abuse. Again one can only wait for the result of the work of this commission.

On a number of occasions, including the interview with Spadaro, the pope has spoken about the role of women in the Church. Women are asking important questions that need to be addressed. The Church cannot be herself without women playing their role. The feminine genius is necessary whenever we make important decisions. The challenge is to think about the specific roles of women in the exercise of Church authority, but the pope has also maintained that women cannot be ordained priests (62–63).

Some have rightly expressed dissatisfaction with the pope's understanding of women and the role of women. He emphasizes the specific gift and genius of women and seems to maintain a view of the complementarity of male and female characteristics. But such an approach comes across to many as a patriarchal view that still makes women secondary. The best example of this was his reference to more women theologians as "strawberries on the cake."[7]

Francis in his interview with Jesuit publications has also stressed the prophetic role in the Church. Vatican II recognized the prophetic role in the Church as distinct from the hierarchical role. Francis points out that religious have an important prophetic role to play in the Church. He certainly would agree with Vatican II that all the baptized share in the prophetic office of Jesus. Francis is realistic about the effects of the prophetic role in the Church. Prophets make noise, an uproar, and some might even say a mess. But prophecy is like yeast in the Church (149). This is certainly a change from all teaching and policy coming down in

222 / *The Ensuing Years*

an orderly fashion from the top in a centralized Church. The pope thus recognizes that the Spirit speaks in different ways in the Church.

Pope Francis solved an institutional problem that seriously riled the Catholic Church in the United States—the investigation of U.S. Catholic nuns. Since 2008, the Vatican initiated two investigations. The first investigation begun in 2008 by the Vatican congregation in charge of religious throughout the world concerned the quality of religious life of nuns in the United States. There was concern mentioned about a certain secular mentality and feminist spirit among the nuns. The long and frequently contentious investigation came to a peaceful end in December 2014 with a generally appreciated report acknowledging the achievements and challenges facing the dwindling number of nuns in this country.[8] The second investigation begun by the Congregation for the Doctrine of the Faith in 2012 involved a committee of three bishops with the mandate of overhauling the Leadership Conference of Women Religious (LCWR) because of concerns the organization strayed from Catholic teaching in its speakers and publications. The Vatican abruptly ended the investigation in April 2015 with the leadership of LCWR meeting with Pope Francis.[9] Both of these investigations evoked strong support for the nuns from many sectors of the U.S. Catholic Church. Press reports indicated the Vatican definitely wanted to settle these issues before Pope Francis's visit to the United States in the fall of 2015.

REFORM OF MORAL TEACHING AND LIVING

There is no doubt that Francis sees himself in general as a reformer, and most people in the Church and broader world agree. In this section the direct focus is on reform with regard to the teaching about the moral life and the living of the Christian moral life. Francis himself is not a trained moral theologian, but he obviously sees himself as a pastor intimately concerned with the moral and spiritual life of the Catholic people. This section will discuss the reform with regard to the teaching about and living of the moral life under three aspects—moral life is much more than just obeying a few absolute moral norms; the relationship between the pastoral and the moral; the possibility for change in the contested moral norms proposed by the hierarchical magisterium, especially in the area of sexuality.

More Than Obedience to Absolute Norms

For Francis, it is obvious that the Christian moral life is much more than the obedience to a few laws. This fits in with his understanding of the priorities as discussed earlier. Too often the Catholic understanding of morality has been seen primarily in terms of this obedience to norms. Francis has strongly differed with such an approach. In his homilies, Francis frequently mentions the call to holiness. Do not be afraid of holiness, of aiming too high. Let yourself be loved and purified by God. We should be enfolded by the holiness of God. Francis cites the teaching of Vatican II that all Christians are called to holiness. The pope also cites the well-known statement of the French writer Leon Bloy that the only real sadness in life is not becoming a saint.[10]

In keeping with Vatican II's contribution of bringing spirituality and morality together, Francis consistently talks about the spirituality of Christians living in the world. The question is: where does the Christian find God? Spadaro's interview has a very long discussion on seeking and finding God in all things (95–109). God is present in the past, because we can see there the footsteps of God's presence. God is also present in the future as promise. But for us, God is above all encountered in the world of today. We need a contemplative attitude in order to find God in all things. In this quest for the presence of God in all things, there is always a great area of uncertainty. If one claims to have all the answers, this is proof that God is not with such a person. Abraham, Moses, and all the great people of faith had doubts. We are all searching for God, and the search is never ending. The pope emphasizes here the importance of discernment (a word very much associated with St. Ignatius) in the whole process. There are always thorns and weeds in our lives and in the world around us, but there is still room there for the good seed to grow.

Note how this model of the spiritual and moral life differs from the older understanding of a moral life in terms of obedience to the law of God. We are seeking for God in all aspects of our life. The primary reality for the Christian is not obedience to God's command but the discernment of God's presence in our daily lives and our response to that presence. Francis, however, still gives the priority not to our efforts to find God but to God's loving gift. When we seek God, we discover God is there to welcome us and to offer God's love. The encounter with God is not something we control. God is the God of surprises. In his addresses and homilies, Francis is not a moral theologian but rather a pastor urging the Christian people to find God in all aspects of life. Pope Francis worries that priorities will be undermined and the beauty of the kerygma will be replaced by a grim sexual morality. When this happens, the moral edifice of the Church is likely to fall like a house of cards. We have to put first things first (78–79).

Pastoral Approach and Moral Teaching

The second area concerns the relationship between the pastoral approach and the moral teaching approach. Francis as a good pastor tries to exhort believers to strive for sanctity and the fullness of the Christian life with its continual growth in love of God and neighbor, but as a pastor of mercy he also recognizes the needs of those who find themselves in very difficult situations. God's mercy is present and acting in both these situations—the upper end and the lower end of the Christian moral life.

Evangelii gaudium addresses this issue. The task of evangelization exists within the limits of languages and circumstances. With mercy and patience a pastor must accompany people through the stages of personal growth as they occur. A small step in the midst of great human limitations can be more pleasing to God than a life that outwardly appears to be orderly. God's mercy spurs us on to do our best (§§44–45).

In the Spadaro interview, Francis expresses the same reality in different words. It is useless to ask a seriously injured person if she has high cholesterol and the level of her blood sugar. You have to heal starting from their particular situation. It is necessary to accompany them with mercy. When that happens, the Holy Spirit inspires the priest to say the right thing (54–57).

The pope in these contexts is not a casuist proposing what specifically should be done in each case, but on the other hand, more could have been said about exactly what is the right thing that the priest should say in this situation. What does such an approach mean for a married gay couple or for a poor single mother contemplating abortion because she is unable to provide for her existing children? What is to be done in these situations?

The pope himself refers to the stages of personal growth. Moral theologians have talked about gradualness or the law of graduality. The Catholic tradition has always recognized the need for growth in the moral and spiritual life. The principle that you cannot ask people to do more than they are existentially capable of doing makes good sense. Francis seems to be saying that the person in need of healing now cannot be expected to fulfill all the particular moral obligations that are pertinent. Accompanying someone on the journey who is in need of healing does not seem to mean that at this stage the person must fulfill all the relevant moral norms.

In Catholic moral theology Bernard Häring distinguishes between the role of moral teaching and the role of pastoral counseling. If a woman who conceives after being raped believes in good faith that she has to abort the child, Häring says she does not have to be told that this is wrong, but he would not tell her that it is a good thing to do. In the light of this distinction between moral teaching and pastoral counseling, theologians have talked about the law of gradualism or graduality. Pope John Paul II accepted such a concept provided it did not mean the gradualness of the law. Even here it is not clear exactly what he meant, but he seems to be putting some restrictions and limits on the law of gradualness. In the light of some comments made by Pope Francis, some members of the synod on the family used the law of gradualness to justify the participation of some divorced and remarried people in the Eucharistic banquet.[11] Both in theory and in practice much work has to be done on the meaning of the law of gradualness.

Pope Francis in the famous interview recognizes another more generally accepted approach in Catholic moral theology—the distinction between objectively wrong and subjectively guilty or responsible. The pope here quotes the *Catechism of the Catholic Church* in support of this important distinction and uses it to defend his comment on the plane returning from his first trip to Brazil. He said then that if a homosexual person is of good will and in search of God, who is he (the pope) to judge such a person. In these instances Francis sees himself primarily as a pastor who is interested in the person. Like God we must accompany people with mercy (56–57).

In concluding this section, two points need to be mentioned. First, it is not totally clear what Francis means in these cases, and there is obviously room for different opinions about what he is saying. Also, Francis is looking at these issues primarily from the perspective of the pastor who is accompanying the person on the journey. But an even more important perspective is that of the conscience of the individual person.

Will Francis Change the Disputed Moral Teachings?

This brings us to the third aspect in this section: will Francis, who is obviously a reformer, change the teachings in the area of sexuality such as contraception, sterilization, artificial insemination, in vitro fertilization, gay marriage, divorce, and remarriage? The two realities involved here are the natural law theory, which is the basis for the sexual teaching and the authoritative papal teaching on these issues. Chapters 5 and 6 have treated these issues in great detail. In reality, the most important aspect is the authoritative papal teaching. In his encyclical *Humanae vitae* (§6) Pope Paul VI recognized the conclusion of the majority of the study commission calling for a change in the teaching on artificial contraception, but he could not accept such a conclusion, because it went against the constant teaching of the Church.

Pope Francis has rightly pointed out these are not the primary or more important aspects of the Christian moral life. For the people involved in these issues in their daily life, however, they are very significant. Some have decided in their conscience they can act against these teachings and still fully participate in the Eucharist and Church life. Others have left the Church because of these teachings. Note the difference with the teaching excluding women from the priesthood. This involves the external forum or the structure of the Church and cannot be solved by the conscientious discussions of individuals. The ordination issue is very painful for many women and men as well.

As already pointed out, Francis has declared himself a son of the Church who supports the existing teaching on sexual realities. He likewise has said that the issue of ordaining women in the Church is not open to discussion. Thus his own words clearly show he is not in favor of changing these existing teachings.

The discussions that have taken place in the synod on the family also indicate there is no support within the hierarchical Church for any change. As noted, the pope has encouraged free and unfettered discussion in the synod, but in the discussion on the family in the 2014 synod there was no discussion whatsoever about artificial contraception. The primary practical issues discussed at the synod was the change in pastoral practice allowing some divorced and remarried people to fully participate in the eucharistic banquet. No one even proposed challenging the teaching on divorce and remarriage. In fact many who supported the pastoral change made it very clear they were still strongly defending the existing moral teaching. There was also much opposition to changing the pastoral practice precisely because for many it amounted to a change in the teaching itself.[12]

Earlier chapters have briefly proposed reasons why the Church should change its teaching, but such reasons have obviously not been accepted by the hierarchical magisterium. The question then naturally arises: why do Pope Francis and other hierarchical teachers in the Church oppose changing these teachings? The primary reason stems from the belief that the Holy Spirit assists the hierarchical magisterium in teaching what is true and the will of God on practical moral issues. Would God ever allow the hierarchical magisterium to teach something that is erroneous and not the will of God? The magisterium aims to help people discover and live out God's will in this world, so it is unthinkable that the hierarchical magisterium could be hurting people rather than helping them.

The credibility of the Church would suffer if the hierarchical magisterium affirms the teaching had been wrong. Who would ever again believe what the Church says on any issue? The Catholics who with great personal sacrifice have lived according to the teaching on contraception, divorce, and gay relationships would rightly be very upset if these teachings were to change.

The Catholic Church has had great difficulty ever admitting that its teachings had been erroneous or wrong, especially when such teachings affect people in their daily lives. Even Vatican II with its reforming spirit could not admit that Church teaching had been wrong on the matter of religious liberty. All recognized that what the Church held in the nineteenth century and throughout the first part of the twentieth century was changed at Vatican II. The primary issue in the debate on religious freedom of Vatican II was this issue of how could the magisterium change its teaching. Was the teaching in the past wrong? No. Historical circumstances change, so the older teaching was true in those circumstances and the newer teaching accepting religious freedom is true in the new historical circumstances.[13] In addition, it is even harder to change on these issues now, because the hierarchical magisterium has so constantly and publicly insisted on these teachings and often engaged in getting some of these teachings written into public law.

All recognize that Catholic spouses use artificial contraception in the same proportion as non-Catholics. Artificial contraception is not a real issue for almost all married Catholics today who have decided the issue in their own conscience. A primary reason for continuing the present teaching is that if the hierarchical magisterium should change its teaching on artificial contraception, it would logically open the door to change on other issues such as gay marriage.

What about the argument that many people have left and are continuing to leave the Catholic Church because of its teaching on these moral issues? One must put this in the proper context. The reality is that a greater percentage of people have left the mainstream Protestant churches in the United States than have left the Catholic Church. The Protestant churches, however, basically accept these moral sexual teachings that the Catholic Church does not accept. These issues, thus, are not the primary reason why people leave the Christian Churches today. The real problem is secularism.

This is not the place to respond to these reasons in depth. This paragraph will summarize what was developed earlier in this volume. It is enough to point out that the problem comes from the claim of the hierarchical magisterium to have certitude on particular moral issues in the area of sexuality. The hierarchical magisterium should have recognized publicly that its teachings here are noninfallible, or in reality fallible. They can be wrong. Some noninfallible teachings in the past were wrong. As pointed out, the problem does not exist in the area of hierarchical teaching on social issues precisely because the teaching did not claim to have certitude on very specific issues. In the long run, to admit change or error in claiming certitude in these areas should help the credibility of the Church. But in the short run, what about those who, with great personal sacrifice, tried to live in accord with these teachings? No doubt this situation would be an important pastoral issue. The

Church would have to ask forgiveness from these people and honor them for their commitments. I remember in the days after *Humanae vitae* a married faculty colleague at the Catholic University was talking with me about this issue. He pointed out that he and his wife lived in accord with the teaching against artificial contraception, but prayed that his children would not have to do so. The largeness of heart exemplified in such a response indicates the best of what it means to be a Christian.

In summary, Pope Francis has already contributed much to the ongoing reform of the Church and the Catholic moral tradition. With Vatican II he insists that all Christians are called to holiness in their daily lives in the world. The primary emphasis and priority frequently given in the past to the observance of some absolute moral norms is misplaced. God's mercy is ever present for all who are striving to live the Christian moral life. The distinction between moral teaching and a pastoral approach has concrete consequences, but the exact meaning of the law of gradualness needs much more development. As a loyal son of the Church, Francis accepts and is committed to what his predecessors have authoritatively taught is of divine or natural law. With regard to the social tradition, he gives priority to the needs of the poor and the importance of peace. Francis also emphasizes care for immigrants, climate control, and ecology. He is strongly committed to see the social mission of the Church as a constitutive dimension of the preaching of the gospel and the Church's own mission.

With regard to methodology, many of his comments such as the recognition that God is present and working in the world today indicate an acceptance of the role of historical consciousness. Recall that chapter 10 criticized the lack of historical consciousness in the teaching of Pope John Paul II on marriage and sexuality. In his understanding of the Church, he does not limit the teaching role only to the hierarchical magisterium. There is a very important prophetic role in the Church, the *sensus fidei* of all the baptized, and popular piety as a *locus theologicus*. These two methodological developments leave the door slightly ajar for some changes in the future regarding the disputed issues.

All in the Church are called to continual reform and growth in our own individual lives and in the life of the Church. Those of us who are convinced that the good of the Church requires a change in some of its specific moral teachings need to continue to work to bring that about.

Notes

1. Pope Francis with Antonio Spadaro, *My Door Is Always Open: A Conversation on Faith, Hope, and the Church in a Time of Change* (London: Bloomsbury, 2014), 78–79. This book is the famous long interview given by Pope Francis to Antonio Spadaro, SJ, which was published in different Jesuit periodicals throughout the world. This interview is the most extensive and most theological of the interviews granted by the pope. When references to this particular interview are made, the page number will be noted in the text.

2. Pope Francis, "Apostolic Exhortation: *Evangelii Gaudium*," at w2 .vatican.va. When the references to this document appear, the paragraph number will be indicated in the text.

3. Pope Francis, *Misericordiae Vultus,* at w2.vatican.va. When references are made to this document, the paragraph number will be indicated in the text.

4. Drew Christiansen, "Listen for This Word 'Synodality,'" at america magazine.org.

5. Thomas Reese, "How the Synod Process Is Different under Pope Francis," at http://ncronline.org.

6. "Pope's Address to Roman Curia," at www.zenit.org.

7. David Gibson, "Lost in Translation? 7 Reasons Some Women Wince When Pope Francis Starts Talking," at www.cruxnow.com.

8. Laurie Goodstein, "Vatican Report Cites Achievements and Challenges of U.S. Nuns," *New York Times*, December 16, 2014.

9. Laurie Goodstein, "Vatican Ends Battle with Catholic Nuns' Group," *New York Times*, April 16, 2015.

10. This and other similar passages are found in the *Church of Mercy: A Collection of Homilies, Writings, and Speeches of Pope Francis* at www .goodreader.com.

11. John L. Allen, "The Synod's Key Twist: The Sudden Return of Gradualism," at http://www.cruxnow.com.

12. John L. Allen, "However Dramatic the Synod of Bishops Was Just the Beginning," at http://www.cruxnow.com.

13. Emile-Joseph de Smedt, "Religious Freedom," in *Council Speeches of Vatican II,* ed. Yves Congar, Hans Küng, and Daniel O'Hanlon (New York: Sheed & Ward, 1964), 157–68.

12. Methodological Approach in Dealing with Particular Social Issues

This chapter appeared in Kristin E. Heyer, James F. Keenan, and Andrea Vicini, eds., *Building Bridges in Sarajevo: The Plenary Papers from CTEWC 2018* (Maryknoll, NY: Orbis Books, 2019).

In this significant conference we are talking about contemporary moral problems we are facing in the world today such as corruption, ecological devastation, and climate change. My charge is to develop what the Catholic moral tradition has to say about these and similar problems. I will often refer to these problems using the broader phrase of justice, peace, and the integrity of creation. I propose that the Catholic tradition at its best has three important considerations that bear on dealing with these moral problems we are facing today. (1) It is not enough just to determine whether an act is right or wrong, but there is a need to make what is right more present in our society. (2) The consideration of the morality of acts is not enough. Attention must be given to the person who can bring about change. (3) Other actors based on the principle of subsidiarity.

DETERMINING WHAT IS RIGHT OR WRONG IS NOT ENOUGH

Catholic moral theology should be understood not only as determining whether acts are right or wrong but also with the need to bring about change so that what is right becomes present in our society and justice replaces injustice. In this aspect Catholic moral theology differs somewhat from moral philosophy or moral ideas. Yes, it is important to be able to show through human reason what is right or what is wrong. But reason or ideas are not enough to bring about change on a particular issue. They are necessary but not sufficient.

Take, for example, the case of bribery that is an important part of the broader issue of corruption and is so present in all parts of the global society today. A bribe is an inducement improperly influencing the performance of a public function meant to be gratuitously exercised. John T. Noonan Jr. years ago published an exhaustive 839-page treatise—*Bribes: The Intellectual History of a Moral Idea*. The title very accurately describes how Noonan deals with the idea of bribes. His concluding chapter discusses the future of the bribe. Noonan concludes that four reasons will likely continue to make sure that bribes are morally condemned. (1) Bribing is universally shameful. (2) Bribery is a sellout to the rich. (3) Bribery is a betrayal of trust. (4) Bribery violates a divine precept. Deuteronomy 10:17 maintains that God does not take bribes.[1]

The Catholic tradition itself has not always recognized the important need to go beyond the morality of acts to attempt to bring about change in a concrete way with regard to existing practices. The manuals of moral theology had the narrow scope of declaring which acts are sinful and the degree of sinfulness. They express no interest in how to change practices such as corruption or bribery. It was enough just to point out what is the law of God about sinful acts.

Catholic social ethics and teaching by their very nature aim at making justice more present in society. Even here the emphasis for some time was heavily on teaching what is the right thing to do, but recently that has been changing. The Pastoral Constitution on the Church in the Modern World decried the split between faith and daily life. There can be no false opposition between professional and social activities on the one hand and religious life and belief on the other (§43). The International Synod of Bishops in 1971 insisted that "action on behalf of justice and participation in the transformation of the world fully appear to us as a constitutive dimension of the preaching of the gospel, or, in other words, of the Church's mission for the redemption of the human race and its liberation from every oppressive situation."[2] Liberation theology recognized the need to free people from social, political, and economic oppression and proposed means to bring this about. The emphasis on sinful structures called for Christians to work concretely to change and eliminate this structural sin.

Catholic social ethics involves not only orthodoxy (right teaching) but also orthopraxis (right practice). The Catholic tradition thus has to be concerned with the concrete ways of overcoming injustice and making justice, peace, and the integrity of creation more prevalent in our local, national, and global realities. Today moral theologians are more conscious of their responsibilities in this area of bringing about social change through more than just teaching what is right or wrong.

In my country, one example of this is the theological recognition of the role of community organizations to bring about change and greater justice in our society. The United States claims to be a democracy, but many people feel they have no power or role to play in our society. They are truly passive and do not participate or become involved, and in fact are estranged from the broader society. For the most part, they do not even bother to vote. They have given up on any possibility of bringing about justice and change. Community organizations attempt to organize the poor and marginalized to show that by their organized efforts they can bring about change and make justice more present. Community organization does not involve privileged people telling the underprivileged what to do. By definition such organizations try to find the local leadership within a community and encourage that leadership to discern among the people what are the primary problems of injustice they are facing. They then discern what are the best ways to try to bring about change. Community organizers recognize that especially in the beginning it is very important for marginalized communities to have the experience that they can bring about such change. Such small successful attempts encourage them to move forward in many other directions. By encouraging the important role of community organizations, Catholic theologians help to show concrete ways in which injustice can be overcome and social structures can be changed in a more just direction.[3]

One can readily see why Catholic social ethics should be concerned about the concrete ways of bringing about justice and overcoming sinful social structures. What has often been called personal ethics such as bioethics is usually distinguished from social ethics and concerns itself with the narrow confines of the discipline. Recently Lisa Sowle Cahill has objected to such a distinction and bifurcation. Cahill calls for participatory discourse in bioethics.[4] Contemporary Catholic bioethics often engages in narrow ethical discourse (Is artificial hydration in these circumstances right or wrong?) and policy discussions about what should be the public policy on these issues. But this is only one sphere of social action open to theological and religious ethics. Heretofore theological bioethics has too readily conceded the playing field to those who define ethics in policy discourse terms that are essentially the terms of liberal democratic personalism. Thus Catholic bioethicists by following the general approach in American bioethics have forgotten about the equally or more important avenues of reform.

Catholic bioethicists must also deal with practices and movements in civil society that can have a subversive and revolutionary impact on bioethics, science, and capitalism. The practice of medicine and the provision of healthcare in our American ethos are generally becoming scientific rather than humanistic enterprises and are primarily directed by marketplace values. Justice in medicine and access to preventative and therapeutic care are increasingly seen in this ethos in terms of individual rights and liberties with their emphasis on autonomy and informed consent. Theological bioethics, on the other hand, even when translated into secular terms and categories, should give priority to distributive justice, solidarity, the common good, and the preferential option for the poor. Participatory theological bioethics must turn its attention more firmly to social ethics and to political grass roots, mid-level, nongovernmental, and governmental levels. Cahill appreciatively describes the role of the Catholic Health Association in working on all these levels for a more equitable healthcare system.[5]

Contemporary Catholic theology recognizes the existence of structural sin that needs to be changed. As structures they are complex realities involving many different aspects. As sinful they are not easily changed. Simply saying that something is wrong will not bring about change.

Bryan Massingale's discussion of racism well illustrates the complex reality of racism and the difficulty in trying to change such structures. The common sense understanding of racism sees racism as personal acts of rudeness, hostility, or discrimination usually against persons of color, but an emphasis on personal attitudes and actions cannot explain the depth of racism and its persistence in U.S. society. Massingale sees race as a cultural phenomenon involving a set of meanings and values that forms the life of a community. Culture provides the ideological foundation for social, political, and economic policies. Racism is a largely unconscious reality developed through cultural conditioning and instilled by socialization. The culture of racism masks the indignities, discrimination, hostility, suspicion, and rejection that black people experience just because of the color of their skin. They are not accepted in the same way as white people are in practically all aspects of social existence in this country. White culture is an often unconscious awareness that accepts whiteness as the measure of what is real, standard, normative, and moral. White privilege involves the uneven and unfair distribution of power, privilege, land, and material resources favoring white people.[6]

To be effective against racism, Catholic ethical reflection must adopt a structural and systemic approach recognizing the social evil as a cultural phenomenon of our underlying color symbol system that justifies race-based disparities and shapes a person's consciousness and identity although usually on an unconscious level. To overcome racism requires changing white privilege, advantage, and dominance.[7] Massingale's understanding of racism provides a very clear understanding of the complexity of structural sin and the difficulties in striving to overcome it.

In discussing immigration, Kristin Heyer recognizes that the best moral and political arguments in favor of the rights of immigrants are necessary but not sufficient.[8] We are dealing here with structural or social sin. Like Massingale, Heyer refers to this reality as scotosis. We need to recognize the unconscious dimension of social sin and the impact unjust structures have on moral agency. There is a dialectical relationship between personal and social sin. Social structures are both consequential and causal in nature. Persons help to create sinful social structures by their actions, but sinful social structures greatly influence human agency.

Socioeconomic, cultural, and political structures opposed to immigration are connected to ideological blindness. Pride, insecurity, ignorance, and group egoism contribute to these structures opposed to hospitality to immigrants. Group egotism, to use Reinhold Niebuhr's phrase, contributes to cultural forces that elevate national or security concerns above moral ones, thus contributing to the rise of human rights violations and callous indifference to immigrants.

These intertwined problems of social sin require repentance, conscientization, and radical conversion. The lens of individual culpability does not address the social sin of opposition to the human rights of immigrants. Radical solidarity is required to reframe immigration as a shared international responsibility and to cultivate conversion from the existing pervasive ideologies.

THE HUMAN ACT MUST ALWAYS BE CONSIDERED IN RELATION TO THE PERSON WHO PLACES THE ACT

In the Catholic tradition, sinful human beings need God's grace in order to act as the children of God. Thus the change of heart is a most important reality for the development of Catholic moral theology. The manuals of moral theology, however, gave little or no consideration to the need for a change in the person with the emphasis always on human actions alone and not on the person. Here there exists a fascinating tension between the older manuals of moral theology and the older manuals of dogmatic theology. The manuals of dogmatic theology defend the thesis that sinful human beings without grace are not able to observe over a long period of time the substance of the natural law.[9] In other words, conversion or a change of heart is necessary for us to live out over time the full requirements even of the natural law. But for all practical purposes the manuals of moral theology paid no attention to this teaching found in the manuals of dogmatic theology.

The Catholic tradition as illustrated in the work of Thomas Aquinas recognized and even emphasized that acts must be seen in relation to the person and the virtues of the person. But even here for many scholars especially in my country in the late nineteenth and the first half of the twentieth century, Thomas Aquinas was seen and studied primarily as a philosopher and not as a theologian.[10] Recently theologians have made the case that Thomas Aquinas was and remains a theologian and not just a philosopher.[11]

Thomas Aquinas developed what is today called moral theology in the *Ia IIae* of the *Summa*. The very last treatise here is grace (qq. 109–14). Grace is necessary to do the works of Christian charity and love. Without grace fallen human beings can do some good acts of the natural law since sin does not totally corrupt human nature, but the human without grace is like the sick person who can do certain actions but not all the same actions that the person in perfect health can do. In other words, even to do the works of the natural law easily and in its totality the human person needs grace. To use the biblical words here, one needs conversion.

Thomas Aquinas is well known for his treatise on natural law. Many volumes and even some libraries are dedicated to Thomistic natural law theory, but Aquinas devotes only one question to natural law (*Ia IIae* q. 94). Very few books on Aquinas's ethics have mentioned the New Law, but the *Summa* devotes three questions to the New Law (*Ia IIae* 106–8). The New Law is not a written law but rather it is primarily the gift of the Holy Spirit dwelling in our hearts.

In addition to the role of grace and the New Law, Aquinas spends most of the *Ia IIae* on the role of virtues, which are the good habits disposing us to do what is right. Aquinas says the virtues modify the basic powers of the human person—intellect, will, concupiscible and irascible appetites to do the good. I prefer to see the virtues modifying the basic human relationships to God, neighbor, world of creation, and self.[12] Here too with regard to the virtues Aquinas sees the important role of the infused virtues enabling the Christian to carry out the supernatural works of charity. One does not have to agree with all of Thomistic anthropology to appreciate the importance for right actions of the human person to be transformed by grace and the infused virtues in order to live out the fullness of the Christian and human life. Contemporary Catholic moral theology has insisted on the important role of the virtues.

The formation of the human person as subject and agent is most basic in carrying on the work of justice, peace, and the integrity of creation. The fundamental change of heart and the virtues relating the individual to God, neighbor, world of creation, and self insist that the human person is not an isolated monad.

In my country the greatest difference between Christian anthropology and the American ethos is the individualism that is so prevalent in the United States. In a classic study, Robert Bellah and coauthors describe two kinds of individualism in the United States. Utilitarian individualism sees all other persons and things simply as means for the good of the individual. Expressive individualism insists on the need for the individual to be free at every moment to express oneself in whatever way one wants. According to this sociological study, the primary language heard in the United States is the language of individualism. So strong and pervasive is the individualistic ethos that even people who in their lives show great concern for others, the poor, and the common good often use the language of individualism to explain what they are doing. They do not have any other way to describe their own broader commitments.[13]

In opposition to such individualism, the Christian ethos insists on the common good, the solidarity of all creatures—human beings among themselves and in relationship to the environment—and the preferential option for the poor. The Catholic tradition today not only recognizes political and civil rights such as the right to freedom of religion, speech, press, and assembly but also social and economic rights such as the right to food, clothing, shelter, education, and healthcare. A major tragedy in the United States is the fact that we are the only highly developed country without universal healthcare. Justice in the United States is usually seen in terms of the relationship of one individual to another, but the Catholic tradition insists on distributive justice involving the relationship of society or the state to the individual as seen for example in the just distribution of material goods in society and legal or participative justice, which recognizes the relationship of the individual to society and the state and that calls for active participation of all in the broader society.[14] Restorative justice from the Christian perspective aims at restoring the relationships in society that have been broken by sin.[15]

From the perspective of Catholic moral theology, individuals striving to live out the love of God and neighbor aided by the appropriate virtues are basic in doing the work of justice, peace, and the integrity of creation. The role of the individual person, however, is necessary but not sufficient. What else is required?

OTHER ACTORS BASED ON THE PRINCIPLE OF SUBSIDIARITY

The Catholic social tradition has developed the principle of subsidiarity, which serves as a guide for how to bring about change in society. The principle of subsidiarity recognizes an important but limited role of government in trying to ensure justice in society. However, between the individual and government are what others have called mediating institutions.[16] The basic Catholic view of society looks something like this. At the very basis of society stands the human person with God-given dignity and rights. The human person is prior to the state and cannot be subordinated to it. Next comes the family, which is the basic unit of society for the development of human beings. On the next level are institutions or structures such as neighborhoods or extended families. We live in and through all these realities. Then come somewhat independent structures and institutions that are necessary for any society. Think, for example, of the role of the press and the media. Cultural institutions of all kinds abound for the higher goods of persons. Educational institutions of great variety exist to foster the education of all the citizens. Religious groups, mosques, and churches bring together people for religious purposes with a recognition that religion also has a role in working for justice, peace, and the integrity of creation. Other groups that people freely join are called voluntary groups such as Doctors without Borders, Union of Concerned Scientists, and Habitat for Humanity. Only then comes the important but limited role of government.

In issues of justice, peace, and the integrity of creation, government has a significant role but not the only role. Governments usually have laws against bribery and corruption. There are also laws to protect the environment and to avoid disastrous climate change. Many governments have mileage and emissions standards for automobiles in order to protect the environment. In addition to laws and regulations, government can provide incentives to influence more people to carry on the work of social justice.

The voluntary associations described in the principle of subsidiarity can promote a culture or ethos to support the work for justice, peace, and the integrity of creation. Such an ethos plays an instrumental role in supporting existing government regulations, but such a culture also has an independent role to play in society. An ethos of honesty and transparency makes it easier for individuals to avoid the temptations of bribery and corruption. A culture of concern for the environment helps individual citizens to become more involved in the work of protecting and sustaining the environment. Voluntary recycling can help motivate others to follow the example and thus make their contribution to the good of the environment.

What are the institutions in society that can help to bring about such a culture? Educational institutions have a big role to play in making society and individuals aware of the important needs in these areas. The free press can promote social justice and serve as a watchdog to point out the problems created by bribery and corruption. Religious groups contribute to such a culture by stimulating their adherents to become more involved in the work of justice, peace, and the integrity of creation. There can be different and at times even conflicting ways to carry out these policies. There might even be a few people opposed to some of these efforts on behalf of justice, peace, and the integrity of creation, but they can and should be drowned out by the vast majority of people who seem willing to support these measures. A very important type of voluntary association that has come to the fore recently involves nongovernment organizations (NGOs). They have already had a significant effect in working for justice, peace, and the integrity of creation throughout the globe.

CONCLUSION

Catholic moral theology has a significant role to play in working for justice, peace, and the integrity of creation on the local, national, and global levels. This role today involves more than just determining what acts are right and what acts are wrong. The struggle for social justice involves the need to make just structures and institutions more present in society. Often such a focus will call for changing existing unjust structures. Structural change by its very nature is complex, involving many different factors and relationships, and consequently is not easily accomplished. From the theological perspective these unjust structures are seen as sinful structures. As a result they are even more difficult to change. Full justice and peace will never be present in this world, but moral theology has a role to play in pointing out the concrete ways in which some progress can be made in these areas.

The principle of subsidiarity in the Catholic tradition provides an approach to bring about such change. The principle of subsidiarity in its own way is a good illustration of the Catholic tradition's insistence on a "both-and" approach. The role of the individual seen in terms of multiple relationships is most fundamental but itself is not adequate. Government too has a significant role to play, but it too is limited. A very important function belongs to mediating institutions and voluntary associations that try to change structures as well as the ethos and culture of society. In short, to carry out the work of justice, peace, and the integrity of creation we need committed individuals, mediating institutions, voluntary associations, and government. But, all these actors need to try to overcome the sinful social structures that support many of the problems facing society today.

Notes

1. John T. Noonan Jr., *Bribes: The Intellectual History of a Moral Idea* (Berkeley: University of California Press, 1984), 702–5.

2. Synod of Bishops 1971, "Justice in the World," in *Catholic Social Thought: The Documentary History*, ed. David J. O'Brien and Thomas A. Shannon (Maryknoll, NY: Orbis, 2010).

3. Jeffrey Odell Korgen, *Beyond Empowerment: A Pilgrimage with the Catholic Campaign for Human Development* (Maryknoll, NY: Orbis, 2005); Bradford E. Hinze, *Ecclesiology and Exclusion: Boundaries of Being and Belonging in Postmodern Times* (Maryknoll, NY: Orbis, 2012), 221–35; P. David Finks, *The Radical Vision of Saul Alinsky* (New York: Paulist Press, 1984).

4. Lisa Sowle Cahill, *Theological Bioethics: Participation, Justice, and Change* (Washington, DC: Georgetown University Press, 2005), 43–69.

5. Cahill, *Theological Bioethics*, 151–55.

6. Bryan N. Massingale, *Racial Justice and the Catholic Church* (Maryknoll, NY: Orbis, 2010), 1–41.

7. Massingale, *Racial Justice and the Catholic Church*, 41–42.

8. Kristin E. Heyer, "Radical Solidarity: Migration as Challenge for Contemporary Christian Ethics," *Journal of Catholic Social Thought* 14, no. 1 (Winter 2017): 87–104.

9. Severino Gonzalez, *De Gratia, in Sacrae Theologicae Summa*, vol. 3, 3rd ed. (Madrid: Biblioteca de Autores Cristianos, 1956), 521–29.

10. For my development of the reasons for the emphasis on Thomas Aquinas as a philosopher, see Charles E. Curran, *The Development of Moral Theology: Five Strands* (Washington, DC: Georgetown University Press, 2013), 54–61.

11. Romanus Cessario, *The Moral Virtues and Theological Ethics* (Notre Dame, IN: University of Notre Dame Press, 1991); Thomas F. O'Meara, *Thomas Aquinas Theologian* (Notre Dame, IN: University of Notre Dame Press, 1997); Servais Pinckaers, *The Sources of Christian Ethics*, trans. Sr. Mary Thomas

Noble (Washington, DC: Catholic University of America Press, 1995); Jean
Pierre Torrell, *Saint Thomas Aquinas*, rev. ed. (Washington, DC: Catholic University of America Press, 2005).

12. Charles E. Curran, *The Catholic Moral Tradition Today: A Synthesis*
(Washington, DC: Georgetown University Press, 1999), 113–30.

13. Robert N. Bellah et al, *Habits of the Heart: Individualism and Commitment in American Life* (Berkeley: University of California Press, 1985), 3–51.

14. Kenneth R. Himes, "Health Care Access for All," *Health Progress* 88,
no. 3 (May–June 2007): 25–39.

15. Eli Saseran McCarthy, "Breaking Out: The Expansiveness of Restorative Justice in *Laudato si'*," *Journal of Moral Theology* 5, no. 2 (2016): 66–80.

16. *Journal of Catholic Social Thought* 2 (Summer 2005) is entirely
devoted to the principle of subsidiarity.

13. Pluralism in Contemporary U.S. Moral Theology

This chapter was published in my *Diverse Voices in Modern U.S. Moral Theology* (Washington, DC: Georgetown University Press, 2018), 249–52.

I started teaching moral theology at St. Bernard's Seminary in Rochester, NY in 1961. The textbook assigned for the course was the moral manual written in Latin by the Austrian Jesuit Hieronymus (Jerome) Noldin (1838–1932). The manual was subsequently brought up to date by two of his successors teaching moral theology at Innsbruck. I used the thirty-second edition published in 1959.[1] Many of the additions made to the original related to developments in canon law and the official documents from the Roman curia, especially the Holy Office, which was later called the Congregation for the Doctrine of the Faith. According to a study in 1962, the Noldin manual was used in more Catholic seminaries in the United States than any other manual.[2]

Thanks especially to the influence of Bernard Häring when I was studying for a doctorate in moral theology at the Alfonsian Academy in Rome, I was dissatisfied with the approach of the manual because it was too minimalistic and legalistic. I produced my own notes for the students as an introduction to moral theology. One year I went to the textbook only on the first of March of the second semester.

My book *Diverse Voices in U.S. Moral Theology* has indicated that the manuals continued in existence even for a time after Vatican II because there were no other texts available. The pre–Vatican II Roman Catholic Church emphasized its catholicity or universality. It was the same Church in all parts of the world and also throughout history. The best illustration of this catholicity was the use of Latin in the liturgy. The Eucharist, which then was often called the Mass, was exactly the same in every country of the world. The teaching of theology in Catholic seminaries reflected the same universalism. The language of theology was Latin. The textbooks were the same textbooks used everywhere in the world. No one was surprised that a text for the practical discipline of moral theology in seminaries in the United States was written in Latin by an author living in a different country and culture.

The narrative developed in *Diverse Voices* shows the dramatic contrast between the situation of moral theology today and what existed just a little more than fifty years ago. What explains such a turnabout? In my judgment, Bernard Lonergan, the Canadian Jesuit theologian who himself taught in Latin in Rome (I was privileged to have classes with him), put his finger on what happened. According to Lonergan, the most significant change that occurred as a result of Vatican II was the move from classicism to historical consciousness. Classicism looked at the world in terms of the eternal, the immutable, and the unchangeable. Historical consciousness gives greater importance to the particular, the contingent, and the historical. Historical consciousness also recognizes that the human subject who is a knower and author is also embedded in and influenced by one's own history and culture.[3] This volume has developed the concept of historical consciousness in greater detail in previous chapters.

The shift to historical consciousness explains the diversity and pluralism of Catholic moral theology today and the importance of *sitz-im-lebèn*. *Diverse Voices* discussed thirteen different approaches to moral theology. John Ford was one of the last manualists. Häring, Fuchs, McCormick, Grisez, and to an extent Cessario responded to the changes of Vatican II and the discussions brought about by *Humanae vitae*. In addition, Cessario brought his Dominican and Thomistic perspective to his work. Feminism strongly influenced the approach of Farley and Cahill as did their respective perspectives of a religious sister and a married laywoman. Isasi-Díaz and Massingale brought their ethnic and racial backgrounds and perspectives to their work. The experience of young Catholic moral theologians at the beginning of the twenty-first century helps to explain the approach taken by the New Wine, New Wineskins group. Keenan's broad interest in many aspects of moral theology and his commitment to recognizing the work of moral theologians throughout the world comes through in many of his writings and in his work with Catholic Theological Ethics in the World Church.

This diversity and pluralism, however, raises the question if there is an identifiable Catholic moral theology still existing today. All Catholic theologians today are heavily involved in ecumenical dialogue as well as a growing interreligious dialogue. What stands out in this volume is the agreement among all the authors on what they oppose. They strongly object to an anthropology that sees the human person as an isolated individual who is free to do whatever one wants. This individualism is especially present in U.S. culture. The U.S. culture insists that the individual person can pull oneself up by the bootstraps and become whatever one wants to become. Success in this country is invariably understood in economic terms. The Roman Catholic tradition, however, has always insisted on the social nature of the human person. We are not individual monads but we exist in and depend upon many different relationships with God, neighbor, world, self, and all that God created.

In my judgment, a fundamental characteristic of Catholic understanding in general and moral theology in particular is the principle of mediation also called the incarnational or sacramental principle. The divine is mediated in and through the human. Catholic ecclesiology well illustrates this approach. God comes to us and we go to God in and through the Church as the community of the disciples of Jesus. The whole sacramental system is based on such an understanding. Thomistic natural law also illustrates the role of mediation. To know what God wants us to do, one does not go immediately to God and ask. Rather our God-given human reason reflecting on what God has made can tell us how God wants the creation to be used. The diverse approaches in *Diverse Voices* well illustrate the Catholic notion of mediation.

As pointed out, pre–Vatican II Catholicism gave great importance to universality. Universality, however, still remains an important characteristic of Roman Catholicism. The authors discussed obviously stress the particular and the changing, but they still hold onto a chastened universality. For example, feminists and minority groups want equality and dignity for themselves and for all human beings.

Mediation and some universality have also contributed to the Catholic emphasis on "both-and" approaches rather than "either-or" approaches. The Catholic tradition has insisted on Scripture and tradition, faith and

246 / *The Ensuing Years*

reason, grace and work, Jesus and the Church. There have been differences and problems as to how the two parts in the both-and approach fit together, but such an approach continues to be characteristic of the Catholic method and is well illustrated by the chapters in *Diverse Voices*.

The negative criticism of individualism pointed out earlier that the Catholic approach to anthropology emphasizes the social aspect of the human person based on both Scripture and reason. In accordance with such an anthropology, the Catholic tradition has given importance to the common good, solidarity, human rights, and an understanding of justice that also includes the relationship of the individual to society and society's relationship to the individual.

The tradition of Catholic moral theology and the authors studied here also recognize the importance of the ecclesial dimension of moral theology. Many of the authors in this volume have dealt with the teaching office of the Church in moral matters. There are, however, many ways in which the Church should carry out its teaching mission, which because of baptism should always involve all those who are members of the Church. The Catholic tradition has insisted on the social mission of the Church, but how this mission is carried out in different situations continues to be an important consideration. Moral theology will always experience the tension between the prophetic role of the Church and its openness to all. The Catholic approach also recognizes that Catholics belong to many other communities and societies and thus moral theology needs to address the role of Catholics in these different communities and in different circumstances.

Thus without going into greater detail there are characteristic aspects of the Catholic moral tradition that are found in the different authors considered in *Diverse Voices*. The Catholic tradition in moral theology is truly a living tradition that involves both continuities and discontinuities. In the future there will continue to be diverse approaches, especially in light of the *sitz-im-leben*, but all these approaches will be influenced and affected by the continuing living tradition of Catholic moral theology.

Notes

1. Hieronymus Noldin, *Summa Theologiae Moralis*, vol. 2, *De Pracep-tis*, 32nd ed. (Innsbruck: F. Rauch, 1959).

2. John C. Boere, "A Survey of the Content and Organization of the Curriculum of the Theological Departments of Major Seminaries in the United States of America," (MA diss., Catholic University of America, 1963), 73.

3. Bernard Lonergan, "The Transition from a Classicist World-View to Historical Mindedness," in *Law for Liberty: The Role of Law in the Church Today*, ed. James E. Biechler (Baltimore: Helicon, 1967), 126–33.

Subsequent Developments

Subsequent developments belong to the future. On the basis of the massive changes that have occurred in the last sixty years, no one should be foolhardy enough to try to predict the future of moral theology. The threefold publics of moral theology—the Church, the academy, and society in all its dimensions—will continue to serve as the parameters for what will occur, but these are very broad parameters. All anyone can be sure of is that change will continue to characterize the work of moral theology.

Looking back, I am most grateful for having the privilege to participate in the development of Catholic moral theology in the last sixty years. Yes, there were difficult and challenging times, but I remain ever grateful for the opportunity to be a part of this history. I have appreciated the companionship of other moral theologians on the journey—ever grateful to those who taught and mentored me and appreciative of the colleagues and students who have accompanied me on the journey. In addition to individual persons, institutions, learned societies, publishers, and editors have contributed to my journey. I hope that all those who pursue the vocation of moral theology in the unknown future will enjoy the journey as much as I have.

Afterword

This book displays fully why and how Charles Curran has been a major, pivotal change agent in the Catholic moral theology of a generation, especially in the United States. The dates on which the book's chapters were originally published span over fifty years (1966–2018). Signature themes of Curran's work—historical consciousness, conscience, and his "relationality-responsibility model," for example—emerge with Vatican II, yet evolve with changing environments, up to and including the global face of twenty-first-century Catholic moral theology. Another key concern, interdependent with these three, is the renegotiation of the Catholic moral tradition's "natural law" approach. This approach was questioned at first from within ("proportionalism"), then exposed to incremental larger critiques as the twenty-first century brought more exposure to diverse cultures and moral traditions, as well as a renewed demand to defend human rights, economic equality, and ecological balance across moral traditions on some common basis.

When Curran began his theological career, both magisterial teaching about morality and its teachers and critics were focused not on global social concerns, but on authoritative pronouncements by the episcopal hierarchy, especially the popes. The most salient and debated issues concerned sex and gender, and it was conformity to "Church teaching" on these above all that defined moral-theological orthodoxy. Most faithful Catholics were obedient to teachings about gender complementarity, indissoluble marriage, and procreative sex, often at great personal and familial cost. The controversy over artificial birth control—as a result of which Curran eventually lost his tenured position at Catholic University—crystallized the painful stresses and strains of Catholics coping with cultural changes occurring more broadly in North America and Europe.

These included growing equality of women, the civil rights movement, LGBTQ activism, rapid advances in technology and communications media, newfound democratic political power that surged in the

249

Vietnam war protests, the unfolding consequences of decolonization, and the increasingly rapid advance of economic globalization. "Westerners" in general—not only Catholics—grew resistant to any form of authoritarianism or traditionalism. In scholarship and academia postmodern, poststructuralist, and postcolonial theories gained influence.

The Second Vatican Council, which offered an open door and a receptive hearing to "the modern world" (though not uncritically), was the Roman Catholic Church's response to these trends. A key point in relation to Curran is that Vatican II both inspired and reflected a "lay liberation" movement, a hunger for spiritual renewal, and a social consciousness that were already emerging in the wider Catholic Church. That Curran (inspired by Bernard Häring) was ahead of the game on these shifts is clear from the first three chapters in this book, especially the 1966 piece, "The Relevancy of the Ethical Teaching of Jesus" (chapter 2).

Humanae vitae (1968) resulted in an ecclesial conflagration not only because of the substantive case for or against artificial birth control. It was also because the Catholic laity and many moral theologians were already questioning the relevance and coherence of the received teaching and expected their views to be heard and heeded. Indeed, by putting lay participation and change on the table, the Papal Birth Control Commission had already prepared many not only to "dissent," but even to walk away from the teaching and its teachers when the collaborative process was short-circuited. Charles Curran is remarkable for his early, incisive, and pathbreaking analysis of *Humanae vitae*'s shortcomings as a piece of moral theology and of pastoral guidance. He is even more remarkable for the integrity, patience, and loyalty with which he engaged over decades, and at great sacrifice, with a teaching with which he so deeply disagreed, and which had in effect already been abandoned by most Catholics. In fact, as he remarks, Curran had wanted to move into social ethics in the 1970s, but the Catholic "obsession" with sexual morality—and with his own notoriety in that sphere—meant that *Humanae vitae* and Curran's practical and methodological subversion of it would decide the direction of his theological career.

In Chapter 6, "Dissent," Charlie remarks that Linda Hogan and I take issue with the way in which he accepts the characterization "dissenting theologian." To my mind, that represents too great a concession to the centrality and authority of the magisterial status quo as defining the terms of engagement. Charlie's critical response to the birth control encyclical has in fact become the status quo as far as the Catholic public's take on "official" Catholic teaching on contraception is concerned, and this has been the case for decades.

It is important here to note, with awe and admiration, that Curran's respect for the officially teaching Church is extended to those among its defenders who specifically repudiate Curran's own proposals. In a remarkable display of character, he has always refrained from any ad hominems or tirades that might further the hostile tone of many *Humanae vitae* disagreements. Instead he summarizes the main concerns and theses of opponents succinctly, while letting his own views speak for themselves. In chapter 5, "Natural Law and *Humanae Vitae*," he even characterizes the "new natural law" of John Finnis and Germain Grisez as "the most creative and innovative defense of the negative moral absolutes proposed by the hierarchical magisterium." This same moderation is reflected in his brief accounts of the phases of his employment dispute with Catholic University (part 2: "Introduction and Context" and "Dissent"), resulting in his eventual relocation to a prestigious position at Southern Methodist University. Something similar happened to Jesus: "no prophet is accepted in the prophet's hometown" (Luke 4:24). I once heard a colleague inquire something along the lines of, "Charlie, why haven't you ever responded directly to the many intemperate attacks on your theology and your character?" The response: "Life is too short." Words to live by, in the age of a polarized and uncivil Catholic blogosphere.

It is appropriate in an "afterword" to move beyond this volume's direct contents, and review or preview happenings its author instigated or predicted, as well as some by which he might have been surprised. In the category of those about which Curran has been prescient and even a participant are the emergence of a more inductive, tentative, and revisable version of natural law, now requiring cross-cultural and interreligious engagement to refine its claims; the turn from laws and absolutes to persons and their relationships, later flowering in a contemporary "virtue ethics"; the recognition, now taking on global dimensions, that relational persons are persons in community and community shapes agency, perspective, and concrete morality; and the strengthening of Catholic moral theology and social ethics in U.S. research institutions with distinctively *Catholic* identities, where critical inquiry is respected and protected by their founding religious orders and "separately incorporated" lay boards of trustees.

As early as 1977 (chapter 3, "Conscience"), Curran saw that "one must honestly admit that white, male, middle-class theologians have not been aware as we should be of the problems of racism, poverty, and sexism in our society," a comment that white, female, middle-class theologians can also take to heart. In the last two chapters of this book (12, "Methodological Approach in Dealing with Particular Social Issues" and 13, "Pluralism in Contemporary U.S. Moral Theology," both from 2018, the first written for an intercontinental conference of Catholic ethicists), many of Curran's earlier insights come to fruition and mark a sea change toward a more diverse, "intersectional," socially oriented, and globally participatory version of Catholic theological ethics. In chapter 12, he addresses the socially embedded and responsible character of bioethics, the "complex reality" of U.S. racism and its structural hold; and the intransigent dynamics of personal, social, and structural sin that hinder just and compassionate immigration policy. Reflecting keynotes of Pope Francis, Curran defines the common good in terms of the preferential option for the poor and the "solidarity of all creatures," demanding restorative and not only distributive justice.

In chapter 13, Curran reaffirms the importance of an "incarnational" and more humble commitment to moral universality in the service of "equality and dignity for all." He also and importantly alludes to the fact that a new and more diverse generation of "young Catholic theologians" will frame these issues differently as they renegotiate Christian belief and practice in a changing world and Church. One of the change factors, of course, is that numbers of Catholics are declining precipitously in the global North and increasingly exponentially in the global South. I believe younger Catholics in the North may be more interested in restoring a strong, even countercultural, Catholic identity and meaningful community around spirituality, prayer, and liturgy, than they are in official repudiation of restrictive sexual norms most already disregard. This development was unanticipated by the Vatican II generation, Curran included, I suspect. Derivative challenges for Church and theology are to make sure Catholic worship and spirituality retain their social-political edge, and bring at least some of the Catholic insistence that sexual relationships be personally meaningful and publicly responsible back to the current realities of "the hook-up culture," 50 percent U.S. divorce rate, and sexual abuse.

Meanwhile the next generation of Catholics in the global South will need more reinforcement than even Pope Francis is currently offering to reform patriarchal traditions that selective readings of the Bible and "authoritative" teaching can so conveniently reinforce, including violence against women and LGBTQ persons. And in the global South (especially Africa), young Catholics need a Church and leaders resistant to the "prosperity gospel," and encouraging of faith-inspired political participation that not only resists pernicious incursions of "Western" culture and economics, but also builds stronger and more just societies that make good on the promise of their long and rich indigenous traditions.

In conclusion, let me turn to a 2016 essay on Pope Francis (chapter 11, "Pope Francis: Reform and the Catholic Moral Tradition") to recapture where Charles Curran has been and is, and where his legacy has gone and might be going from here. If there is one cause that has defined Charles Curran's theological vocation in the public eye, it is his insistence that official Catholic sexual teaching must change, on the basis of its accountability to the Church as a whole, and on that of the lived testimony of the majority of its people. In his chapter on Pope Francis, he commends the pope for his humility, simplicity, approachability, and his "endearing" personal presence and outreach. Francis's calls for reform, consultative approach, Church of the poor, and priority on mercy have brought new life and heart to the Church. Nevertheless, questions Curran, "Will Francis change the disputed moral teachings?"

Curran has always been committed to a direct retraction of the specific content of *Humanae vitae*, and he still is. But in his pursuit of this goal over five decades, he has himself contributed to a Catholic ethos in which the "faithful" exercise their consciences more independently on sexual and familial matters, taking into account their relationships, responsibilities, and contexts. The teaching Church has now come to agree with Curran's own conviction in the 1970s that Catholic identity and theology should center on the preferential option for, solidarity with, and empowerment of the poor. Pope Francis in particular has turned the teaching Church into a listening and consultative Church, just as Curran has long demanded. This too is a surprise, and a welcome one. And it is true not only of *Evangelium gaudium* (as noted by Curran), but also of

Laudato Si' (mentioning at least seventeen local bishops' conferences and calling for popular mobilization); and even more strikingly of the two-stage 2014–15 Synod on the Family, the questionnaires that went out in advance of it, and the open and fractious public discussions of episcopal differences on sex and gender; and the follow-up apostolic exhortation *Amoris laetitia*. The latter referred more contentious issues (such as communion for divorced and remarried Catholics) back to the local churches and discernment by couples and pastoral advisers.

To my mind, this already represents a change in disputed teachings, as well as a structural reform, and an encouragement of conscientious discernment by people actually in difficult or nontraditional familial and marital situations—on a "relationality-responsibility model" where "natural law" certainties make way for contextual evaluation. This is not to say direct and specific revisions of teaching would not be salutary or welcome, especially to those who experience exclusion, violence, or internalized stigma in the name of Catholic morals. Yet as debates and polarizations among Family Synod participants made clear—and as *Humanae vitae* had already de facto taught—it is no longer possible to expect top-down dicta by Catholic pontiffs and hierarchs to produce conformity and obedience on any moral issue. The more likely result is a split in the Church, something Pope Francis seemed concerned to avoid at the Family Synod.

Yet, in effect, Pope Francis opened the door to a reformed method of moral discernment and learning that could have landmark significance for Catholic moral theology and its magisterial iterations. It also bears a good deal of similarity to Curran's earlier advisories concerning historical learning and relational responsibility. This seems confirmed by powerful media images and first-person reports of Francis's meetings with gay and transgender Catholics; as well his 2014 Vatican welcome and marriage ceremony for twenty couples who had already been living together, some with children; and the message of *Amoris laetitia* that God's grace can be found even in "irregular" families and marriages. These papal interventions do not amount to a perfect picture. Pope Francis still has a problematic profile on gender and "gender ideology," for example. Yet papal edicts and actions should be viewed through a twenty-first-century lens, and not in light of the assumptions by or about the papal magisterium that set the terms of the *Humanae vitae* wars. In contrast, Pope Francis's teaching model is strikingly "bottom up" (consider the 2019 Synod on the Amazon), collaborative, and revisionary. He rarely presents his own opinions as the only or final word. His meetings with gay and transgender persons radiate humanity and hospitality. As Francis said of transgender people, "Life is life, things have to be accepted as they come....Not to say that it's all the same, but in each case. Welcome, accompany, study, discern and integrate. This is what Jesus would do today."[1]

To attract new Catholic membership, or reattract those that have already left, it is necessary to do much more than rewrite any obsolete teachings still "on the books" of the moral magisterium. It will be essential to reinvent Catholic community that is spiritually centered and liturgically profound yet inclusive. It will be essential to ground a committed and "holy" way of life in a vibrant relation to a transcendent Creator who is present to us in the risen Jesus and the Spirit. That this kind of faith and commitment has inspired Charles Curran's own theological creativity and his "faithful dissent" over a lifetime theological vocation in turn inspires his many friends and followers, as I trust it will the coming generation of Catholics and Catholic moral theologians.

Lisa Sowle Cahill
J. Donald Monan, SJ, Professor of Theology
Boston College

Notes

1. Airplane interview with reporters, return from Georgia, October 1, 2016, cited by Inés San Martín, "Pope Says Walk with Trans Persons, but Fight Gender Theory," *Crux*, October 2, 2016, https://cruxnow.com/global-church/2016/10/02/pope-says-walk-trans-persons-fight-gender-theory/.